How To Write
Powerful
Catalog Copy

Books by Herschell Gordon Lewis:
Direct Mail Copy That Sells
*How to Make Your Advertising Twice as Successful at Half the
    Cost*
How to Write Powerful Fund Raising Letters
How to Handle Your Own Public Relations
The Businessman's Guide to Advertising and Sales Promotion
*More Than You Ever Wanted to Know About Mail Order
    Advertising*
Herschell Gordon Lewis on the Art of Writing Copy
As co-author:
Spirit of America: Norman Rockwell
Everybody's Guide to Plate Collecting

How To Write
Powerful
Catalog Copy

Herschell Gordon Lewis

Bonus Books, Inc.

94   93   92   91   90   5 4 3 2 1

Library of Congress Catalog Card Number: 89-81587

International Standard Book Number: 0-929387-10-4

Bonus Books, Inc.
160 East Illinois Street
Chicago, Illinois 60611

Printed in the United States of America

Distributed by

Contents

Preface   vii

Acknowledgments   ix

1.   What "Kind" of Copy? We Have Lots of Choices   1

2.   Who Hired This Guy, Anyway? We Have Lots of Words, So Why Doesn't Our Copywriter Use the Good Ones?   39

3.   I'm Awfully Tired Today, So Please Don't Challenge Me   61

4.   The Clarity Commandment Revisited   73

5.   What's on Top of the Copy-Block?   85

6.   "Let Me Make This Absolutely Clear"   95

7.   Should Catalog Writers Have to Take Literacy Tests?   105

8.   Why Not Tell 'Em What It's For?   121

9.   Give Them a Reason   131

10.   Lovely? Useful? Unique? Prove It!   141

11.   The Ultimate Explosive...and Other Overused Oddities   153

12.   "Why Should I Pay You That Much?"   165

13.   Positioning: A Key to Higher Response   181

14.   Turning on the Reader's Toggle-Switch   193

15.   Describing the Complicated Item... Explaining the Deception Perception... and Other Matters   205

16.   The More You Know...the More You Can Say   217

17.   The Law of Absolute Confusion   231

18.   A Little Enthusiasm...and a Little More Clarity...Please!   247

19.   The Negative Rule of Partial Disclosure:
      Don't Leave Them Hanging There!   257
20.   OVERfamiliarity: Is It the Cause of Your
      UNDERdescribed "Shadow Copy"?   267
21.   "Hit-and-Run" Copy: Why Not Use Words
      That Turn the Reader ON?   281
22.   At Last! A "Can't-Miss" Copywriting
      Instrument: The Benefit/Benefit/Benefit
      Principle   295
Appendix A   309
Appendix B   317
Index   325

Preface

"A copywriter is a copywriter, right?"

"Rules for catalog copywriting don't differ from rules for space ads or mail order packages, do they? I mean, if you can write one you can write another, can't you?"

"A catalog copywriter who can write about plastic pipe should be able to write about women's fashions, don't you think?"

One of those statements is true: the last one.

It's true because catalog copywriting is a combination of a special *discipline* (one I wish all copywriters had) and the ability to jump from one item to another without having to re-dress for radical surgery.

Somebody is leafing through your catalog. Here's a picture. It grabs attention.

Now what?

The page-flipper has become a live prospect. It's your turn. The cosmic moment—whether the metamorphosis becomes complete, page-flipper to live prospect to actual buyer, is in your hands...or, rather, at your fingertips, because those fingertips are on the keyboard.

Are those fingertips trained salespeople or dull sales clerks? Do they just describe or do they start the salivary glands churning? Effective copywriting isn't an accident.

In this book I identify 14 kinds of catalog copywriting. If you think 14 kinds represent a lot of stylistic differences, consider: These are the *major* kinds. A complete list might be twice as long...or endless.

As we approach the year 2001, specializing our approach to both our craft and our target-readers, the professional copywriter who moves from job to job may have to re-learn the copy approach with each new job. Already, high-fashion copy, copy aimed at young people, electronics copy, hi-fi copy, and many areas of business-to-business copy use a jargon all their own.

In this madhouse, where are some beacons shining into the murk, guiding copy into a response-pulling haven?

I'm counting on this book being one of those beacons. That's because rules of catalog writing for the 1990s transcend any aberration of style. A professional catalog copywriter *can* write for The Sharper Image one month, Bloomingdale's the next, Mainframe Computer Peripherals the next, and Farm Supply Company the next.

That writer may need a list of terms. But what that writer doesn't need is a new persuasion-in-print education.

Why not? Because with the information in these pages, glued tightly to a professional attitude, that writer can switch gears as easily as trading in one automobile for another.

A suggestion, if you're seriously involved in catalog copywriting:

This book has 22 chapters plus two appendices. For the next month read a chapter a day, twice. For the extra days, re-read the chapters you think affect you the most.

Will you be writing better copy? I *think* so. But even if you don't, I can guarantee you a few laughs as you see what some of the others—even the giants—are doing wrong!

Herschell Gordon Lewis
Plantation, Florida, 1990

Acknowledgments

The origin of this book lies not with me, but with two dear friends.

I'm deeply indebted to Charles I. Tannen, chief executive officer of Catalog Management Resources and former publisher of *Catalog Age*. Chuck convinced me to become the copy columnist for that influential magazine's first issue...and beyond. Many of the concepts in these pages stem from those columns.

I've never had a book achieve such effortless publication. My thanks and admiration to the production experts at Bonus Books.

The editors of *Catalog Age,* too, have been both helpful and cooperative. I treasure my relationship with the publication.

It will be no surprise to those who know how I live and work to know who has been my right arm in the preparation of this manuscript: my wife and business partner Margo, who not only compiled most of the exhibits but whose knowledge of catalog salesmanship far surpasses mine (and that of anyone else I know). Her mark is on every line of every page, and her unerring eye is responsible for many of the principles codified here.

Thank you all. And especially you.

CHAPTER *1*

What "Kind" of Copy? We Have Lots of Choices

FIRST, *YOU* TRY IT!

Your assignment: Your assistant gives you this catalog description of a pair of sandals:

> Alp Sport Sandals offer you comfort and fit. They're waterproof, so you can wear them anywhere. $29.95.

You tell your assistant: "You've written 'minimalist' copy. Our catalog uses 'snob appeal' copy. Your description doesn't fit our image, so change it."

Your assistant looks perplexed, then says, "Give me the first few words and I'll take it from there." So you write a "snob appeal" opening.

Take 30 seconds. No longer than that.

What was your opening? Did you refer to the *Jet Set?* Did you rename the shoe the "St. Moritz"? Did you write "These lovely waterproof sandals are as much at home on the beaches of St. Tropez as they are in the casino at Monte Carlo?" If you wrote any of these...

...Congratulations. You're a catalog copywriter.

Change Our Image? To What?

"Let's change the image of our catalog."

In a meeting...over lunch...at a session of the board of directors ...by edict or memo...this declaration generates the reaction, "To what?"

The other guy's catalog is always greener. You've been writing straightforward product descriptions. One competitor has been writing chest-thumping copy. Another has been writing "down home" copy. Each envies what the others are doing. The versatile writer has to be ready to switch gears.

The Fourteen Kinds of Catalog Copy

I suppose if we were to divide and subdivide and pick hairs and nits, we could come up with 50 types of catalog copy. But in broad categories, we can isolate 14 varieties:

1. "Jes' folk" copy.
2. "Down home personality" copy.
3. "You-you-you" copy.
4. "Shout" copy.
5. "Quietly upscale descriptive" copy.
6. "Image all the way" copy.
7. "Touchstone" copy.
8. "Narrative" copy.
9. "Minimalist" copy.
10. "All the facts" copy.
11. "Informational/educational" copy.
12. "Snob appeal" copy.
13. "I am the greatest" copy.
14. "Plain vanilla" copy.

We might recognize sub-categories such as "Good guy" copy, "Golly, gee whiz!" copy, and "More than you want to know" copy, but I figure we have to end the list somewhere.

(At the end of this chapter are samples of each category. Numbers correspond to category numbers. For example, Figure 1-9 is an example of no. 9, "Minimalist" copy.)

"Jes' Folk" Copy

Jes' folk copy is easy to read. Most copy blocks are first person—"I" or "we." You'll seldom see an uncontracted expression where a contraction is possible, so it's always "I'm," not "I am"; "We're," not "We are"; "didn't," not "did not."

(In my opinion this approach makes sense for 13 of the 14 categories. Exception: Some versions of no. 12, "Snob appeal.")

Jes' folk copy is the first cousin of the second category, "Down home" copy; but the difference is clear to both writer and reader.

A jes' folk description might begin this way:

> I went all the way down to Matamoros to sample this 'Tex-Mex' salsa, and danged if it isn't hotter than an El Paso afternoon. We don't call it "Hell-Fire" Sauce for nothin', and if it don't give your taste-buds a pretty strong bite, you got us beat before we start.

Some jes' folk writers would use "ain't" instead of "isn't"—a dangerous game. Maintaining a P.O.C.B. (plain ol' country boy) pace is tough enough without entrapping yourself in jargon.

The benefit of jes' folk copy: It's highly readable and entertaining.

The drawback of jes' folk copy: After a couple of pages it gets cloying and too cute to generate solid buyer-response. The reader *remains* reader, not buyer.

"Down Home" Copy

Down home copy borrows the personalized "I" approach from jes' folk copy, but it limits itself to conviviality, never lapsing into hay-chawin' folksiness.

The writer tries to draw the reader into a "you and I are a family" attitude—not possible with jes' folk copy except on the very lowest economic levels (with the very lowest buying power).

The down home writer would attack the salsa copy block this way:

> My aunt Maria vacationed in Mexico and was so excited she phoned me. "I've found the hottest 'Tex-Mex' salsa I've ever tasted," she said. "It's wonderful. I bought a case, and I think you ought to have it in the catalog." Aunt Maria isn't often wrong, so we made an exclusive arrangement with the small Mexican company that makes "Hell-Fire" Sauce. If you're brave...or if you love *real* Mexican sauce...you have to get some.

Down home copy can include straight talk without seeming "preachy." But when the copy lapses into "You'd better..." or "You really should..." it can alienate readers—without their quite knowing why they're alienated.

The benefit of down home copy: The reader feels the copy is aimed at him or her, which means benefit *has* to be present.

The drawback of down home copy: After a few pages, it seems forced. How many relatives, how many trips, how many problems-to-be-solved does this cataloger have, anyway? The writer can be trapped in the device.

"You-You-You" Copy

Advertising writing classes in schools of journalism teach a safe dogma: You the writer can't go wrong by emphasizing *you* the reader.

In catalogs, this sometimes works and sometimes doesn't, because a catalog parallels a solo mailing in only one respect: It's part of the direct marketing family. "You," revisited hundreds of times in a 32-page or 64-page catalog, becomes wearisome and repetitive.

The you-you-you writer would describe the salsa this way:

> You think you've tasted hot pepper salsa? Oh, no, you haven't. That is, you haven't tasted the *real* salsa until you've dipped a spoon into our "Hell-Fire" Sauce and sprinkled a little on your salad. Your tongue will tell you: You never knew a hot sauce could be this good.

In that single paragraph we have the word "you" nine times. Reader-involving? You bet. Too heavy a pace for a whole catalog? You bet. And in those two sentences we have the core of benefit and drawback.

The benefit of you-you-you copy: The reader *can't* feel left out. Copy is aimed like a blunderbuss straight at him or her.

The drawback of you-you-you copy: Reader interest buckles under the fatigue caused by artificially heavy involvement.

"Shout" Copy

Shout copy is the easiest of all to write. In a great many instances it's the strongest-pulling copy, because the shout usually centers around one image: "Bargain!"

A key rule, *THE YELL-OUT-BARGAIN RULE:*

> When you're shouting "Bargain!" play up price. The very act of shouting implies a price lower than competitors charge, even when it may not be true.

Lots of exclamation points, please! Who ever heard of a quiet shout? But except for the schlockiest copy, don't use more than one exclamation point after any one exclamation.

The writer charged with the responsibility of writing shout copy for the salsa would grind out something like this:

> A Hell-Fire Deal on "Hell-Fire" Salsa!
> 14-Oz. Bottle $2.49!

- Enjoy the hottest of the hot!
- Make a real 'Tex-Mex' dinner—for pennies!
- Concentrated—a little goes a long way!
- Never before at this low, low price!

You can see the emphasis: It isn't on product; it's on bargain. (Don't mistake me. Shout copy can't abandon its responsibility for telling the reader exactly what's for sale. What changes is emphasis, not the informational core.)

"Quietly Upscale Descriptive" Copy

Quietly upscale descriptive copy was more popular during the early 1980s than it is now, probably because the "yuppies," its principal and most logical targets, are past their status-seeking phase.

Still, clever catalogers looking for a marketing niche can settle into this posture with some confidence, because often the target who responds to quietly upscale descriptive copy won't buy from any other source.

Quietly upscale descriptive copy usually has a long headline. Salsa copy might look like this:

> **For your next party, this unusually hot sauce with the unusually hot name can be the evening's hottest topic of conversation.**
> "Hell-Fire" isn't for everybody. In fact, we don't recommend its daily use, because it makes every other sauce seem so tame. . . .

The writer has to keep the leash on quietly descriptive copy at just the right amount of tension. That's why this approach requires the professional laying on of hands.

"Image All the Way" Copy

Image all the way copy differs from quietly descriptive copy in its less-subtle approach to exclusivity. Like its first cousin, "touchstone" copy, image all the way depends on a tie to a known and accepted comparative base.

Image all the way copy for the salsa might read this way:

> If J.P. Morgan and John D. Rockefeller came to your home, they'd know whether to stay for the

> authentic Mexican dinner you've prepared. "Hell-Fire" on the table means genuine 'Tex-Mex' on the palate.

Image all the way usually has longer sentences than other types of catalog copy. It doesn't use bullets, because excitement and image aren't in the same corner.

"Touchstone" Copy

Touchstone copy ties whatever we're selling to a known base. Touchstone theory is logical: The reader accepts the touchstone . . . and automatically accepts whatever is tied to the touchstone.
Touchstone salsa copy might read like this:

> If you had been in the Alamo, you'd have had the opportunity to sample real 'Tex-Mex' food. You weren't there, but the secret of good, hot 'Tex-Mex' salsa is back . . . with "Hell-Fire."

Touchstone copy isn't easy to write and it isn't always pertinent. An advantage is its adaptability: You can intermix touchstone copy with any other type and not destroy the coherent tone of the catalog.

"Narrative" Copy

Narrative copy tells a story. Depending on the narrator's story-telling expertise the reader is intrigued or turned off.
So an effective narrative catalog copywriter has to be a good yarn-spinner. Ability to add a little malarkey to the mixture doesn't hurt, but inserting fiction doesn't work in today's "the reader knows more than we do" marketplace.
Narrative copy for the salsa would read something like this:

> In 1912 the Mexican bandit and folk hero Pancho Villa escaped to the United States. After his triumphant return in 1913 he formed the famous *División del Norte*. One of the prizes he brought across the border was a recipe for a salsa unlike any tasted before: "Hell-Fire." When Villa became governor of the state of Chihuahua, he served this unique hot sauce to special guests at his dinner table. Now you can serve it to your special guests.

Writing *workmanlike* narrative copy isn't as exacting a task as writing touchstone copy; a competent writer with a competent set of reference books or notes from the company's buyer can do a competent job. Writing a catalog filled with engaging narratives requires more showmanship than most journeyman writers can bring to the arena.

"Minimalist" Copy

Minimalist copy is the standard for many digest-size catalogs which have eight or ten items on a page. Description is bare-bones.

Minimalist copy for the salsa:

> Famous "Hell-Fire" Salsa—the very hottest. 14-oz. bottle, $2.49

Photographs accompanying minimalist copy, like the words themselves, have to be no-nonsense.

"All the Facts" Copy

All the facts copy regurgitates any and every scrap of information about the product. The two assumptions: 1) The more the reader knows, the more likely the reader is to buy. 2) The more you tell, the more the reader believes you.

These assumptions become truer in business-to-business catalogs than in consumer catalogs, because the business buyer may have to justify the purchase to someone else—and we don't know who that someone else might be or what minor fact might trigger approval.

In defense of all the facts copy in consumer catalogs: Some of our customers are catalog "readers" who resond to heavy copy. An example of all the facts copy about salsa:

> **"Hell-Fire" Salsa**—Bottled in limited quantities in Matamoros, this authentic 'Tex-Mex' salsa combines red peppers, jalapeños, green chili peppers, peeled and chopped beefsteak tomatoes, scallions, and a touch of cilantro. Our peppers are transplanted from their original site in French Guiana to a private orchard outside Matamoros, where parallel climate ripens them to produce the hot capsicum extract. Our master chef Pablo grinds the pepper to a fine powder, soaks them in brine to "loosen" the flavor, then marries them to the tomatoes in our special sharp vinegar....

Obviously all the facts copy demands space. If we were actually selling a $2.49 salsa, it's unlikely a lengthy description would justify a heavy dedication of space.

"Informational/Educational" Copy

Informational/educational copy is a specialty. To maintain its integrity, this type of copy dares not lapse into hard sell.

The writer has to pick and choose logical subject-matter for informational/educational copy. Probably salsa couldn't qualify for this treatment, but if it did the copy might read:

> **Cilantro** is the fresh leaf of the coriander plant. This delicate fragrant-pungent leaf is one of the oldest spices known to man. When the Romans used finely-chopped cilantro to season their bread, the spice already had been known for thousands of years. Each 14-oz. bottle of "Hell-Fire" Salsa includes both cilantro and . . .

You can see the value of informational/educational copy for computer software, garden supplies, electronics, and chemicals. Properly written, this copy approach will attract readers who don't respond to exhortation; but it can repel readers who do.

"Snob Appeal" Copy

Snob appeal copy is making a comeback. From about 1975 to 1987, only a few catalogs dared risk the accusation of outright snobbery. But now, as *need for approval* rejoins the other four great motivators (*fear, exclusivity, guilt,* and *greed*), snobbery is in.

The problem with snob appeal copy isn't writing the copy itself—although I certainly wouldn't turn loose a beginner on this copy. Rather, it's the need for an exquisite matchup of copy, layout, and illustration. If any of the three falter, the effect is one of stupidity rather than status.

Snob appeal copy for the salsa might be:

> **Only 1,200 bottles . . . ever, this entire year.** Our exclusive "Hell-Fire" Salsa is made from such rare herbs, under such rigidly controlled conditions, that only 1,200 bottles will be available this year. We must limit any purchase to two bot-

> tles (subject to availability, of course). Each numbered bottle carries the Seal of Elegance. Handsomely gift boxed for your favorite gourmet who cannot obtain this elsewhere. 14 ounces, twenty-nine dollars.

Much snob appeal copy spells out the price. That's why, to the would-be snob, "twenty-nine dollars" has greater verisimilitude than the more pedestrian $28.95. You say the price should be just $2.49? Forget it.

"I Am the Greatest" Copy

A supercilious approach will attract some of the status-seeking buyers who want reassurance.

Unlike snob appeal copy, I am the greatest copy makes a flat statement of superiority. The believing reader buys; the nonbeliever doesn't buy. Gradually the catalog builds a house list of customers for whom the flat statement of superiority becomes a reason to buy. (Once disillusioned, the customer is gone forever.)

I am the greatest copy for the salsa:

> THE BEST SALSA. In comparison tests, our Kitchen Board rated this salsa superior in consistency, palatability, and flavor. Unlike other sauces tested, "Hell-Fire" contains genuine tomatoes and fresh spices, producing a greater degree of effectiveness when applied to both tortillas and salads. $2.49, unconditionally guaranteed.

The hedging in I am the greatest copy turns me off because of the inevitable weaseling—"Superior" to what? "Unlike other sauces *tested*"? Which sauces, better than "Hell-Fire," didn't you include in your tests?

Still, no one can argue with the ability of I am the greatest copy to sell merchandise. Even recognizing the weasel, I've bought from such catalogs.

"Plain Vanilla" Copy

An experienced copywriter with lexical imagination is overtrained for plain vanilla copy.

Actually, plain vanilla—copy unadorned with hyperbole or puffery—is a pleasant relief after wading through the thick, adjective-rich rhetoric we see in so much contemporary catalog copy. Plain vanilla copy for the salsa rids itself of all but distilled essence:

> **"Hell-Fire" Hot Salsa**—14-oz. bottle. Ingredients: red peppers, jalapeños, green chili peppers, beefsteak tomatoes, scallions, cilantro. $2.49.

If yours is a catalog of exotica—and "Hell-Fire" Salsa would qualify—plain vanilla copy is too bland to do a competitive selling job. Plain vanilla is the floor under all catalog copy; its primary value is in multi-product catalogs of household staples.

We don't see much plain vanilla copy any more. The closest in everyday use is what we might call "vanilla ripple"—a touch of sell mixed into the plain description, with an occasional exclamation point added as a rhetorical moisturizer to prevent dryness.

Making the Choice

Can you combine copy types within the same catalog?

My answer is an unequivocal *yes*. There's an *if:*

To intermix a copy approach which differs from the rest of the catalog, set up a section—four or eight pages. It's like a special boutique (or even bargain basement) within a department store. Border the pages differently. Tell the reader this is a special section; don't cause confusion by forcing the reader to wonder whether the printer has bound some wrong pages into the good old catalog.

If your sales have reached a plateau. . . if your universe seems to be shrinking. . . if you have to pass up items because they don't match your "image". . . then consider a section of "different" copy. You just might attract a whole new cadre of buyers.

Figure 1-1A

"If I had a dime for every time I've..." is classic "Jes' folk" copy. Logic isn't a factor—if he ran out of batteries a hundred times he'd have ten dollars, hardly enough to retire. "Jes folks" establishes the image of being a good guy; that's what this copy does.

Sports Enthusiasts: Now You Can Tape Outdoor Action Without Worrying About Weather, Water, or Whales ...

I learned my lesson the expensive way. We were 2 miles off the Maui coast in a 19' Zodiac searching for humpback whales. It was February, prime whale watch season in Hawaii, so I brought along my Sony Pro 8mm camcorder. Already I could imagine zooming in on a mother and calf, great tails arching skyward before slipping beneath the surf. I checked my Sony Pro one last time, then heard the Captain bellow "Thar she blows!." Every pair of eyes on board swung to port, and sure enough spotted the distinctive plumes of vapor on the horizon. The Captain turned into the wind, and then disaster struck.

The $1500 Wave! *— As we came about, the rubber Zodiac's blunt bow slammed into a wave, and our side of the craft caught a heavy spray. It was kind of fun, until I noticed the water droplets on my camcorder. As the Zodiac raced towards the whales, I stared anxiously through the Sony's viewfinder — nothing! I wiped it, shook it, blew it off, and still it wouldn't respond. Here we were, 250 yards from a herd of humpbacks, and I had a dead videocamera!*

A Spectacular Show *— Well, the whales were in rare form that day, rolling, diving, blowing, and yes, jumping, as if there were no tomorrow! Of course I couldn't entirely enjoy it, thinking about the tape that might have been, and my lifeless Sony Pro. After a good 45 minutes of whale frolicking, the Captain proudly proclaimed that we'd witnessed the best showing of the season, a once in a lifetime experience!*

Sony's 8mm Sportscam is the camcorder I *should* have taken to Hawaii, and it's the only one we now own. With a rugged, water-resistant sports body, you can get right in the middle of outdoor action without fearing for your camera's safety! You can't submerge it, but Sportscam easily withstands the splash and spray you'll encounter on a boat, dock, or by a pool. An extensive system of O-ring seals, plugs and control covers means you can get great tapes in foul weather, and along a windswept beach, where salt spray and blowing sand would cripple lesser cameras. Sportscam also takes a punch, with a thick Lexan case that's a lot more shock-resistant than ordinary cameras.

No Sacrifices — Sportscam delivers all the sophistication of Sony's top-end videocameras, plus some neat features of its own. Autofocus 6:1 power zoom lens (w/macro) spans a 9-54 mm range perfect for panoramic landscapes as well as close-ups. A variable high-speed shutter (1/60-1/4000th/sec) captures the fastest motion. Low-light performance is extraordinary, needing minimum illumination of just 4 lux for good reproduction. Sony's newest ½" CCD image sensor with true RGB color process gives sensationally vivid hues. And impressive crystal-clear special effects let you study details in slow motion, freeze-frame, or frame-by-frame, all with no "snow" whatsoever! (great for golf swings!). Pivoting electronic viewfinder even lets you shoot from the hip!

The Only Camera You'll Need! — With its comprehensive list of features (ie. flying erase head, advance edit search and insert, date/time generator, 2-page digital graphics superimposer), Sportscam will do everything that its less-athletic syblings will. But while the others stay home, Sportscam can join you in the rugged outdoors! Complete outfit includes: padded case, rechargeable battery, RF adaptor, antenna switch, and extended battery case (gives 2¼ hrs. of continuous operation!). *Weight 3 lbs. 9 oz.; 5¼" x 5¾" x 12⅝"* **#V540 Sony Sportscam (8mm) — $1599.00** 13

Figure 1-1B

This description *starts* as a "Jes' folks" episode. The writer (wisely) decided the artifice wouldn't sustain a lengthy description of a $1599 camcorder and switches to "All the facts" copy.

Go Ahead and Give This Auto-Everything Zeiss/Yashica 35mm Camera to Your Wife — She May Let You Use It!

My father gave this slick rangefinder to my mother for their anniversary (such a romantic!). It has auto-focus, auto-load, auto-wind/rewind, auto-flash, auto film-speed setting (ISO 64-1600) — you name it. Perfect for someone who likes fine photography, but doesn't want to fool around with lenses and exposure settings. So imagine my surprise when I caught Dad shooting roll after roll with Mom's camera! Now, my father worked 30 years for Eastman Kodak (and for Bachrach Studios before that). He owns more SLRs than I do, including a new $2400 Leica R4. So why the fascination with the Zeiss/Yashica T3?

Zeiss Optics — The T3 is the only autofocus camera with optics by Carl Zeiss, the incomparable West German lens maker. Unlike cheaper point and shoot cameras that use plastic lenses, the T3's 35mm f2.8 lens consists of 4 glass elements in 3 groups, all with costly Zeiss Tessar T*multicoating. As a result, pictures taken with the T3 exhibit outstanding color tone and balance, with sharpness that pleases even the most critical eye (like my father's!). To protect those Zeiss optics, the power switch is cleverly integrated with a sliding lens shield, so when you're not shooting, the lens won't collect dust and scratches.

An Engineering Marvel — Auto film-loading ends the hassles of jamming the film leader into the take-up spool. Auto-wind takes you to the next shot — at end-of-roll, the T3 even rewinds automatically! Auto-focus (from 20 inches to infinity!) uses an active infra-red beam for accuracy. Silicon Photo Diode (SPD) instantly measures lighting for perfect exposures every time. Auto flash fires by itself in low light, indoors or out; recycles in just 0.6 sec. And a 10 second self-timer LED flashes so you know when to smile!

With its high degree of automation and small size, the T3 is a quick-reacting camera that lets you capture spontaneous events you might otherwise miss with your SLR. And because it's completely splash and water-resistant, you can safely use the T3 in rain, snow, or on your boat (but *not* underwater!). It doesn't come in pastel colors, and doesn't have a catchy name, because it's a serious camera for those who appreciate fine photography (which of course explains my father's fascination). And it does make a perfect gift for the woman in your life!

#P855 Zeiss/Yashica T3 — $259.00 (requires 6V lithium battery not included)
#P857 Lithium Battery (6V) — $12.95   #P858 Padded Case — $14.95
#P856 Zeiss/Yashica T3 w/Data Back — $289.00 (imprints date or time on photos)

Figure 1-1C

The first sentence identifies this as "Jes' folks" copy. The reader may be skeptical about the writer's father using this camera, which doesn't even have basic SLR, when he has a $2400 Leica sitting on the shelf.

Bath COMFORTS℠

A. Running out of hot water in the middle of a shower is frustrating, to say the least ... but, since we've installed this *energy saving shower head*, the amount of hot water in our tank goes much further AND we save money on heating costs, too. While

Guaranteed to pay for itself in water savings

Our water-saving shower head

2½ gallons per minute

Conventional shower head

6 gallons per minute

reducing water flow up to 70%, it increases velocity giving you the benefit of a *full-bodied spray* (which adjusts easily with fingertip control). The easy-mount shower head plugs into all standard showers, in minutes. Includes lifetime, non-clogging guarantee. Made in England.

#B5287 ENERGY SAVING SHOWER HEAD $20.00

B. Since I put this triple magnifier mirror on my medicine cabinet door, I don't have to put my glasses on to see as I floss my teeth and put on make-up. My son, Bill, thinks it's just wonderful for shaving. It holds on to any clean, smooth surface (tile, too!) by means of 3 powerful suction cups. The lucite-framed mirror measures 9½" in diameter. P.S. The 2X magnified (6" in dia.) size is great for travel.

#B4026 STICK-ON MIRROR (9½") $25.00
#B4027 STICK-ON MIRROR (6") $12.00

C. Thanks to my 85-year old mother, I realized that she and many others find it difficult both sitting and rising from the normal toilet seat height. This 5" high elevated polyethelene seat really helps. It sits right on the bowl and has a special bracket that slips under your existing toilet seat to secure it against tipping or sliding. No tools or clamps are needed and it removes easily for cleaning. Since she cannot be without it, I had a nylon (moisture repellent lined) carrier bag specially designed for her to travel with discreetly. *Not for elongated seats.*＊▣

#B2409 SECURE-HOLD RAISED TOILET SEAT $28.50
#B2009 CARRIER BAG $19.00

D. Being able to take care of yourself *by yourself* is a wonderful thing — especially when it comes to bathing and personal hygiene. The new open design of this chair allows you to cleanse more effectively and independently. You can reach **all** areas, *even while seated*. The "vinyl on foam" cushion provides a supportive padded surface and eases contact pressure. The legs easily adjust in height by push button from 15½" to 20" and have non-slip rubber tips. The chair is corrosive resistant and is also available without a back. A special chair for special needs with new features well worth the cost.＊▣

#B1064 OPEN BATH SEAT $98.00
#B1065 OPEN SEAT (without back) $71.00

E. Having to wipe up the wet floor everytime somebody takes a shower is frustrating. Splash Enders close the gap between shower curtain and wall. You get two molded corner inserts made of durable white plastic and a tube of caulking. Simple instructions are included for quick and easy installation. End bathroom mop up at last!

#B8510 SPLASH ENDERS $15.00

F. The last time I slipped while bathing, I vowed that I would never enter the tub again without a safety mat. I found this oversized mat which is 30% longer and larger so it *covers more slippery surface* than ordinary mats. Dome-shaped suction cups create a strong anchor, provide a soft cushion of air for your body and feet, and also create a "toe grip" foothold for an extra measure of protection. Made of high quality vinyl and machine washable. White only.

#B1852 NON-SLIP BATH MAT (15½" x 40¾") $15.50

NEW! Soft Foam Cushion Construction

COMFORTABLY YOURS℠ 　　＊No Gift Wrap Available 　　▣ Federal Express Not Available

Figure 1-2

Six items on this page. A, B, C, and F are pure "Down home personality." D and E, although not first person singular, are written in the same style. Don't you get the feeling you're part of this writer's family? That's the common thread joining "Jes' folks" and "Down home personality"; the two techniques differ in "Down home's" relating episodes to what the catalog is selling.

Makes Cellular Safer by Silencing Your Stereo When the Car Phone Rings!

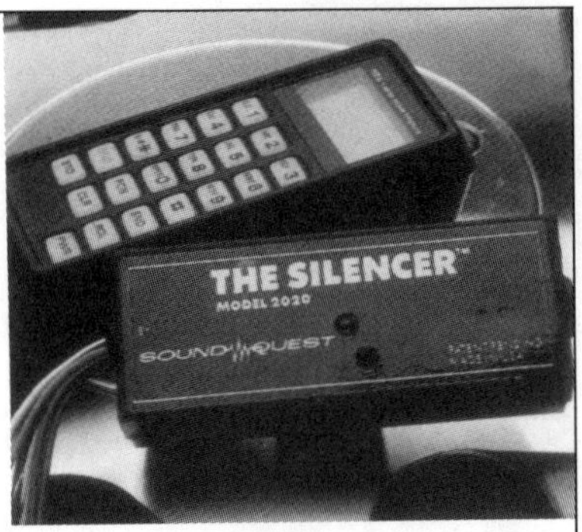

If you've ever played your car stereo above moderate levels, you know how easy it is to miss an important call. And how distracting (and dangerous) it can be to answer the phone, reach for the radio, and drive, all at the same time! Our solution is the Silencer, an easily installed relay that detects incoming calls, *just before* the phone starts to ring, and automatically turns your stereo off while the phone is in use. So you won't have to take your eyes off the road, or your hands off the wheel! Hang up, and the Silencer automatically turns your stereo back on. Works for both incoming calls and dialing out.

#M624 Cellular Silencer — $39.95

Figure 1-3

Variations of the word *you* appear nine times in this short copyblock. *You* is the safest word we have, not just in catalog copy but in the entire world of force-communication. "You-you-you" copy can breed antagonism if it's obviously forced; this well-written copy isn't.

Figure 1-4A

"Shout" copy emphasizes bargain pricing. Neatness can actually damage the effectiveness of shout copy. This retail catalog cover screams its giant word "Sale!" and terms such as "limit 6 boxes" and "stock up."

Figure 1-4B

This two-page spread shouts, but not stridently. Every item has a "Save" sticker (in red on the original), and the big oval at top left shouts, "$10–$122 off!" Historians please note: See the "Good," "Better," "Best" on the chairs? This is the labeling technique Sears used during its golden days.

FURNITURE SPECTACULAR!

✔ **SHIPPED VIA UPS.** All chairs are shipped by economical UPS to save you money on shipping charges.

✔ **MEET RIGID SPECS!** Chairs shown are BIFMA (Business and Industrial Furniture Manufacturer's Association) approved.

THIS IS THE BEST MULTI-FUNCTION TASK CHAIR FOR AROUND $130 WE'VE EVER SEEN!

THIS QUILL EXCLUSIVE HAS 5 CONTROLS!

SAVE $10 off regular price

Shown in Blue— also in:
Brown · Grey · Sand

Shown in Mauve— also in:
Beige · Lt. Brown · Grey · Black

Shown in Grey— also in:
Brown

[5] **BETTER** — SAVE $101 off manufacturer's list — List $251.00 SALE PRICE **149⁸⁸** each

[6] **BEST** — SAVE $116 off manufacturer's list — List $296.00 SALE PRICE **179⁸⁸** each

A QUILL EXCLUSIVE!

Reg. $129.99 SALE PRICE **119⁸⁸** each

HAVE 3 (OR MORE) CONTROLS

(5) DELUXE SERIES (BETTER)

Has all the features checked above, plus a full array of adjustments to give you complete control over your seating. You can instantly adjust the seat height with the gas-lift lever. You can adjust the pitch of the chair back and front-to-back tilt. The tilt tension and chair back height adjust by turning a knob. The padded back has extra contours to provide you with complete lumbar support; the extra-large seat is 2½-3¼" thick with medium density foam padding for best comfort, back is 2-2½" thick. All foam is fire-retardant for safety. The seat and back are covered with comfortable Herculon/Nouvelle fabric. Seat measures 20Wx19"D. Seat height adjusts from 18½-23½". Back measures 16Hx16½"W. Shpg. wt. 26 lbs. Shipped UPS. F.O.B. Tennessee or California factory (shipping charges additional). Allow 15 working days for shipping, plus normal transit time.
306-S-981-* .... Sale Price, Each $149.88
*Specify Color: Blue—BE; Sand—SA; Brown—BN; Grey—GY.

DELUXE SERIES (BETTER) WITH ARMS

Has the same quality features as the 981 chair shown above, plus molded and padded armrests for style and comfort. Shpg. wt. 34 lbs. Shipped same as chair above.
306-S-981A-* List $302.00
Sale Price, Each $179.88
*Specify Color: Blue—BE; Sand—SA; Brown—BN; Grey—GY.

SAVE $122 — SALE PRICE **179⁸⁸** each

(6) DELUXE SERIES (BEST)

Our best gas-lift chair is designed to cradle you in comfort and fight fatigue even for extended periods of time! Has all the features checked above, plus controls that adjust the chair seat up and down, as well as adjust the chair back up and down, forward and backward. Seat and back tilt together. Extra-large seat and back provide more comfortable operating. Herculon/Nouvelle fabric in your choice of colors. Pneumatic gas-lift mechanism gives you instant seat-height adjustment from 18½-23½". 5-strut base has molded plastic caps that cover and protect chair legs; dual wheel casters that roll easily on any floor surface. Seat measures 19Wx17½"D. Back measures 11½Hx16"W. Seat is 3½" thick; back is 2½" thick. Shpg. wt. 27 lbs. Shipped UPS. F.O.B. Tennessee or California factory (shipping charges additional). Allow 10-15 working days for shipping, plus normal transit time.
306-S-801-* .... Price, Ea $179.88
*Specify color: Mauve—MV; Light Brown—LTBN; Grey—GY; Beige—BG; Black—BK.

CREATE A NEW OFFICE LOOK WITH OFFICE PARTITIONS SOLD ON PAGE 46.

DELUXE GAS-LIFT CHAIR

Designed exclusively for Quill to be one of the most value-packed chairs on the market today! All chair adjustments can be made from a seated position (no need to turn or handle the chair in any way). The large cushioned and contoured seat and back are fire retardant and foam covered with a wool/polyester fabric. The stable 5-strut base adds stability and support. Bellows style seat and back supports add a touch of distinction. Seat measures 17½Wx15¾"D. Back measures 10Hx16"W. Seat is 2¾" thick, back is 2" thick. Shpg. wt. 30 lbs. Shipped by economical UPS, usually within 8-32 hours of receipt of order. F.O.B. Quill (shpg. chrgs. add'l.).
306-S-Q699-GY—Grey .... Each $119.88
306-S-Q699-BN—Brown .. Each $119.88

TOTAL ADJUSTABILITY!

(1) Pitch of chair back adjusts with a turn of a knob

(2) Front to back tilt adjusts with a lever, allows free floating motion, and locks in any position

(3) Chair tilt tension adjusts with a knob

(4) Seat height adjusts from 18½-23½" with a touch of the pneumatic gas-lift lever

(5) Chair back height adjusts with the turn of a knob

⑪

19

Figure 1-5A

Is this "quietly upscale" or "snob appeal" copy? A sentence such as "The sumptuous bouquet and velvet texture of fine mature red Burgundy seems to demand a more round and open bowl for its develop-

ment than even the noblest Bordeaux" (copy block D) could be either. Because this copy appears in a wine-lover's catalog, we categorize it as quietly upscale. If it were in a department store catalog, it probably would be snob appeal. You can see how the *type* of copy can change automatically as the *type* of catalog reader changes.

Furniture designer and third generation Californian Robert Ferguson originally built this bench to commemorate the cottage garden cultivated at the Sausalito Woman's Club. His design complements the architecture of the turn-of-the-century clubhouse, a work by architect Julia Morgan. The bold, linear design of the bench and chair echo Morgan's concern for honesty, simplicity and functionality in architecture. Even the detailing, the exposed mortise and tenon joinery and the geometric beveling, is rooted in function, giving this furniture an enduring quality. Made of cedar, a durable wood used in greenhouse construction, the furniture will weather to a silvery grey. The bench is shown weathered; the chair is shown new. A table designed to complement these two pieces is available (see Specifications pages 28 and 29.)

■ BENCH 5'   #5784 $450
■ ARMCHAIR   #5785 $325
■ TABLE   #5786 $210

415-383-2000 17

Figure 1-5B

For "quietly upscale" copy to achieve the proper image, illustration has to match. Placing the bench in a tailored garden gives this tableau the look of a classical painting. Long sentences, which have a calming effect, match the upscale description. Quietly upscale copy matches a specific reader-demographic. The bargain buyer would be puzzled and quickly bored by references to Robert Ferguson and Julia Morgan.

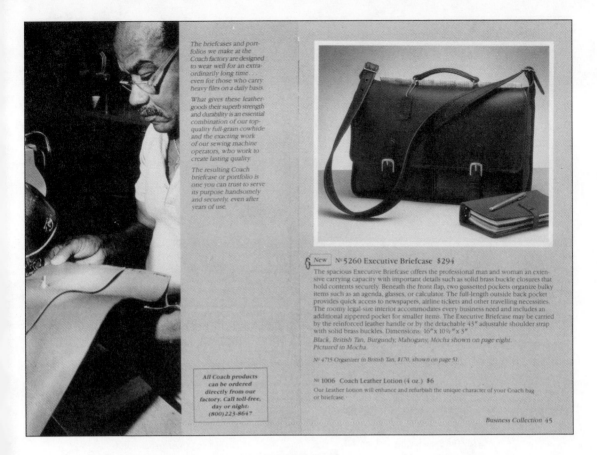

The briefcases and portfolios we make at the Coach factory are designed to wear well for an extraordinarily long time... even for those who carry heavy files on a daily basis.

What gives these leathergoods their superb strength and durability is an essential combination of our top-quality full-grain cowhide and the exacting work of our sewing machine operators, who work to create lasting quality.

The resulting Coach briefcase or portfolio is one you can trust to serve its purpose handsomely and securely, even after years of use.

All Coach products can be ordered directly from our factory. Call toll-free, day or night: (800)223-8647

New Nº 5260 Executive Briefcase $294

The spacious Executive Briefcase offers the professional man and woman an extensive carrying capacity with important details such as solid brass buckle closures that hold contents securely. Beneath the front flap, two gusseted pockets organize bulky items such as an agenda, glasses, or calculator. The full-length outside back pocket provides quick access to newspapers, airline tickets and other travelling necessities. The roomy legal-size interior accommodates every business need and includes an additional zippered pocket for smaller items. The Executive Briefcase may be carried by the reinforced leather handle or by the detachable 43" adjustable shoulder strap with solid brass buckles. Dimensions: 16" x 10½" x 3"
Black, British Tan, Burgundy, Mahogany, Mocha shown on page eight.
Pictured in Mocha.

Nº 4715 Organizer in British Tan, $170, shown on page 51.

Nº 1006 Coach Leather Lotion (4 oz.) $6
Our Leather Lotion will enhance and refurbish the unique character of your Coach bag or briefcase.

Business Collection 45

Figure 1-6

"Image all the way" copy emphasizes the company at least as much as whatever the company is selling. Image eats up space, which explains why some catalogers who might want to use the approach feel the laws of economics make it impossible for them. For years this catalog has used whole pages for pure image...suggesting the major dedication of space has worked successfully.

Figure 1-7A

Accuracy is no novelty in today's quartz-watch ambience. The "touchstone" of tying the watch to Swiss trains in both copy and illustration (see the timetable under the watches?) is a clever way to establish uniqueness in a competitive marketplace.

Figure 1-7B

Whatever you think of the Beatles, you can't seriously compare them with Bach. That's what makes this "touchstone" so charming. In less-sure hands, copy for a recording *not* by the Beatles (nor Bach), but by a relatively unknown "coterie" musician, would have had little selling-power.

Easily Scoop Rock-Hard Ice Cream With The Original Zeroll® Server

Invented in 1935, the *patented* Zeroll Ice Cream Scoop is an American-made marvel of simplicity and clever engineering. As you grasp its contoured aluminum handle, the warmth of your hand is transferred by a sealed internal fluid to the scoop. Even the *hardest* ice cream dishes out easily and releases instantly from the scoop.

Honored by New York's Museum of Modern Art design collection, it remains one of the most effective ice cream scoops ever created.

#582115 **Zeroll® Ice Cream Scoop $14.95** *(1 lb.)*

Figure 1-8

"Narrative" copy tells a story. This description of a mundane item—an ice cream scoop—does it well. Suppose *you* had the job of justifying a $14.95 price for an ice cream scoop. Would you have been able to sidestep the problem as nimbly as this writer did?

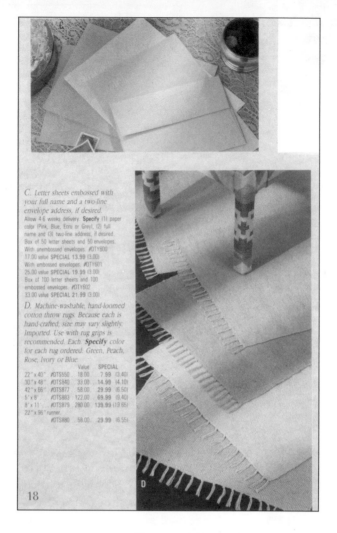

Figure 1-9

Bare-bones "minimalist" copy peels away the frills: "Just the facts, ma'am." This *doesn't* give the copywriter latitude to omit pertinent selling facts; the technique supposedly forces focus on subject rather than adjectives. In my opinion minimalist copy is flat, but some catalogs use it and seem to be thriving.

Figure 1-10

Heavy copy? You bet. "All the facts" copy empties the fact-basket. It's best used in situations such as this, in which the difference between similar items lies in facts the knowledgeable reader will ferret out.

Figure 1-11A

When a catalog introduces an item whose use and benefit may not be known to the reader, copy has to educate as well as sell. "Informational/educational" copy is the right way to present "Hello on hold" to this catalog's readers. Will some readers think it's too much copy? Will some turn the page, muttering, "Why didn't they get to the point?" Sure. But would those readers have bought anyway?

ROSE 'Princesse de Monaco' - ('Princess of Monaco')
A Wayside Exclusive Introduction

One of the most spectacular and interesting hybrid tea roses to have been bred in Europe in many years, and one we are proud to have introduced.

The tragic passing of Princess Grace of Monaco emphasized the touching personal history of this rose. Since the 1956 wedding of Prince Rainier and Grace Kelly, there developed a close friendship between the royal family and the House of Meilland, for years one of the world's leading rose hybridizers. Francis Meilland presented roses to Princess Grace on her wedding day and received a gold medal from the royal couple in memory of the occasion. In 1973, Meilland dedicated a new rose to the young Princess Stephanie, and in 1976 a rose garden was dedicated to Francis Meilland by Monaco, which in 1981 hosted the first International Rose Show.

Among the new roses that the Meillands exhibited at that show was a bicolor with rouge and cream buds which opened into perfect, full blooms of rich ivory, tinged with a deep pink blush (the colors of the Principality). Each was displayed to perfection against the dark, glossy foliage. Initially exhibited under the name 'Preference', its credentials were enhanced by having the worldfamous 'Peace' as an ancestor. Princess Grace immediately declared it her favorite, and Alain Meilland decided to rename it 'Princesse de Monaco' in her honor.

'Princesse de Monaco' is now proving an exceptionally fine rose for the show table. Already an international award winner, it has proved its versatility — ideal as a bedding subject, its prolifically produced blooms are also perfect for exhibition, cutting and arranging. Blooms are produced all season and are weather resistant, holding their distinctive color despite heat. Although it is sometimes slow to break dormancy, once started, this rose produces blooms all season.

450-887   Each $10.75, Three $30.00, Six $56.00

ROSE 'Royal Velvet' - *A Wayside Exclusive Introduction*
Roses should be red, and this is one of the reddest ever! Originated by Marie-Louise Meilland, of the famed House of Meilland, this glorious Hybrid Tea is unsurpassed for its prodigious display of bright, clear red blooms — a truly spectacular display in the garden. The high centered, nearly black buds open to huge blooms of clear, bright red, with no touch of blue whatsoever. The center remains high, while the outer petals roll back, never showing the white markings so common in other red roses. Flower production is continuous and generous, with blooms held well above the foliage on strong stems. Plants are vigorous with excellent base branching and strong canes. Foliage is glossy dark green . . . the large leaves clothe the plants nearly down to the ground. In addition, 'Royal Velvet' also displays excellent winter hardiness. Truly breathtaking in the garden and an excellent cut flower variety.

451-017   Each $9.00, Three $25.00, Six $45.00

ROSE 'Michelle Meilland' - *Exquisite!*
Truly a rose for the connoisseur! Flowers of dainty appearance are light pink, sometimes showing a faint tinge of lilac — other times subtly marked coral or yellow. Flowers are held on long, sturdy stems, excellent for cutting. There is a unique, porcelain-like quality about the blooms which gives them unmatched pristine beauty. Francis Meilland, the hybridizer, who developed many world famous roses, including 'Peace' (offered on page 52), considered it to have the aura of perfection found only among aristocrats. Truly outstanding among roses, but slow to propagate, hence quite rare and in extremely limited supply. For sheer perfection of form and color, delicacy and grace, this rose has no equal!

450-837   Each $12.75, Three $35.00, Six $67.00

Rose 'Princesse de Monaco' - Chosen by Princess Grace of Monaco as her favorite at the First International Rose Show in Monaco, June, 1981. An Exclusive Wayside Introduction

'Royal Velvet' - A glorious red, red rose!

'Michelle Meilland'

Michelle Meilland at the Meilland test garden in Lyon, France.

Figure 1-11B

Rose-lovers will read every word of this "informational/educational" copy. It actually tells a story, making it the first cousin of "narrative" copy. Will *non*-rose lovers respond to such heavy copy? Who cares?

Figure 1-11C

"Informational/educational" copy is often the best way to sell a mechanical or electronic device whose value may not be apparent. Without the informational first paragraph (which in my opinion should be separated into at least three paragraphs), a prospective buyer would be considerably less likely to consider buying one of these sprayers.

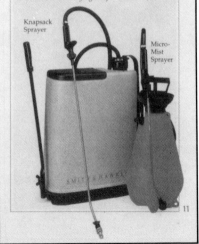

SMITH & HAWKEN

SMITH & HAWKEN SPRAYERS

Many organic pest control products are best applied with a sprayer. Ours are designed and engineered specifically for garden use, utilizing a micromist spray technique: liquids are vaporized into a fog to penetrate foliage, leaving just the minimum of treatment solution on plants. Far superior to most sprayers, ours offer three distinct advantages. First, their positive shutoff valves absolutely eliminate leaks and drips. Second, clogging, which can make inexpensive sprayers worthless, is overcome with removable filters. And third, our sprayers are made of durable lightweight polypropylene for structural strength and complete corrosion resistance.

KNAPSACK SPRAYER

This professional sprayer holds up to five gallons, with a form-fitting design and straps for comfort. The jet-action agitator insures positive mixing, and the quick-pressurizing pump allows continuous spraying with little effort. The pump lever is switchable for left- or right-handed use. Comes with a 48" hose, brass extension wand and fully adjustable brass nozzle.
#8063 **$124**

MICRO-MIST GARDEN SPRAYERS

Available in two sizes, the Micro-Mist Garden Sprayer is best suited for home gardening where planted areas are not expansive. Every bit as rugged as the professional-size Knapsack Sprayer, it features an innovative teardrop design for stability, a funnel top for no-spill filling, a quick-pressurizing pump for easier operation, an extralong, 48", hose with a brass extension wand for maximum reach and chemical resistance, and a pressure relief valve for safety and ease of unloading. Two nozzles are standard: one for straight-stream and ultrafine misting; and a second for flat, fan-type spraying, for optimal coverage.
1¾ Gallon (shown below, right) *#8061* **$44**
3 Gallon, with carrying strap *#8062* **$58**

Knapsack
Sprayer

Micro-
Mist
Sprayer

11

30

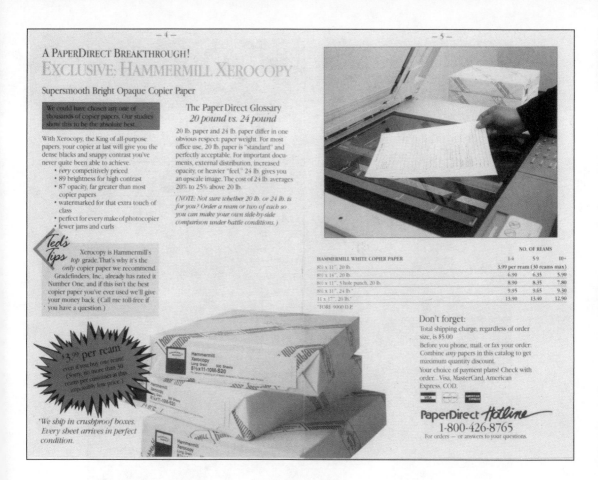

Figure 1-11D

This spread from a digest-size paper catalog is near-perfect use of "informational/educational" copy. The block headed "The Paper-Direct Glossary" describes the difference between 20 lb. and 24 lb. paper—and makes the logical suggestion: "Not sure whether 20 lb. or 24 lb. is for you? Order a ream or two each so you can make your own side-by-side comparison. . . ." *Useful* information is the logical base for asking for an order. It's the height of the art of informational/educational copywriting.

21A-C. For many, if they could only own one bag, it would be by Louis Vuitton. Vuitton creations set a style in the 19th century, and still do. 21A. The double-handled tote, 15 × 22", 175.00 (4.00). 21B. The curved-top handbag with zipper closure, shoulder strap, 12½ × 9½", 295.00 (4.25). 21C. The famous double-handled satchel, with lock and zipper, 7 × 10", 150.00 (3.90). All are made of vinyl-impregnated Egyptian cotton canvas. The Vuitton Boutique.

Figure 1-12A

The very name Louis Vuitton is synonymous with "snob appeal," and this catalog description makes the most of it. The first few words are a pure appeal to snobbery. (A prop giving a clue to the size of these bags would have aided clarity.)

ARISTOCRATIC ELEGANCE
Time Honored Magnificence - a Rare Find - a typical Renaissance Home nestled in a Beautiful Tropical paradise between the ambience of Boca Raton and the sophistication of Fort Lauderdale within easy access of International Airports, Exclusive Shopping, all of the Arts, yet sequested from it all in your own Kingdom by the Sea. Dock your yacht at your door in a "No Wake Zone".
Offered at: $1,650,000.

Figure 1-12B

"Snob appeal" here is underscored by words such as *aristocratic* and *elegance* and *ambience* and *sophistication.* Just one thing wrong with this picture and one other thing wrong with this description, in a catalog of expensive homes. Picture: Where's the house? The picture shows a row of houses, not one of them close enough to be recognizable. Description: Specifics? Zilch. If I were plunking down $1,650,000 for a house I'd at least want to know how many bedrooms it has.

OLIVE OIL
NO FOOD CONNOISSEUR
WILL WANT TO BE
WITHOUT

Today's interest in foods that are pure and true has led to a new popularity for olive oil – once revered by the ancient Etruscans for its rejuvenating qualities. Now, many of us are finding that the taste and bouquet of the oil are just the touch needed to enhance the flavour of a steamed vegetable or a bowl of salad greens.

When selecting olive oil it is important to remember that it is graded by quality. Only Extra-Extra or Extra-Virgin comes from the first pressing of the olives which makes this top grade oil more difficult to find.

California Cold Pressed Extra-Virgin Olive Oil
Made from the first pressing of tree-ripened California Mission olives exclusively, it's cold pressed and Extra-Virgin quality. Intense and fruity in flavour, it reminds one of the best olive oils of Provence and Tuscany. To accompany your steak, use in a classic salad dressing combined with a Thomas Garraway™ Dijon Mustard and Red Wine Vinegar. Also a distinguished steak marinade.

| 90280 | California Cold Pressed Extra-Virgin Oil | 12 fl. oz. | $9.95 |

THE SOPHISTICATED
SHALLOT

California Dried Shallots
The premier onion for serious cooking, these beautiful shallots are intense in taste, yet sweet and delicate. Chopped fresh and freeze dried, they are extremely convenient when making a Béarnaise, Beurre Blanc or deglazing a sauce, and are a sophisticated substitute for onions in many recipes.

| 90166 | California Freeze-Dried Shallots | .40 oz. | $2.70 |

15

Figure 1-12C

$9.95 for 12 ounces of olive oil? Why not, if you're a status-seeker. This "snob appeal" copy succeeds despite its failure to tell us what "Extra-Extra" or "Extra-Virgin" really means. It "comes from the first pressing of the olives"? That's a start, but how is that better? And why did the writer list extra-extra first, if what the company sells is extra-virgin? (Note the impressive snob-appeal words in the "shallot" description.)

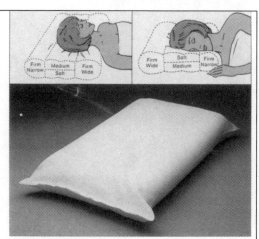

The Best Orthopedic Pillow

Based on a survey of orthopedic physicians and chiropractors conducted by the Hammacher Schlemmer Institute, this unique four-in-one orthopedic pillow was rated best for maintaining the spine's natural alignment to eliminate abnormal posture during sleep. Unlike other orthopedic pillows, its unique design combines soft and firm sections that provide stable support while cradling the neck at a precise therapeutic angle. Made of non-allergenic open-celled polyurethane and polyester fibers. Fits any standard pillow case.

33522W . . . . Postpaid $39.95

The Best Cordless Phone

THE BEST CORDLESS PHONE. In tests conducted by the Hammacher Schlemmer Institute, this cordless telephone was rated best for its unsurpassed sound quality, superior range and ease of use. In an outdoor location, this model achieved the greatest distance, transmitting clear voice signals over 900 feet from the base. Unlike other models with only one or two channels, it operates on any of the 10 FCC approved channels to eliminate interference from other cordless phones. Also unlike other models, the base unit has its own keypad, speakerphone and sliding volume control for placing calls without the handset. The memory stores nine frequently-called numbers; automatic redial; two-way intercom. NiCad battery pack (included) recharges when handset is replaced. Base plugs into household outlet and modular phone jack. High-impact plastic housing. Base height: 2½ inches. Width: 6½ inches. Length: 10 inches. Weight: 3 pounds.

35616T . . . . . . $189.50 Postpaid and Unconditionally Guaranteed

Figure 1-13

Any description beginning "The Best..." is about to launch itself into an "I am the greatest" competition. Being rated "best" by the company selling it is an act of salesmanship, not statesmanship. These two items from a well-written catalog exemplify this type of salesmanship. The cordless phone "achieved the greatest distance," 900 feet; many cordless phones advertise 1500 feet. Most now have the multi-channel capability. The analytical reader asks, "What other phones did they test against?" But that reader isn't likely to buy anyway.

Reading about "The Best Orthopedic Pillow," eyes of most readers are likely to slide acceptingly past the "survey of orthopedic physicians and chiropractors conducted by the Hammacher Schlemmer Institute." The cynic might ask, how many physicians and chiropractors? Come on, do you really test orthopedic pillows? How many others did you test? Does the description describe differences from a number of pillows with similar characteristics?

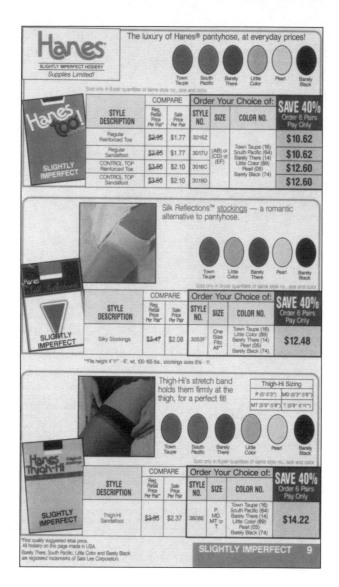

Figure 1-14A

Descriptions on this digest-size page are "plain vanilla." When price is the sole basis for sales argument and no description is necessary for comprehension, no description is necessary at all.

36

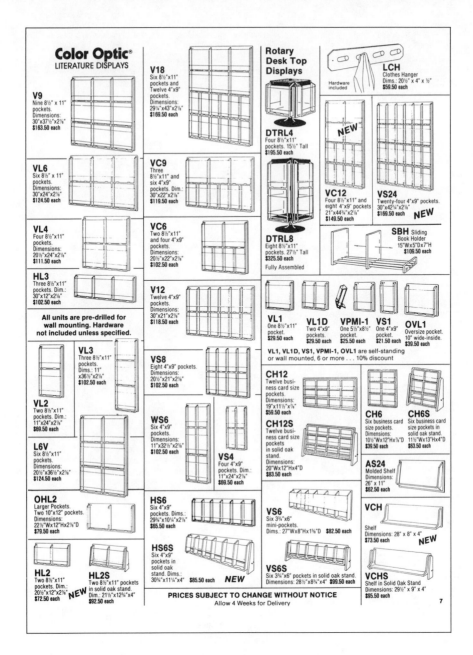

Figure 1-14B

Find one word of puffery, one enthusiastic adjective, on this page. In business-to-business catalogs, "what it is" may not only suffice as a description; puffery can irritate the prospective buyer, whose product-knowledge may exceed the catalog writer's.

CHAPTER 2

Who Hired This Guy, Anyway? We Have Lots of Words, So Why Doesn't Our Copywriter Use the Good Ones?

FIRST, *YOU* TRY IT!
Your assignment: Supply an adjective for a terry-cloth robe
you'd slip on after a swim or shower.

Take 30 seconds. No longer than that.

What was your word? *Absorbent?* Or, if you're struggling for a
superlative, *super-absorbent?* How about *spongy?* The word does
have a different ring, but it doesn't work because it doesn't really
suggest absorbency.

Did you bypass the problem with waste-of-space copy such as
the finest terry-cloth robe? Shame on you! You aren't writing catalog copy; you're just excreting nondescript words.

If you came up with *thirsty*—whether you had to lean on the
thesaurus or not—you're a catalog writer. Sure, writers have used
thirsty for half a century, describing towels. The word generates
just the right image for a terry-cloth robe.

Want proof? This is the word the catalog writer used in the actual catalog description. See Fig. 2-5.

Nondescript Descriptive Words

Every catalog writer has done it—dozens, maybe hundreds of times.
We look at our description of something we're selling, and our brains
stagger out of gear. So we give up. We use the word "beautiful" as a
descriptive word, which if we were untainted we'd admit it isn't.

"Beautiful" and "Lovely" and "Ultimate" and "Wonderful" and
"Luxurious," and their ilk, are archetypical *non*descriptive descriptive
words. You may have had as an exercise in a primitive creative writing
class this project: Write a letter to a friend and don't use the word "I"
in it. Okay, try writing a women's fashion catalog without using the
word "beautiful." See? You have to labor to leave it out.

Write in Color, Not in Black-and-White

Give the typical jaded catalog-writer the job of writing a single descriptive paragraph about sheepskin slippers and you'll get back copy
with the archetypical descriptive words: "comfortable" and "luxurious." Sure, these are adequate adjectives, but they're typical of black-
and-white descriptions which don't trigger an emotional firing-pin.

More to the point professionally, these knee-jerk-response words are reinforcements for the argument mounted by non-writers that catalog writers are hacks, mindlessly grinding out copy as though it were hamburger.

That's why the catalog writer who wrote this simple, clear, uncomplicated descriptive sentence—*in color, not in black-and-white*—has my admiration:

> Customers have told us that wearing these slippers is like going barefoot on a fur rug.

The simile strikes home. In my opinion this copy is infinitely superior to "Comfortable, toasty-warm slippers you'll scarcely know you're wearing," acceptable but uninspired copy the typical writer would have ground out.

Okay, let's try another. Let's suppose you're writing the inside-the-cover letter for a 33-year-old, family-operated catalog business. To excite and inspire the reader, would you write your message in these words?

> This season we celebrate our 33rd year of bringing you the best for your casual (or elegant) living style. We're a small, caring, family business, with the efficiency that comes from these years of experience.

I hope you *wouldn't* have written this message. Why? Because except for the word "caring," this is boiler-plate copy. The writer can pour this kind of copy out of the word-can without knowing anything about the company. That's the clue to copy which has no effect on the reader's attitude.

I'm looking at the heading over a copy-block in a consumer catalog:

> Swissmass Is The Ultimate
> Massager From Sweden

Now, let's not do what we usually do. Let's not slide around that headline, accepting it as unimaginative puffery. Suppose for once we *don't* accept the statement at face value. Suppose we say to the writer, "All right, my friend, you've said this is the *ultimate* massager. Mr. Webster says that means no massager ever will match yours. This is as far as massagers can go."

So what's the first sentence of body copy?

> You'll imagine you're being professionally mas-
> saged by the skillful touch of a trained masseur.

If that's so, and if that's the comparative benefit of this device, the headline not only misuses the word *ultimate;* it misses the boat by using generalized puffery as the point of emphasis instead of specifying what this is and does. Buried in the copy is the key—the unit has five 1-inch finger-like nodules that simulate the action of human fingers.

The effectiveness of the copy is blunted by the tired puffery of the headline, which draws no word-image to help convince the reader and ignores the unique selling-point.

A catalog writer's total description of a necklace made of semi-precious stones:

> Blue lapis is enhanced with the finest touches
> and 14K gold lustre.

What if the person paying this writer said, "Hey, hold it. What does 'enhanced with the finest touches' mean? Rewrite that description to make it descriptive." *Whatever* would have resulted would have been an improvement.

Don't Overcomplicate Your Copy

Describing an item within a predetermined amount of space is a discipline...but not necessarily a talent.

That's why so many writers can write acceptable catalog copy but stumble when they shift to some of the more dynamic forms of force-communication. It also explains why some writers who have powerful creative talent but little professional discipline can't write effective catalog copy.

"The Clarity Commandment"—Friend or Foe

Anybody who supervises the creative process for a catalog has faced this dilemma:

It's catalog writer hiring time. The company runs an ad or posts a notice, and candidates troop in to compete for the job. Each has samples, which may or may not be indicative of personal talent.

So we give the candidates a standard writing test. They know, as they sit at a foreign keyboard, how much of their future lies in the hundred or two hundred words they'll write.

What they *don't* know is what we want them to do, unless we give them samples.

Like most who read these words, I've been a lot of different people at the keyboard. I've written catalog copy so deliberately pompous it wears a monocle. . . "Y'all be good naow" P.O.C.B. (plain ol' country boy) copy worded on a level far less sophisticated than "Jes' folks" copy. . . no-nonsense here's-what-it-is-and-you-make-up-your-own-mind copy. . . poetic and rhapsodic copy. . . hi-tech copy. . . artificially bright copy. In each case my goal was to match copy into a four-piece jigsaw puzzle.

> Piece 1: Buyer demographics.
> Piece 2: Our intended position, actual image, and
>   history.
> Piece 3: Production limitations.
> Piece 4: Corporate or CEO ego.

Within all these strictures and limitations, a battle-scarred copy chief still has to warn the beginner: Keep your massive vocabulary in check.

Why? Because the job-applicant usually feels he or she will lose unless copy shows the potential for spectacle. Out comes copy which violates *THE CLARITY COMMANDMENT:*

In force-communication, clarity is paramount. Don't let any other component of the communications mix interfere with it.

Then whoever administers the writing test draws a conclusion: This person is too vocabulary-conscious to write catalog copy. The conclusion is logical only if proper instructions preceded word-regurgitation.

A Modest Proposal

If your copy tests have been one-string fiddles, I suggest this modest change:

Ask applicants to write the same copy-block at least two ways—"straight" and lyrical. It's been my experience that: 1) a copywriter who can write lyrical copy can, with minor deprogramming, write straight copy; 2) the copywriter who can write straight copy but who stumbles when writing on-demand lyrical copy has about a fifty percent chance of ever being able to make the switch if needed; 3) left alone without instructions, copywriters will write (or try to write) lyrical copy because they think it's a better exemplar of their talent.

While I'm ranting about copy tests, three other suggestions:

1) Always prescribe the copy-length of the test.

2) Ask the writer to describe two unlike items, to prevent disqualification based on lack of product-familiarity.

3) Show an example of the kind of copy you're looking for.

Is it a sad commentary on our profession that the most dependable catalog copywriters are parrots? I don't think so. The copywriter who changes the entire face and image of a catalog isn't a copywriter at all; that person is a copywriter-*plus*. Catalogs such as *Inmac,* which in a business-to-business ambience achieve the near-impossible miracle of producing a thoroughly down-to-earth yet entertaining compendium of product descriptions, aren't the result of an individual copywriter saying, "And now for something completely different."

Mud Isn't a Clarifier

Here's the opening of a one-paragraph copy-block for a mailbox:

> It's copper. And it will have your name and a scene of landing ducks embossed on it, both sides. And, fittingly, it's big...21" long, 12" high, 8" wide. What isn't gleaming copper is steel enamelled in earthy green. It will last long and weather beautifully, to a lovely soft patina.

Well, so the writer used "lovely." It's a second-echelon word, after all; it might have been "beautiful." My question is about two other components. First, why *fittingly?* What prior reference makes this "fitting"?

Second, "what isn't gleaming copper" is a negative way of putting a positive thought. In this era of word processing and instant corrections, we no longer can justify writing ourselves into a corner. While we're chewing on that description, "steel enamelled in earthy green" reads wrong. We read *steel enamelled* as a unit, which we couldn't do if the writer threw in a comma after *steel.*

Business-to-consumer catalogs don't have a lock on muddy writing. In business-to-business catalog writing, "I know something you don't" arrogance and "I'd rather entertain you than sell you something" insecurity eliminate a host of potential buyers, who just don't know what the writer means.

An example is this catalog copy for—well, you guess what it's for:

> WHEN THINGS GO BUMP IN THE NIGHT,
> *MIGHTY MO* DOESN'T EVEN HAVE AN A.C. BLINK
> You may have milliseconds to waste, but your micro doesn't. *Mighty Mo* keeps micros up to snuff with power on when power's off. Old Jim Watts lent his name to the *Mighty Mo* 400 and the *Mighty Mo* 800, depending on how many goodies you hook into your micro's guts.
> Want ultimate protection? Want to sleep, even sitting at the board? *Mighty Mo* just might keep you from becoming "mighty po'!"

The CIA's cryptography department helped decode this message. "Micro" stands for "micro-computer," and *Mighty Mo* is an uninterruptible power supply. Once you know this, figuring out the Jim Watts reference is duck soup. It's James Watt (not Watts, but don't we wish this were the only flaw in the copy?), whose name is immortalized as the measurement of electric power; so *Mighty Mo* 400 gives us 400 watts of power and *Mighty Mo* 800 gives us . . . aw, what the heck, who cares?

If you're of a mind to defend this copy, saying, "At least it's different," I point out that painting your face purple and your hair green also is "different," but please don't come to my dinner-party.

What's Wrong with "An Elegant Gift"?

What's wrong with this, the total description of a designer scarf?

> "An elegant gift that's certain to be appreciated and used with pride."

Right. It's more of that boiler-plate copy some infernal artificial copywriter-maker is excreting. Proof? Try it on just about anything you're describing in your catalog.

This gives us another component for a catalog copywriting test: Look for boiler-plate copy.

Turning this mild tip inside out, we have, for journeyman (journey-person?) catalog copywriters, *THE BOILER-PLATE AVOIDANCE PROPOSITION:*

> The possibility of depersonalized, inter-changeable nondescriptive copy de-creases in exact ratio to an increase of usable fact presented to the writer.

To validate the Proposition, try writing two parallel pieces of copy. For the first, you have bare bones information—colors, sizes, and a product photograph with no cutline. For the second, you have all the information the buyer would give to the department manager of a re-tail store.

Sure, the second piece of copy is easier to write. But that isn't the way a catalog-recipient keeps score. The second piece of copy invari-ably has more meat in it, and that's a powerful way to keep score.

The catalog writer who lazily uses the first available word is just as unprofessional as the cabinetmaker who uses the first available scrap of wood, whether it fits or not.

The catalog writer who egocentrically says, "Let me entertain you," had better tie a string around every finger that might hit the keyboard, as a reminder of *THE CATALOG COPYWRITER'S FIRST CHARGE:*

> The purpose of catalog copy is to sell the item you're describing. *Every* other facet of creative copywriting is subordi-nate to this, except maybe the Clarity Commandment, without which copy isn't copy.

We Have Catalog Copywriters... and Catalog CopyWRITERS!

Catalog writers instinctively take a competitive, comparative view of the copy in other catalogs. It's almost a Pavlov's Dog reaction.

Maybe that's why we seize upon nondescript and ineffective words-mithy and let good copy slide past us. On an educational level, rewriting a random copy-block from a competitor's catalog is an effective exercise. Recognizing, admiring, and emulating a colorful or powerful piece of copy is just as effective an educational procedure—and probably more advanced.

Are They Good Writers? We May Never Know.

Only a select few catalog writers achieve celebrity status. This isn't necessarily because they're the only ones who can write stirring prose. No, I don't doubt for a moment that deep in the catacombs of many catalog houses are writers who have "the gift" but who are trapped in *format.* When we have six lines of forty characters to empty our verbal baskets, how poetic can we be?

So the titans of catalog writing—the Babe Ruths, the Bo Jacksons, the Michael Jordans—invariably are those whose good fortune or talent lands them at The Sharper Image or Herrington or Alsto Handy Helper or maybe Bloomingdale's. There they can stretch their creative muscles to match the stretched-out copy-blocks which tight little catalogs don't make available.

How many free spirits are trying to pop the cork out of their restrictive six-line-forty-character bottles and show us how much talent they really have? We'll never know.

A Different Set of Yardsticks

Our counterparts who write solo mailings and space ads might list these as professional requirements:

```
Salesmanship . . . . . . . . . . . . . . . . . . . . . . . . . . . .30%
Vocabulary . . . . . . . . . . . . . . . . . . . . . . . . . . . . . .20%
Grammar. . . . . . . . . . . . . . . . . . . . . . . . . . . . . . . .15%
Writing discipline. . . . . . . . . . . . . . . . . . . . . . . . . .15%
Knowledge of relationship to graphics  . . . . . . . .10%
Speed  . . . . . . . . . . . . . . . . . . . . . . . . . . . . . . . . . .10%.
```

I've omitted product knowledge, because this is impossible to measure. As hired Hessians, we'd better be able to write effective copy for insurance one day, insecticides the next day, and insulated underwear the next. That's why salesmanship tops the list.

Because we have to kill with one blow, our copy for solo mailings and space ads depends heavily on our ability to match vocabulary with our targets. That's why vocabulary ranks second.

Every word is "Page 1" in a solo mailing, so grammar is significant. (Actually, I don't ever see a need to justify decent grammar as a starter-requirement for *any* writer.)

Writer discipline isn't a big deal. Yes, we have to get the mailing package out in time. But nobody expects us to hammer away at the keyboard for eight solid hours a day. That, too, is why speed isn't a major consideration. Mailing dates often are flexible.

Usually, an ad or mailing piece has art direction. So the writer has a companion in the hotseat, figuring out the graphics.

Now let's assemble a similar list for catalog writers, *excluding the copy-heavy catalogs.* In my opinion the ratios would be:

Writing discipline	35%
Speed	25%
Salesmanship	15%
Vocabulary	10%
Grammar	10%
Knowledge of relationship to graphics	5%.

If you don't believe this shift, apply for a writing job at the typical catalog house and see how long you last without writing discipline and speed. This is why ex-catalog writers can increase the departmental output but may stumble over the salesmanship barrier when they're appointed creative directors at mail order companies: They're more discipline-oriented.

If we move those writers over to copy-heavy catalogs, we see an obvious change:

Writing discipline	25%
Salesmanship	25%
Speed	20%
Vocabulary	15%
Grammar	10%
Knowledge of relationship to graphics	5%.

Salesmanship moves up and discipline slacks off, because although they still have catalog deadlines, these writers don't struggle inside the strait jacket of having to grind out an eight-item page. And with one or two items on a page, salesmanship surges forward; without it, the page won't pay for itself.

"A HAND PUSH Lawn Mower? You're Kidding!"

With those ratios as yardsticks, I'll pay homage to some catalog writing I regard as superior.

I can't comment on speed, because I wasn't there with a timer. I'm taking discipline for granted, because this *is* catalog copy. But salesmanship—no question about the talent.

Most of us, asked to write catalog copy for a hand push lawn mower, would snort, "You're kidding! My grandfather had one of those." Not the writer of this gem, who knew the magic equation:

Successful salesmanship = projection of benefit.

The heading:

The Hand Push Lawn Mower is perfect for small lawns, trimming tight corners, and a little peace and quiet on a Sunday afternoon.

What an elegant headline! It's pure benefit, relating to the reader, not the manufacturer (and that's a welcome relief after some of the chest-thumping braggadocio copy we see).

When you get to chapter 22, remember this example because it's two-thirds of the magical benefit/benefit/benefit principle described in that chapter. (The entire text is Fig. 2-6.)

I have a simple way of judging copy: Would I be proud if an outsider asked, "Did you write that?" and I could answer, "Yes."

Is It Because the Copy Attacks a Specific Prejudice?

I'm looking at another copy-block I admire. The heading:

Why You Should Spend $125 for a Golf Bag That Weighs a Mere 2-lbs., 15 oz.!

I don't understand why the writer stuck a hyphen between "2" and "lbs." and not between "15" and "oz."—but, heck, we're being picky; it isn't as though the writer used "it's" for "its." And we only rate grammar at 10 percent anyway, for this kind of writing.

The copy immediately attacks our negative reaction, which is based on human prejudice against something lightweight costing more than similar items weighing considerably more. The very first sentence isn't descriptive; it's the smooth opening of a salesman who knows he can't establish rapport until he dissolves implicit prejudice:

> Based on cost-per-pounds, our Balance Bag™
> may be the most expensive golf bag you can buy.

The next word, of course, is *but*. (See Fig. 2-7.)

Can YOU Do It?

Can *you* sell a hand push lawn mower for $86.80? Can *you* sell a lightweight golf bag for $125? Can *you* sell a standard-looking clay pottery figure for $350? And can *you* get this copy out of the printer by deadline-date?

Then you're the most desirable of all catalog copywriters, the magical amalgam of salesmanship and discipline.

Innocent Until Proved Guilty

Anyone who reads catalog copy with a critical eye will agree: Catalog copywriters are guilty of many sins. Sloth, dullness, and an accordion-like imagination that either puffs itself full of air or goes flat are a few.

Consider, though: Before you blame the copywriter for all the communications-sins, ask around. You have three logical questions:

> 1. Did the copywriter get as much selling weaponry as the buyer or product manager had at hand?

> 2. Has corporate policy stifled the copywriter's ability or capability of asking for information that surely exists but wasn't included?

> 3. Who hired this guy, anyway?

If your copy is strong-selling *and* clever, may the Lord bless and keep you. But if it sacrifices salesmanship for cleverness, may you spend eternity re-stocking the shelves of catalog houses who knew better and hired writers to whom moving merchandise is a more worthy goal than showing off.

The Classic Collection of porcelain bath accessories by Lenape turns the ordinary into the extraordinary. Choose from a beautiful selection of florals and solids. Glazed, high-fired vitreous porcelain in white, bone or grey; and 3 delicate patterns: blossom on white, blossom on bone or blue flower on white.

Finishing touches

G-P. Clip-on Accessories.
Easy to install with a Fastick® strip. #31025, $2
G. Towel ring. #31018: solid, $15; decorated, $16
H. Toothbrush/tumbler holder. #31019: solid, 12.50; decorated, $14
J. One-piece shelf. 22" wide × 5" deep × 3" high #31028; solid, $59; decorated, $69
K. Corner shower caddy (does not need Fastick® strip). #31022: solid, $15; decorated, $16
L. Soap dish. #31020: solid, 12.50; decorated, $14
M. 24" towel bar. #31021: solid, $25; decorated, $27
N. Toilet tissue holder. #31023: solid, $18; decorated, $20
P. Double robe hook. #31024: solid, $10; decorated, $12

Q-Z. Freestanding accessories.
Q. 26" × 17" oval mirror. #31026: solid, $149; decorated, $159
R. Tumbler. #31027: solid, $7; decorated, $8
S. Pedestal soap dish. #31029: solid, $10; decorated, $12

T. Wastebasket, (not shown). #31030: solid, $40; decorated, $45
U. Porcelain cat. #31036: solid, $40; decorated, $50
V. Boutique tissue box. #31033: solid, $22; decorated, $24
W. Soap/lotion dispenser. #31031: solid, $10; decorated, $12
X. Toothbrush/tumbler holder. #31032: solid, $10; decorated, $12
Y. Vanity soap dish. #31034: solid, $6.50; decorated, $7.50
Z. Toilet brush holder with brush. #31035: solid, $29; decorated, $35
Matching cabinet knobs and drawer pulls, page 27; matching switch plates, page 30.

Available in Blossom on white, Blossom on bone or Blue flower on white. Also white, bone or grey. Please specify.

K23G

Figure 2-1

What's your opinion of the generic copy at mid-left? Here's mine: I wouldn't hire this writer. Why? Because "turns the ordinary into the extraordinary" creates no image at all, and "Choose from a beautiful selection" is semi-pro description.

Words are our only weapons. Let's keep them honed.

Clean Marine
Slime off the
Bottom of Your
Hull in Just Minutes
— Without Getting Wet!

Too good to be true? That's what everyone thinks, till they actually use Dri-Diver. With its large 3' long flexible scrubbing pad and 6' extension handle, Dri-Diver actually cleans the crud off any boat, power or sail, up to 40' in length, and up to 15' in beam. While you stand on your dock, or even on your boat's deck! The key is the natural flotation power in the closed-cell foam scrub pad. When submerged, the bouyant pad provides a steady 12 pounds of upward scrubbing pressure (about twice the pressure you exert if you dive under your boat and begin scrubbing by hand!). As you guide Dri-Diver along your boat's length, the flexible pad shapes itself naturally to the hull's contour, removing all marine growth in its path as it strains upward against your hull, trying to reach the surface. With total length of 9', Dri-Diver easily reaches your boat's centerline; then switch sides and do the other half. You'll do a 20' boat in about 15 minutes! Power Boat model uses brushes (shown) in order to clean between, and on both sides of, lifting strakes common to fiberglass hulls. Sail models use scrubbing pads better suited to smooth hulls, and will remove early-growth barnacles too. Scrubbing pads last dozens of cleanups and are easily replaced. Uses no chemicals or hoses.

DECK   DOCK   DINGHY

Dri-Diver:
#B602 Sail Boat Model (up to 30') — $49.95   #B603 Power Boat (up to 40') — $69.95
#B604 Large Sail Boat Model (up to 40') — $89.95
Replacement Pads and Brushes:
#B606 Power Boat Brushes (4) — $24.00   #B605 Sail Boat Pads (3) — $9.95 (for regular cleaning*)   #B618 Barnacle Pads (2) — $14.95 (for barnacles only*)
*fits both sail boat models.

Figure 2-2

Visualize this description with "Clean Dirt and Oil" instead of the vivid "Clean Marine Slime" and you can see how graphic descriptions grab and shake the reader's interest. "Slime" and "crud," which appear within the copy-block, usually aren't salesworthy words; here, they give just the proper negative "Ycch!" image.

Finally, You Can Outdrive that Gorilla in Your Foursome!

The Pirate 432 deserves its name, and its growing reputation. It's the outlaw ball that cannot be used in USGA sanctioned tournaments. The reason? The Pirate will add 20-25 yards to your drivers — **illegally**! Engineered by noted ball designer Troy Puckett, the man who designed both the Wilson Pro Staff, and the MacGregor MT Tourney used by Jack Nicklaus himself. Puckett's Geodesic Dimple Design of 432 triangulated dimples gives the Pirate less drag, and more distance, than USGA regulations permit. The Pirate is regulation size, but is precisely 4 grams heavier than USGA guidelines, so it really bores through the air! Play even the longest courses as they were designed to be played, even if you don't hit the ball as far as the pros! The added distance off the tee usually gets you two clubs closer than normal, so you can hit a 7-iron instead of a 5. And since medium irons go about 10 yards farther, the Pirate can make a three club difference on your second shot — imagine what that can do for your score! The Pirate employs durable two-piece construction, with a "hot" rigid core that produces a high spin rate for bite on greens. Specially blended Surlyn cover won't cut, yet the Pirate clicks crisply when struck. Why not try a Pirate on your course? **We guarantee you'll hit your driver at least 20 yards longer than your regular ball** (whether Titleist, Maxfli, or Top Flite), **or we'll refund your money!**

The Pirate 432:
#G335 (doz.) — $24.95   #G336 (2 doz.) — $46.00   #G337 (6 doz.) — $119.00

Figure 2-3

Can you think of a more descriptive heading to sell this golf ball? I can't. What if the headline referred to "that Heavy Hitter in Your Foursome"? Would you be as likely to read the description as you are because of that wonderful trigger-word "Gorilla"?

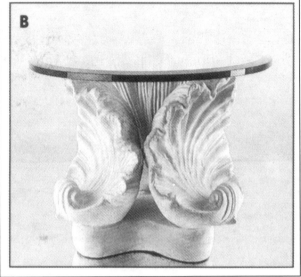

B. TRIPLE SHELL COFFEE TABLE. Sea-washed motif of three sculpted shells makes a fine focal point for coffee or cocktails. Plaster with an antiqued(1)* finish. Shown with a 30" beveled edge(B) glass. 17½" high, 17" diameter top. 85 lbs. #210 $285.00 (Freight Collect)

B

Figure 2-4

This description loses me for two reasons: 1) "...a fine focal point for coffee or cocktails" draws a muddy image, because *fine* as it relates to *point* isn't what the writer means; 2) what does the "(1)*" before "finish" mean? It may be explained elsewhere, but looking elsewhere isn't what catalog copy-blocks are supposed to ask the reader to do. (I couldn't find it elsewhere.)

SPA FACE 26   SPA BATH 29   SPA GEAR 34   SPA SPORT 38

S P A   S T Y L E

For a Spa Style summer, you'll find these La Costa Spa Collection products essential to the season: For sun time — a tube or two of SPF Sun Treatments, a sleek Spa swimsuit, a terrific Velour Lounge Towel and our new Remoisturizing Skin Balm. For true Spa Style, look for our new jade Spa Wear and our lots of dots women's collection in the comfort of 100% cotton. This summer — grab the energy of the season with Spa Style.

Cover Look. Spa Cardigan Dress, see back cover.

Kimono Robe. The official guest robe of The La Costa Spa was recently selected as the Number One hotel robe in the state by California Magazine! And with good reason—our plush velour robes are constructed of the highest quality 100% heavyweight cotton available. The traditional kimono style is generously cut for comfort and features a self-tie belt and front patch pockets. Each robe has a thirsty looped terry interior, a plush velour exterior and our embroidered La Costa Spa logo. One size fits both men and women. White 5-270-US, Black 5-275-US $80.00

Robe Monogram. Up to three initials embroidered on the sleeve. Allow 3–4 weeks for delivery. Sorry, monogrammed items are not returnable. $10.00

Swim Goggles. Dive into summer fitness with our competition quality goggles. They feature permanent anti-fog optical lenses, soft closed-cell foam seal for a water tight fit, center split molded rubber headstrap and an adjustable nosepiece. Royal blue with clear lenses. 8-140-20 $17.50

Lycra Swim Cap. For a sleek swim. Our royal blue nylon/lycra swim cap controls your hair and keeps it out of your face for free breathing. One stretch size fits all. 8-140-00 $7.50

Figure 2-5

Good copy: "thirsty looped terry interior." A strain on credulity: Can you imagine a bunch of judges sitting around a smoke-filled room, voting on which will be "the Number One hotel robe in the state"? Only in California!

The Hand Push Lawn Mover is perfect for small lawns, trimming tight corners, and a little peace and quiet on a Sunday afternoon.

Of all the modern conveniences that engineers and scientists have given us, the gas powered lawn mover has certainly been one of great luxury. But what was once a harmless, inexpensive piece of equipment has now become a self-starting, self-bagging, self-pushing, turn-on-a-dime, 400 lb., padded-seat piece of toe-lopping machinery that costs hundreds of dollars and yet can still accomplish only the same simple task of trimming your grass. Progress is progress, but it doesn't have to mean elimination. These first-class quality hand mowers offer a low noise, low investment alternative. They're virtually maintenance free and give a superior cut to power mowers because reel type blades snip the grass instead of ripping or tearing. Both models have 5 bladed reels made of tempered, high-carbon steel, 10″ diameter cast-iron rim wheels, a 16″ cutting width, and three-position cutting height of ⁵/₈″ to 2¹/₄″. The grass catcher with durable canvas sides and a galvanized steel bottom is optional for both mowers. For many lawns and situations, the Hand Push Mower will always be a better choice. Sometimes it's just impossible to improve upon a good idea.

F-4259500	Standard Mower	$86.80
F-4259600	Deluxe Mower	99.80
F-4259700	Grass Catcher	19.80

Figure 2-6

This near-perfect copy justifies a product most readers would think is obsolete, and as it does it gently damns those roaring goliath mowers that replaced it. Are blades that "snip the grass instead of ripping or tearing" really better? After all, grass isn't our hair. But we cringe a little at the well-chosen words and don't even think of analyzing the sales argument. *That's* salesmanship in print.

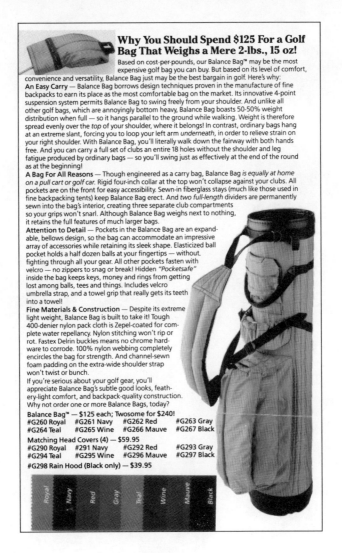

Why You Should Spend $125 For a Golf Bag That Weighs a Mere 2-lbs., 15 oz!

Based on cost-per-pounds, our Balance Bag™ may be the most expensive golf bag you can buy. But based on its level of comfort, convenience and versatility, Balance Bag just may be the best bargain in golf. Here's why:

An Easy Carry — Balance Bag borrows design techniques proven in the manufacture of fine backpacks to earn its place as the most comfortable bag on the market. Its innovative 4-point suspension system permits Balance Bag to swing freely from your shoulder. And unlike all other golf bags, which are annoyingly bottom heavy, Balance Bag boasts 50-50% weight distribution when full — so it hangs parallel to the ground while walking. Weight is therefore spread evenly over the *top* of your shoulder, where it belongs! In contrast, ordinary bags hang at an extreme slant, forcing you to loop your left arm *underneath*, in order to relieve strain on your right shoulder. With Balance Bag, you'll literally walk down the fairway with both hands free. And you can carry a full set of clubs an entire 18 holes without the shoulder and leg fatigue produced by ordinary bags — so you'll swing just as effectively at the end of the round as at the beginning!

A Bag For All Reasons — Though engineered as a carry bag, Balance Bag *is equally at home on a pull cart or golf car.* Rigid four-inch collar at the top won't collapse against your clubs. All pockets are on the front for easy accessibility. Sewn-in fiberglass stays (much like those used in fine backpacking tents) keep Balance Bag erect. And *two full-length dividers* are permanently sewn into the bag's interior, creating three separate club compartments so your grips won't snarl. Although Balance Bag weighs next to nothing, it retains the full features of much larger bags.

Attention to Detail — Pockets in the Balance Bag are an expandable, bellows design, so the bag can accommodate an impressive array of accessories while retaining its sleek shape. Elasticized ball pocket holds a half dozen balls at your fingertips — without fighting through all your gear. All other pockets fasten with velcro — no zippers to snag or break! Hidden *"Pocketsafe"* inside the bag keeps keys, money and rings from getting lost among balls, tees and things. Includes velcro umbrella strap, and a towel grip that really gets its teeth into a towel!

Fine Materials & Construction — Despite its extreme light weight, Balance Bag is built to take it! Tough 400-denier nylon pack cloth is Zepel-coated for complete water repellancy. Nylon stitching won't rip or rot. Fastex Delrin buckles means no chrome hardware to corrode. 100% nylon webbing completely encircles the bag for strength. And channel-sewn foam padding on the extra-wide shoulder strap won't twist or bunch.

If you're serious about your golf gear, you'll appreciate Balance Bag's subtle good looks, feathery-light comfort, and backpack-quality construction. Why not order one or more Balance Bags, today?

Balance Bag™ — $125 each; Twosome for $240!

| #G260 Royal | #G261 Navy | #G262 Red | #G263 Gray |
| #G264 Teal | #G265 Wine | #G266 Mauve | #G267 Black |

Matching Head Covers (4) — $59.95

| #G290 Royal | #291 Navy | #G292 Red | #G293 Gray |
| #G294 Teal | #G295 Wine | #G296 Mauve | #G297 Black |

#G298 Rain Hood (Black only) — $39.95

Figure 2-7

Some of the sentences are uncomfortably long, and too many words are italicized. But that's a small price to pay for copy which sweeps past any possible objection to a $125 price for a golf bag weighing less than three pounds.

CHAPTER *3*

I'm Awfully Tired Today, So Please Don't Challenge Me

FIRST, *YOU* TRY IT!

Your assignment: Rewrite this headline for communication—connecting with your readers—assuming your targets are up-scale consumers who don't have a lot of technical background.

**Acoustic Masses Parallel
Room-Dominating Speakers**

In place of massive vibrating woofers you'll find in expensive production-line speakers, the Olaf Acoustrong OA-67X Speakers use two acoustic air masses to reinforce the bass while reducing harmonic distortion. Omnidirectional 2" wide range speakers work anywhere in the room.

Okay, what's your first decision?

Right! You're going to tell the reader what you're talking about . . . which is . . . what?

Speakers? If that's your decision, you're selling metal, not romance. The alert copywriter asks himself: What interests the *reader*?

Fig. 3-1 is an actual copy-block for the speakers (I changed the names for our copy-test), and even though the layout and sub-heads help this description you may (as I did) find it hard slogging. BEFORE YOU LOOK, at least suggest a headline.

Take 30 seconds. No longer than that.

What's your headline? If it's something like "Big Speaker Sound" or "Technological Breakthrough," you're safe. But you aren't on the main line, because you're just repeating a tired cliché. Here's a different tune, a dialogue:

— "Close your eyes and listen."
— "Hmmm. I'd guess it's a 15-inch woofer."
— "Nope. The whole speaker is 2^1/$_2$ inches."
— "You've gotta be kidding!"

You can't even consider a heading such as this unless you have the kind of space Fig. 3-1 allows. In small space, how about:

In 2001
Your Neighbors Will Have These Speakers Too.

"Lip Service" Isn't Service to Clarity

Do you, struggling through the day's catch of catalogs, sometimes feel as I do...the writer is daring you to clarify the muddy message?

A single constant theme, running throughout this book, is my slavish worship of *THE CLARITY COMMANDMENT.*

> In force-communication, clarity is paramount. Don't let any other facet of the copywriting mix interfere with it.

Catalog copy is as grass-roots force-communication as any copywriting could ever be. Catalog copywriters, who have smaller space and fewer words than advertising, direct mail, or editorial writers, have to brand the Commandment on their foreheads.

I really hope this isn't like a seat-belt law, which gets lip-service from drivers who then ignore it.

Add to the Clarity Commandment another venerable maxim, *THE WHOSE MESSAGE IS IT ANYWAY? RULE:*

> Your message should operate within the experiential background of the message-recipient, not within your own experiential background.

Together, these stainless, rustproofing principles will lead a catalog writer through the muddy rhetorical waters of overwritten, over-colorful, and self-contradictory copy.

Overwriting, over-colorful word use, and copy engendering an "Is it 'A' or is it 'B'?" reaction didn't exist when Sears, Ward's and Alden's were the only catalogs most of us saw. Those were companies that took the long view; their product-lines, though extensive, were slow to change; description was paramount and benefit was left to the buyer's imagination (which in those bygone times was far more self-corruptible than the writer's).

Sophistication Grows... Clarity Goes

What could be clearer than the classic Sears "Good, Better, Best" labeling? When catalog merchandise is competitive only with itself, clarity is recognized as the asset it is.

In these darker days, with our tables and desks covered inches deep with catalogs, competition is external, not internal. Each catalog fights for its life in one of the most brutally competitive marketplaces the wily brain of man could invent. An endless fight makes clarity a victim, like a pedestrian crossing an expressway which has no stop-lights, no speed limit, no lane markers, no direction-signs.

Our job: Preserve the victim.

Why Clarity Suffers

Clarity suffers because of...

1. The fight for attention;
2. The fight for item-by-item desirability;
3. The fight for reader-involvement;
4. The fight for colorful word-use.

How far we've come down the muddy road! The struggle to create clarity in the midst of the raging maelstrom of rhetorical tricks isn't at all parallel to sweetly innocent product descriptions.

(Nor should it be. We couldn't be content with 1930-ish catalog writing, any more than we'd be content with 1930-ish novels or movies or luxury cars. They're charming curios, not dynamic competitors.)

So clarity becomes a petunia in an onion patch. It's out of place when the writer, after the fact, tries to go back into copy-blocks created for a different purpose—flair, corporate image, ultra-high fashion—to bring clarity bubbling to the surface. Copy is skewed because clarity wasn't a primary intention of the original message-mix.

Proofreader, Where Are You?

Fashion catalogs are especially prone to sacrificing their descriptions on the "We're Different" altar. Probably this is because this is the toughest field in which to stand apart not only from competitors but from internal competition within the catalog's own pages.

That's where proofreading should become a factor.

A copywriter falls in love with a phrase and unconsciously overuses it. Days or even weeks may elapse between product descriptions, but the reader sees them in one piece.

So we have, on page 10 of a fashion catalog:

```
Fresh pastels weave their fashion magic in this
versatile braided cotton belt. . .
```

and on page 12, same catalog:

```
Fiesta-bright colors weave their fashion magic in
this cotton braided belt. . .
```

Okay, it's possible that fresh pastels and fiesta-bright colors both weave fashion magic. But don't the two descriptions *detract* from each other's impact? (I didn't scan the catalog for other fashion magic weavers, but they may have been there because obviously nobody said, "Hey, we've used that phrase before. Make up another description.")

"Who Cares If You Know the Words? I'm the Writer and I Know Them."

The Whose Message Is It Anyway? Rule popped into place when I heard one woman I regard as knowledgeable in fashion ask another, "What's a dobby pattern?" Neither knew. They guessed a "nobby" or "nubby" pattern, but the product photograph didn't bear them out.

I thought—if it shows horses, maybe it's a *dobbin* pattern. It didn't show horses. The copy read, "Our pleat-front cotton blouse has a dobby pattern, Peter Pan collar and concealed button front." No clues there.

That's one of the no-clarity keys: Hit-and-run description, using a word and telling the reader, "If you're not fashion-wise, you don't deserve to understand my copy." Uh-uh. Copy should say, "Dear, Sweet Reader, This is for you, and because you feel comfortable and secure with my description you'll buy." (More on hit-and-run in chapter 21.)

The dictionary gave us the definition of *dobby:* "A spirit like a brownie, but often malicious." I don't want that pattern in my house.

Okay, I'm being wry. But how difficult would it have been for the writer of this medium-price fashion catalog to say, "*I* know what dobby means, but maybe some of my readers don't. So I'll inject a four or five word description: "Our pleat-front cotton blouse has a dobby pattern (SHORT EXPLANATION). . . ."?

66

Mis-Mix and Mis-Match

Should we be upset by these two references from the inside-the-cover letter from a recent fashion catalog?

> Turn to page 5 for the New Romantic look, in our red calico suit . . .

> Remember, you can find your size—whether it's Misses, Petites (5′4″ and under), Women's or Half Sizes. Our new △ emblem makes shopping for your size range even easier.

Page 5 had a red suit which *probably* was calico. But nowhere in the description did the word *calico* appear, making letter and description a mismatch for those who may not have a one-on-one knowledge of calico other than the childhood poem about the calico cat.

And how does the △ emblem make shopping for a size range easier? Scouring the catalog, we do see an occasional wedge, usually facing the other direction, with phrases such as "Also petite" and "Also women" set inside. Wouldn't it have been gracious of the copywriter to tell us *how* the emblem (that word also bothers me: it isn't an emblem) works, explaining that it appears when the range of sizes is expanded? "Makes shopping easier" is the muzzy phrase that throws us. (See Fig. 3-4.)

The Adjectival Morass

As usual, it's the adjectives and adverbs, not the nouns and verbs, that cause copy to grunt and heave instead of flowing smoothly. Read this product description:

> F. *Shrimp basket.* Georgia artist Kate Lloyd has created yet another virtually irresistible basket of natural reed and papier-maché. The pale peach basket is freshly decorated with coral-colored shrimp and highlighted in blue and green. Hand painted and signed by the artist, our shrimp basket is just as comfortable in traditional settings as it is at the beach . . .

Colorful writing causes kinks here. Our "How's that again?" reaction isn't generated by "coral-colored shrimp"; we know perfectly well, and the photograph verifies, they're painted on, not real. What raises the first question in comprehension is "freshly." How does that word fit? How does it enhance the description? We'd understand "decorated with fresh, coral-colored shrimp," but "freshly decorated with coral-colored shrimp," suggesting wet paint or fresh shrimp, is hard to compute.

Then we hit "just as comfortable in traditional settings as it is at the beach." Does that mean we've been wrong? It's a *real* shrimp basket? No, it can't be, because it's papier-maché, and that means fragility.

Conclusion: It's a case of overwriting, stemming from emphasis on colorful rhetoric rather than the Clarity Commandment and the Whose Message Is It Anyway? Rule.

How Sweet It Is

The writer who says, "Here's mud in your eye," and the writer who struggles like Hercules in the Augean Stables (see the next paragraph) for word-color can damage the catalog-reader's desire to buy. What a paradox! It's exactly the reverse of what the writer is paid to do.

(If you don't know the story of Hercules and the Augean Stables, consider: If I'd used the reference in catalog copy, I'd have killed you off. Even in a trade book, showing off for no purpose makes the reader uncomfortable, doesn't it?)

Like a virtuoso violinist who makes impossible fingering seem easy, a good catalog writer creates descriptions so clear and appealing the casual reader doesn't recognize the talent behind it. The writer has done what he or she is paid to do—call attention to what's being sold, not *how* it's being sold.

This near-perfect piece of copy, in lesser hands, might have repelled the reader instead of attracting her:

> STRIPED TUNIC
> In India, where temperatures often reach scorching, unbearable heights those in the know on how to keep cool wear the traditional tunic called a "kurta." We've designed ours in 100-gram *Bengal Silk*, to keep you cool in the sizzling days of summer, and glide just as easily into autumn's chillier clime. With deep, gusseted armholes, pullover placket front, and . . .

Yes, I know a comma is missing and I know the phrase "those in the know on how to keep cool" is a shade tortured. What I admire is the writer's restraint in not hitting us in the eye with the word *kurta*, bragging at once, "I know something you don't, dummy."

Effective force-communication often demands vocabulary *suppression*. If this bothers you, write textbooks.

Figure 3-1

We can't fault the writer's knowledge of speakers. What we *do* fault is the headline, which says flatly: The speakers are invisible. They aren't. Instead, they're tiny. Then the headline says the speakers will fill the room with sound. A "boom-box" does that. It's unpleasant, but it's filling.

"Latest triumph in Bose research" suggests the writer doesn't give a hoot about the *reader's* experiential background. Ask 1,000 recipients of this catalog: "Who or what is Bose?" The electronics hounds—and, yes, this catalog does have a lot of them within its reader-mix—will know. The average person won't. (My guess: Of the 1,000 readers, 200 will, 800 won't.)

Even electronics hounds aren't moved by the running-in-place sub-head "Latest triumph in Bose research," which not only suggests Bose does this all the time but also projects no benefit for the reader. How much easier salesmanship becomes when the salesperson says to the customer, "Here's why you should own this."

Figure 3-2

What's a "Cat Lovey"? Oh, on second reading we know it's the writer's cat, Lovey. But why couldn't she put in a comma to help us out? If you're bewildered by the notion of a cat tripping around on a canvas (and the nearby carpet?), pressing award-winning art into the painting-to-be, you aren't a cat-lover. Conclusion: In a cat-lover catalog—where this was—no problem. In a general catalog, it might not pay for the space.

Figure 3-3

The generic but specific headline isolates the proper target-group. Each of the four items fits within the special interest frame. I don't agree with the subhead "Give them the gift of a lifetime," nondescript wording suggesting the writer ran out of steam.

shopping international®

Dear Friend,

You're on the move! Soon, winter will be giving way to the promise of spring. Let Shopping International help you make that change with a variety of natural fabrics, in traditional—and not-so-traditional—designs.

Turn to page 5 for the New Romantic look, in our red calico suit. You won't have to hunt hard to find safari fashions scattered throughout the book, and you'll love the brass Patina Jewelry (page 23) in this year's new jade-green color.

Remember, you can find your size—whether it's Misses, Petites (5'4" and under), Women's or Half Sizes. Our new ◁ emblem makes shopping for your size range even easier. You'll find shoes in hard-to-find sizes, too. As always, our service is prompt, courteous, and guaranteed, because your order is important to us.

Shopping International

Figure 3-4

What if this weren't an inside-the-cover letter? What if it were a speech? The spokesperson holds up a card with a right triangle on it and says, "This new emblem makes shopping for your size even easier. " Wouldn't you raise your hand and ask, "How?" That's probably what a lot of people who read this noncommunication asked. The worst part of this gaffe: Reader *frustration* is in ratio to reader *interest* in whatever this company sells.

CHAPTER 4

The Clarity
Commandment
Revisited

FIRST, *YOU* **TRY IT!**

Your assignment: Replace this headline, which actually ran, page after page, on an upscale catalog:

The Season of Quintessence

Before replacing these four words with one to ten *clearer* words, ask yourself: What was this writer trying to transmit?

Yes, the impression is one of a beginner who learned a new word and has to launch it at every target he/she can find.

If we look up *quintessence* in Merriam-Webster's, we get little help:

> *1.* The fifth or last and highest element in ancient medieval philosophy. The ancient Greeks recognized four elements, fire, air, water, and earth. The Pythagoreans and Aristotle added a fifth, ether. Heavenly bodies were said to be composed of this additional element. *2.* The essence of a thing in its most concentrated form. *3.* The most typical example.

How do we tie any of this to *season?* We don't. . .and not just because it's a wild stretch. No, we don't tie it to *season* because we, as clarity-seeking copywriters, wouldn't use *quintessence* at all. What percentage of our readers know the word at all? What percentage won't buy from us because we've made them feel uncomfortable?

So let's have your replacement.

Take 30 seconds. No longer than that.

Okay, what do you have? "The Heavenly Season"? Great. "Procession of the Ultimates"? Much as the word *ultimate* is overused, it's an improvement. In fact, I'll bet four dollars *anything* you created is an improvement.

Form Over Substance: A Dangerous Direction

Depending on whose catalog you're writing, you have lists of rules, constraints, and no-nos at your elbow.

"You can't say this." "You have to put it this way." "You can have only twelve words of two syllables or more in a copy-block." "The first word has to be a verb."

What's wrong with every one of these rules?

Right! They emphasize form, not substance.

But *we* know better. We have The Clarity Commandment. It's at our elbow, pasted onto our keyboard, scrolled on the doorposts of our house, and etched onto our foreheads.

With The Clarity Commandment in place, emphasis shifts to where it should be: communicating on the reader's level.

The Benefits of Clarity

Clarity adds a key ingredient to the catalog copy-mix: The reader knows what you mean.

Ever travel to Europe without your voltage adapter and unwittingly try to plug your electric appliance into a wall-outlet? It didn't fit without an adapter.

The same problem confronts the catalog writer who tries to plug his rhetoric into the reader's consciousness. Unless the writer is equipped with a rhetorical adapter, it won't fit. No current flows through the line because the rhetoric isn't plugged in.

Okay, enough metaphor. The adapter is The Clarity Commandment, and if it hovers in the background ready to strike at a violation, copy can only be improved.

Another benefit: You'll cut down returns and white mail, because what you ship will be what you've described.

What Is It?

I'm looking at a catalog page describing scrimshaw pocket knives, money clips, belt buckles, and other novelties.

You and I know: We can find two types of scrimshaw. The first, the expensive type, is hand-carved ivory. The second, the inexpensive type, is molded plastic. Which are these?

This writer ignored the Clarity Commandment. Copy says, rather cleverly, "...original scrimshaw designs..." and "...carefully etched and hand-finished..." The word "ivory" appears, but its use could be interpreted as a color, not a medium—which may be a sly attempt to *avoid* clarity.

Might this be a trade-off? We'll attract some buyers who don't know the difference...and handle forthrightly any complaints from buyers who think they're getting real ivory.

Had The Clarity Commandment been in effect, the writer could have served both God and Mammon by phrases such as "In the tradition of..." and "...the look and feel of..." I recommend this only because, having read the copy three times, I'm still only 99 percent sure it *isn't* real ivory, and without the key we won't open as many doors.

Vol-Au-Vent and Other Puzzlers

Quick! What does *vol-au-vent* mean?

If you answered, "It's pronounced 'vol-oh-vahn' and it's pastry filled with meat or vegetables," skip this section.

If you answered, "Huh?" you parallel every person I asked, except one, whose guess was oblique to the target but close enough to qualify ("It's some sort of prepared food, isn't it?").

Copy for this item, in a catalog of cookware gadgets, reads:

> Our new *VOL-AU-VENT CUTTERS* are such fun! Use on puff pastry (frozen works just fine) to make patty shells for creamed chicken, shrimp, or vegetables. So easy, it's a wonderful way to add elegance and excitement to a meal! Four great shapes, each approximately 4¼" in diameter. Made in the USA.

The copy isn't bad; the picture does show the item. Defense might be, "If they don't know what it is they aren't our prospects anyway." Ah, but the catalog was addressed to "H. Lewis," who, even with a superficial knowledge of French and kitchens, couldn't pinpoint this. Are we mailing catalogs to those who don't understand the copy in the catalog?

Too, replacing the generic "So easy, it's a wonderful way to add elegance and excitement to a meal!" with a *specific* could only help clarity *and* salesmanship.

On to another question: What does the word "Fingerpaint" mean to you?

I tried this one on the same group, and answers without exception referred to kindergarten scrawls. So this headline—

FINGERPAINT MUGS

—didn't prepare any of us for the pleasant but mismatching descriptive copy:

> Set of two prettily decorated earthenware mugs
> handpainted in bright springtime colors. A re-
> freshing look. Set of two, 10 oz. each. Gift boxed.
> #01265 – two fingerpaint mugs $10.95

Looking at the mugs, I can see they're hand painted. But, at least *within my experiential background,* they aren't fingerpainted. In no way could a finger, however well-trained, create those designs.

Get those words: *within my experiential background.* It's inconsequential that the writer knows what he or she means. What matters is whether the *reader* knows.

If you think I'm being too harsh, consider: Why should any catalog copywriter *ever* violate The Clarity Commandment? Whatever the writing style, whatever the admonition from on-high, whatever is being sold to whomever, no one ever perished from an overdose of clarity.

And about Those Line-Breaks . . .

When you're writing text-type headlines, why not give the reader a break, by breaking lines at logical points?

For example, which of these is easier to read?

> A Charming Pictorial Treasury of the Many Images of the
> Jolly Gentleman with the Red Coat and White Beard

—or—

> A Charming Pictorial Treasury
> of the Many Images
> of the Jolly Gentleman
> with the Red Coat and the White Beard

The second version breaks the message into chewable bites. That's one step toward clarity. A more profound stride is elimination of the word-barrier caused by that strange break: "of the" leads nowhere. If we have just two lines, we can add quick comprehension by changing the line-break this way:

> A Charming Pictorial Treasury of the Many Images
> of the Jolly Gentleman with the Red Coat and White Beard

Take a keyboard breath where you'd normally take a speaking

breath and you're less likely to fluster the reader. A flustered reader is less likely to buy.

As I said, no one ever perished from an overdose of clarity.

MILITARY EQUIPMENT

D. U.S. ARMY SPECIAL FORCES M-1984 WATERPROOF BOOT

Specially created for U.S. Special Forces, this all-climate, all terrain, multi-purpose boot incorporates the most sophisticated materials, design and construction features modern technology can provide. Rugged outer shell of silicone-saturated cowhide in combination with lightweight, high abrasion nylon Cordura is significantly lighter than all leather boots.

Inner lining of long-lasting absorbent, non-woven Cabrelle, in combination with the microporous Gore-Tex membrane bonded to the inner lining provides a totally waterproof, breathable shield and some insulation against heat and cold.

Also features: Ski-binding, lands on the sole and heel grooves; removable washable saran mesh sack lining; protective stainless steel plate for additional firmness required in mountain scaling, rappelling and skiing; three layered super-resilient box toe for long wear and barrel style speed hooks to facilitate rapid donning and removal of the boots. Made in the U.S.A. Color: Black. Sizes Available: 7 to 13 (Whole Sizes Only) in Regular and Wide Widths.

Q89-11   SF M-1984 Waterproof Boot $89.95

Figure 4-1

Copy reads: "Rugged outer shell of silicone-saturated cowhide in combination with lightweight, high abrasion nylon Cordura is significantly lighter than all leather boots."

What did the writer mean by "all leather boots"? "All-leather boots," meaning boots made entirely of leather? A hyphen would clarify. "Any leather boot," which a minor word change would clarify? No, don't tell me it makes no difference. We're supposed to be wordsmiths. A blacksmith who puts any piece of curved metal on a horse's hoof isn't a professional; neither is wording which puts vague information on a description.

While we're at it, what does "high abrasion nylon" mean? Does it mean "high abrasion-*resistant* nylon"? If so, say so.

There is no
time limit to real style.

19A-C. Beautiful fabrics, neutral in color, have always given the wearer a style of aplomb. **19A.** The pure cashmere sweater, white with a diamond-intarsia yoke of beige and grey. Sizes S,M,L by William Kasper. 200.00 (4.60). **19B.** Barry Bricken's fine worsted wool gabardine pants, superbly classic. Available fully lined, in winter white as shown. Sizes 2-16. 128.00 (3.25). Not shown: **19C.** The same pants as above; unlined, in black. In sizes 2-16. 118.00 (3.25). Both, Sport Shop.

Figure 4-2

The first sentence: "Beautiful fabrics, neutral in color, have always given the wearer a style of aplomb." Well, the words all are spelled right, but what does it mean? Items on this page are white, beige, and grey, and the pants are available in black. Are all these neutral colors? I'll bet my aplomb the writer could have written more clearly if form weren't paramount over substance.

Figure 4-3

8A. Lavishly large, manmade
Baroque pearls are interspersed
with faceted, iridescent cylinders of glass in a mutable purple
and blue mixture. An N-M exclusive, by Pierre Cardin. The
necklace is 30″ long. 130.00
(3.00). Costume Jewelry.

8A

We're rolling along nicely with this description until we hit the word *mutable*. The
dictionary says that word means "Capable
of change or being changed in form or na-
ture." Oh. I see. Now, what is it we're describing? Iridescent cylinders of glass?
They're mutable? Okay, if you say so. By
the way, what does that mean they do? I
wish you'd told me.

25A. Drop the relaxed shape of this knit tunic in cotton and silk over any bright idea—shirts, skirts, pants. The tactile blending of fibers mixes medium to pale shades of neutral beige and ecru. The sweater is hand-knit, with tubular edging detail. An N-M exclusive, in sizes S, M, L. 78.00 (3.25). From the Sport Shop.

25B-D. Coordination in cotton. **25B.** The sweater vest, with "paper doll" intarsia. S-L. 96.00 (3.25). **25C.** Ruffled blouse of cotton and linen, in hand- kerchief weight. 4-12. 110.00 (2.75). **25D.** Long, pleated plaid skirt in pima cotton shirting. 4-12. 116.00 (3.25). All, colors as shown. Sport Shop.

Figure 4-4

If you write headings such as "The interplay of pattern and textures changes style as you mix the elements," you probably love puzzles. What if the reader doesn't? Analyzing the sentence clears away some of the murkiness, but who will take the time to perform an analysis? Why not nail the reader with a headline picking up image-generating words in the body copy, such as *relaxed shape?* For that matter, why not keep a relaxed and *conversational* tone instead of showing off with phrases such as *tactile blending?* Ask a panel of your customers to de- scribe *tactile blending* and I'll bet you won't use that phrase again.

CHAPTER 5

What's on Top of the Copy-Block?

FIRST, *YOU* TRY IT!

Your assignment: A family clothing catalog has a generic heading:

Squall Jacket. . . $69.50

Add more copy to *position* the squall jacket. We want a headline—obviously longer—which not only tells us what it is but gives us a quick explanation of what it does.

If you can make this lengthened headline lively, you're all the more professional. But don't lapse into deep romance. That's another assignment altogether.

(Warning: Don't change *Squall Jacket* to *Rain Jacket.* That's evolution in reverse.)

Take 30 seconds. No longer than that.

What's your solution? "Let It Rain, Let It Pour. You're Snug and Dry in This $69.50 Squall Jacket"? Okay. Not inspired, but you're completely workmanlike. If you want to see the brilliant heading for this item, from the fastest-growing family fashion catalog in the business, take a look at Fig. 5-1.

The Six Types of Headings

Analysis shows us two key families of headings—

- ► Nominative
- ► Descriptive

Nominative headings are simple categorizations such as *Dress, Cordless Telephone,* and *Radio.*

Descriptive headings replace the name with what that name represents, such as *For An Evening Out, Twirl as You Talk,* and *AM/FM Cube.*

Within each family we have three copy choices—

- ► Basic
- ► Romantic
- ► Positioned

Basic headline copy is a no-nonsense, unassailable approach: *Red Jersey Dress*. Romantic headline copy attempts to superimpose an emotional reaction: *The Paris Salon Look*. Positioned copy replaces product with product-in-use: *Perfect for Office or for Evening Out*.

So actually, we can choose from six headline types:

> ► Basic nominative
> ► Romantic nominative
> ► Positioned nominative
> ► Basic descriptive
> ► Romantic descriptive
> ► Positioned descriptive

So what?

Match Headings to Your Readers

So this: By matching headings to your readers you're more likely to get an order.

Why? For two reasons:

First, it's possible to promise too much, just as it's possible to promise too little. Either way, you've disconnected the thin line of rapport you're hoping for as the recipient flips through the first few pages of your catalog.

Second, business-to-business catalogs take a calculated risk when they depart from basic nominative. That risk can pay off, by either adding enough romance to generate an impulse-buy or by positioning the item so the reader becomes an unwitting convert; or the risk can turn off the energy-flow. That's the challenge of this business!

Is it profitable to romanticize the headline so far the reader has to stop—reconnoiter—then check the picture again to be sure he or she has understood what you're selling? Headline copy becomes a game of Russian Roulette.

"Contemporary" catalog writing leans toward romanticization without touching either a nominative or descriptive base. This is a bleed-over from the most upper-crustish catalogs, and it seems to have filtered down to all levels. Sometimes it's a way for the writer to show off, and that's when it gets dangerous, because the reader just can't follow the writer into the byzantine maze of nondescriptive words.

(The whole issue doesn't exist in catalogs that don't use headings at all. They have to grab with the first few words of body-copy . . . or with an overpowering illustration.)

A catalog headline says:

Strike it Rich!

The picture shows a miniature replica of an oil derrick (positioned, for some reason, against a venetian blind, which makes the derrick hard to see). Body copy doesn't implement the heading or follow through on the "Strike It Rich" romance:

> These 18K gold-plated oil derricks are perfect
> conversation pieces for home or office...

Sure, we know the phrase "Strike It Rich"—we'd also capitalize *It*—can relate to an oil-strike. (And sure, you or I wouldn't have intermixed plural and singular in the description, which continues, "To turn it off...") But if we're romanticizing *without* a nominative or descriptive base, do we intrigue or confuse?

An indication of how the heading affects the tone of the whole copy-block is this description of a necklace:

> *Rondo a la turquoise:* neo-classic variations on a
> theme of silver circles, with a touch of the blues.
> Counterpoints by Jay Feinberg. Faux turquoise
> necklace of antique-looking silver discs in a
> jazzy progression of sizes.

Interesting. *After* Jay Feinberg we have a solid description of what the item really is.

Safe Isn't Always Best

You don't really need a catalog writer for basic nominative headings. In fact, catalog-houses whose copy stems from product managers defend this type of heading on grounds of "descriptive integrity." They have a point: It's hard to exaggerate or make a phony claim in a basic nominative heading.

But safe isn't always best. A powerful writer can bring a mundane item to life with a bright headline that romanticizes or positions.

Can you intermix heading types? You bet. Try doing it. At worst, you'll stretch some rusty creative muscles. At best, you'll add wallop to some rusty descriptions.

We're all victims of neatness complexes. We set a pattern for description-headings, and then we're stuck with that pattern throughout the catalog.

Our theory is sound—the catalog gains coherence—but our execution of the theory may cost us some orders.

Polarplus® lining gives warmth without bulk, shakes dry

Thinsulate® gives extra warmth in the sleeves

Raglan sleeves give you room to move, let you add a sweater underneath

A storm flap underneath the zipper keeps wind out

Zippered handwarmer pockets keep small items secure. Inner pocket is zippered too

Rugged Supplex® nylon shell is treated with Durepel® to repel wind, rain. It wears like iron, feels soft as cotton

Rib-knit waistband and cuffs won't "pill"

Our famous SQUALL JACKET fights off wind, rain, even a dunking. Then shakes dry (like a dog). Costs just $69.50!

Now tell us, who do you think makes a better "element fighting" jacket? A sportswear designer or a maker of sailoring gear?

We think you should go with the latter. (That's us. We first made our famous Squall back in the days when we sold mostly to sailors. And we tested it on the open seas!) Read about the features over there to the right. Then order one and let us prove ourselves to you. Machine wash. Made in USA.

Mn's *Red, Sunburst, Royal, Teal, Charcoal.* Mn's Regular in S 34-36, M 38-40, L 42-44, XL 46-48. 8829C27 **$69.50** Mn's Tall in M 38-40, L 42-44, XL 46-48, XXL 50-52. 8828C21 **$79.50**
Wm's *Red, Sunburst, Royal, Teal, Grape* in S 6-8, M 10-12, L 14-16, XL 18. 8827C26 **$69.50**
Youths' *Red, Sunburst, Royal, Teal, Grape* in S 6-8, M 10-12, L 14-16. 8826C20 **$49.50**

Teal Grape

Royal Charcoal

Red Sunburst

90

The term "Squall Jacket" is itself light-years more salesworthy than "Rain Jacket." Lands' End, an innovator in many areas of catalog copywriting, stretches the *basic nominative* headline as far as it can go without becoming *romantic nominative.* Even if you aren't looking for a jacket, doesn't this above-the-norm description of *what it is* make you want to buy?

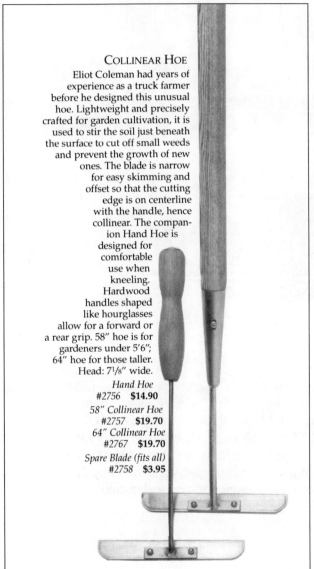

COLLINEAR HOE

Eliot Coleman had years of experience as a truck farmer before he designed this unusual hoe. Lightweight and precisely crafted for garden cultivation, it is used to stir the soil just beneath the surface to cut off small weeds and prevent the growth of new ones. The blade is narrow for easy skimming and offset so that the cutting edge is on centerline with the handle, hence collinear. The companion Hand Hoe is designed for comfortable use when kneeling. Hardwood handles shaped like hourglasses allow for a forward or a rear grip. 58" hoe is for gardeners under 5'6"; 64" hoe for those taller. Head: 7⅛" wide.

Hand Hoe
#2756 **$14.90**
58" Collinear Hoe
#2757 **$19.70**
64" Collinear Hoe
#2767 **$19.70**
Spare Blade (fits all)
#2758 **$3.95**

Figure 5-2

This headline is basic nominative, with a twist: What's a "collinear" hoe? That adjectival noun turns the two-word heading not quite halfway toward positioned nominative. For those who know the word, it *is* positioned nominative. Illustration shows us an unusually-shaped hoe, so "collinear" must refer to this shape. The single word "Hoe" would have been too spartan a heading, even for basic nominative.

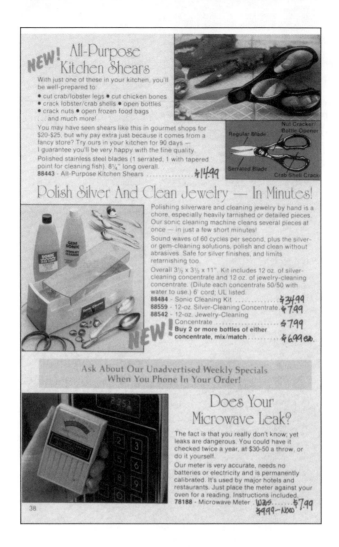

Figure 5-3

Can you intermix heading styles? This digest-size catalog page proves you can. "All-Purpose Kitchen Shears" is pure basic nominative. "Polish and Clean Jewelry—In Minutes!" is romantic descriptive. "Does Your Microwave Leak?" is positioned descriptive. (If you're wondering how silver polish can be romantic, your scope has been too narrow; you've been thinking of fashion, beauty aid, and food copy. Romance is a copy approach, not an appendage to particular commodities.)

Figure 5-4

We discussed plain vanilla copy in chapter one. Here are plain vanilla headings. They're basic nominative, of course. Do they force a plain vanilla description? Certainly not. Item "D" uses the word *snappy,* an excellent adjective for a lapel pin. One headline is *romantic* nominative. Which one? Right! "Glamor Sweatshirt." The difference one extra word makes is in our labeling, not in the writing. The single word "Sweatshirt" would have been an inappropriate heading, because it wouldn't be descriptive: The garment isn't an unadorned sweatshirt.

CHAPTER 6

"Let Me Make This Absolutely Clear"

FIRST, *YOU* TRY IT!

Your assignment: You supervise the copy department at a catalog house. You sell sports, diving, and upscale automobile equipment. One of your writers, a recent college graduate, has handed you a piece of copy with these words in it:

```
turgid
minimal
incongruity
bifurcated
maturation
plethora
utilize
haut monde
pulchritudinous
```

You decide: Which of these words belong in catalog copy? Which words don't?

Take 30 seconds. No longer than that.

I hope your decision is *none* of these words belong in catalog copy. We're supposed to be communicators. The catalog writer who practices vocabulary *suppression* is the professional communicator. Save your massive vocabulary for the crossword puzzle.

(What's wrong with *utilize?* It's pompous. Why utilize *utilize* when you can use *use?* If you're hiring writers and an applicant uses *utilize,* beware!)

"Yipes!"

I was in the less-than-fortunate position of moderator at one of those "panel discussions" on copywriting.

Instead of being able to assume the anticipated role of mentor and kindly dean, I found myself defending what seems to be an increasingly uncommon (and even unpopular) approach to copywriting. One of my fellow panelists had made this brave conjecture:

> "The copywriter's role is to teach, to instruct. We aren't just parrots. We're leaders. The reader has a responsibility, just as we do. If we write on an eighth grade level, that's as far as our readers' learning level will reach."

The other panelist agreed:

> "Yes, that's the only hope we have if we want others
> in marketing to take us seriously. We can't just use
> the words everybody knows without looking up if we
> want to justify our profession."

My own reaction—"Yipes!"—was drowned in a sea of acceptance by those present. The sentiment was unmistakable: This group, at least, sees the copywriter's role in a different light from the rose-colored lamp I've been shining on my keyboard.

I long have preached: One key to successful copywriting is vocabulary *suppression*. My "Yipes!" reaction stemmed from my ongoing fight to clarify what we have to say by using as many one and two syllable words as possible. Then the flashes of color come from *colorful* words, not from *incongruity* and *plethora*.

When I challenged the logic of assuming the casual reader would stay with us through an exercise in intellectualized terminology, one of the attending group answered, "Readers appreciate learning something new. They have dictionaries, just as we do. If we use a word they don't know, they'll look it up."

Will they, now? My keyboard has a lot of scar tissue that says otherwise. So my conclusion that afternoon, philosopher that I am, was... Okay. Until the mob leads those copywriters to the rhetorical guillotine, let them eat cake.

Why the Reader's Dictionary Won't Budge Off the Shelf

We have every right to expect our catalog-recipients to know the word *cat* and the word *free*. But how about these words, each of which was thrown at me in hit-and-run copy within the pages of three catalogs addressed to an anonymous me:

> tumid
> zonal
> disparity
> optimal
> bifurcated
> nonpareil
> brachial
> dulcet
> potpouries

umbels
tractable
cavalier

As it turns out, I know the meanings of all the words exept umbels. (Want to know what it means? Look it up, as I did. Hate the writer, as I did.) In fact, I'm literate enough to see that *potpourris* (plural of pot-pourri) is misspelled. And what does that prove?

As a catalog browser, I'm not going to jump into the arena and engage in a battle of wits with the copywriter. For heaven's sake, by what divine edict does a writer arrogate the right to *demand* the reader's parallel knowledge?

Don't *you* resent someone you don't know (and don't care about) testing your knowledge? Wouldn't you sidle away from a dinner guest who used *brachial* and *zonal* in conversation?

The reader's dictionary will stay on the shelf and your description won't generate any reaction other than annoyance *unless* the illustration is such a barn-burner the reader feels a driving need to know more about what you're selling. But consider: Is the writer who uses illustrations as a crutch a true professional?

But If You HAVE to Use an Unfamiliar Word...

Let's be charitable.

Let's embrace this supposition: You *have* to use a big word. The manufacturer has said, "If you don't tell them this is *aqueous-nonadhering* canvas you don't get any co-op money."

How do you handle it?

Simple: Your description incorporates what the manufacturer wants you to say...*and* what the reader's eye accepts. Your copy would open something like this:

> NEW! Aqueous Nonadhering Canvas
> Aqueous nonadhering means water won't pene-
> trate. No matter how wet and blustery the
> weather, this haystack cover will...

Key "tie-words" such as *means, is named for,* or *our way of telling you that,* or even a definition within a pair of parentheses will help the reader through the maze.

We're in Their Ballpark

Maybe we'll reach a dim day when a) all catalogs except one have gone out of business, and if you want to read catalog copy it's this one or nothing; or b) some goofball offers a test-plus-prize for being able to define all the bizarre words in the catalog. Until that day, I'll stick with my belief that somebody whose catalog-readership is casual, not forced, doesn't give a hoot how big a vocabulary *we* have.

The ability to simplify—what a lovely, useful talent! Those with that talent can write catalog copy without ever developing a case of foot-in-mouth disease. Their copy won't win the William F. Buckley lexicographer's award. They're true communicators, operating inside the reader's experiential background instead of their own.

An unswerving opinion: The catalog copywriter who says smugly to the victim reading his or her words, "I know something you don't," is in the wrong profession, marking time until Scrabble becomes a career instead of a game.

Figure 6-1

The last sentence of the heading: "Nothing is simpler or more sophisticated." I have a different suggestion for a final sentence to this obfuscation: "Nothing is more nebulous." Just below is "The quintessential gentleman's sweater." Are you a quintessential gentleman? Am I? How do we find out if we qualify? And while we're investigating, why do we have the word "Merrick" in quotation marks, with no further explanation?

G WARING BLENDOR®
Waring's 50th anniversary model is our favorite. The quintessential design has all the best features of the 1935 model — heavy 40 oz. glass container made from the original mold, integral stainless steel blades, chromed steel base and a heavy duty, commercial 2-speed motor. 15½" high.
#02-279406 $98.00

Figure 6-2

To match our quintessential sweater, let's get a quintessentially-designed blender. Does the writer mean this is a "classic" design? What? When using words such as *quintessential,* ask yourself cold-bloodedly: Am I adding selling-value to the description?

'MONDRIAN' CREWNECK

a. A masterpiece of the knitter's art, made in Scotland of lightweight cashwool with the soft, smooth appeal of cashmere. Intarsia blocks of brilliant color make a strong statement against a solid navy back. Sizes M, L, XL.
U2436 $185

b. The Six-color Stripe Tie gives you color and texture for maximum versatility. A great tie for travel, handmade in Canada of chevron weave pure silk. U1686 $50

c. The Sea Island Pinpoint Oxford Shirt, in the lustrous cotton renowned for its silky smoothness. Pink, blue, or white, with pearl buttons. 14 ½ (32-33); 15 (32-34); 15 ½ and 16 (32-36); 16 ½ and 17 (33-36); 17 ½ (34-36). U2081 $98

Figure 6-3

This attractive sweater is a " 'Mondrian' Crewneck." Since the writer had room for puff copy such as "A masterpiece of the knitter's art," mightn't he have included an explanation such as "in the style of the artist Piet Mondrian, with blocks of vivid color at 90-degree angles"? Mightn't he explain the word *intarsia* (which means, if you look it up as I did, "inlaid"—a far more comprehensible word)? This copy is a "grabber" for those who know who Mondrian was. For the others, let them buy from somebody else. Who needs them?

HANDY BURNER COVERS LET STOVE CLEANUPS WAIT! Now, keep your stove looking smart and neat, even when you don't have time to clean up! Just place sturdy covers over burners. Decorative, vine-patterned covers hide mess, "dress up" older stoves . . . help tidy up your kitchen! Set of 4 steel covers—small, 8″ diameter; large 10¼″. Your choice of white or gold.

Set of 3 sm., 1 lg.   Set of 2 sm., 2 lg.
K1345 White ... **$6.99**   K1347 White ... **$6.99**
K1346 Gold..... **$6.99**   K1348 Gold..... **$6.99**

TURN ANY FAUCET INTO A SWIVEL SPRAYER-AERATOR with Spritzer®! It sprays—aerates—rinses—and swivels a full 360°! Reach every corner of your sink as you rinse vegetables, dishes; wash hair, etc. Change at a touch from a splashproof stream—to a strong, steady spray. Tough white delrin head won't heat up with hot water. Fits any standard threaded faucet—no tools needed. Great kitchen helper!
K1207 Spritzer® **$4.49**

ELEGANT RETURN ADDRESS LABELS are personalized in lustrous raised gold! Distinctive self-stick identification for letters, packages, books, etc.—labels cling to anything at a touch. Your name and address in gleaming raised gold letters on lovely matte-finish white. Set of 250 labels in handy box; ¾x1¾″. *Please print* name and address—up to 4 lines, 26 letters and spaces per line. One of our most beautiful labels!
P6177 Raised Gold Labels *(Name/Address?)* **$2.98**

SPACE-SAVING CAN RACK stores up to 60 cans in less than 1 square foot of space! Organizes vegetable, soup, tuna and sauce cans in cabinet for easy slide-out selection. Adjustable shelving and dividers accommodate different size cans and let you find what you need at a glance. Holds soda pop cans neat and handy in your refrigerator just like those used in convenience stores! Sturdy, vinyl-coated steel; 10x14x10½″.
K1531 Can Rack...................... **$18.99**

FROZEN FOOD LABELS. Identify every package in your freezer with these special self-stick labels. There's a place to write contents, date frozen and weight. Makes finding the right package easy . . . lets you use food before time steals freshness and flavor. Pack of 100 self-stick labels, 2x1⅛″. Special glow-green paper for easy finding and reading. Buy freezer pen, too . . . special ink has freezer staying power!
S2066 Frozen Food Labels, 100 .... **$1.00**
S3037 Freezer Marker Pen .... **98¢**

DELUXE HOLIDAY RETURN ADDRESS LABELS add a merry touch to every card, letter and package you send! Each white, self-stick label features your name, address and zip in bright red printing . . . highlighted by red and green holly, and a cheerful "Merry Christmas!" Boxed set of 250 labels, cling to anything at a touch! Each a big 2¼x⅝″. *Please print* 3-4 lines, 22 letters and spaces per line.
P6108 Holiday Labels *(Name/Address?)* ... **$2.98**

80

Figure 6-4

This quiet little page from a digest-size catalog has few words of more than two syllables. See how easy it is to read? See how clear the descriptions are? No, not every word-diet has to be this bland. The point of this illustration is: The Clarity Commandment works. Can you say that about copy-blocks resulting from a struggle to display the writer's vocabulary?

CHAPTER 7

Should Catalog Writers Have to Take Literacy Tests?

FIRST, *YOU* TRY IT!

Your assignment: You're the proofreader at a catalog house. A copywriter delivers this description:

> AN HISTORIC FIRST!!
> There's many kinds of rainware for ladies. But not one of them are like *Miladys' Coat-ture!* This coat feels like silk but actually breaths, you won't feel hot and uncomfortable. It's velcro fasteners let you zip up quick and easy. S-M-L, $49.95

Clean up this copy.

Take 30 seconds. No longer than that.

If your first move wasn't to change "An Historic" to "A Historic," your background has some phony pomposity in it. And did you get rid of the second exclamation point? Good for you, because two exclamation points are weaker than one.

Now to the serious stuff. Let's list the problems:

> 1. The writer always has a stronger way to start a sales argument than "There is..." or "There are..."
>
> 2. The first sentence has a singular verb (*is*) and a plural subject (*kinds*).
>
> 3. *Rainwear* is misspelled.
>
> 4. The next sentence has a singular subject (*one*) and plural verb (*are*).
>
> 5. *Milady's* has the apostrophe in the wrong place, but because this is a trade name we might pass responsibility for this illiteracy on to the manufacturer.
>
> 6. The word *breathes* is misspelled.
>
> 7. Two sentences are hooked together with a comma ("This coat feels like silk but actually breaths, you won't feel hot and uncomfortable.")

8. *Its* as a possessive never has an apostrophe. Terrible!

9. The final qualifiers should be adverbs, not adjectives—*quickly* and *easily.*

Did you get them all? You can be my proofreader. Did you miss some? Uh-oh. Don't write catalog copy until you brush up on spelling and grammar.

The Plumber Has His Tools. The Writer Should Have His Literacy

Back in the antediluvian days when the Sears catalog was the standard training-ground for catalog copywriters, the question of writer-literacy didn't exist.

Why? Implicit in being a *writer* was being *literate.* The plumber had his tools; the writer had his literacy.

Here we are, pushing the year 2001, and many plumbers don't carry tools. They're consultants, making a disgustingly stratospheric living by charging for estimates.

A lot of catalog writers seem to have an empty tool-chest, too. Is it because their background isn't formalized? What a wonderful society! Anyone can proclaim: "I'm a writer." Voila! He's a writer. Ready or not, here we come.

"And What's Wrong with That?"

When a catalog marketer asks me to share my usual set of cynical comments about copy, the company is forewarned: I take a hard look.

So I welcomed the opportunity to sail into an assemblage of the eight-person creative staff, plus a dozen assorted executives, of a giftware cataloger. It wasn't my fault that right there on the inside cover was this copy:

AN HISTORIC ISSUE

I thought my chiding was mild. *Everyone* knows it's "A historic..."—or *does* everyone know it?

Apparently not.

"What's wrong with that?" The question came from the copy chief. No damage below the water-line yet.

But then the head of the company piled on. "Yes, what's wrong with that?"

The questions were edged, almost triumphant. Had they caught me in a wrongful accusation?

Now, here's the point of all this mini-hullabaloo:

I had two backups with me—books on grammar by respected authorities. Both said flatly: no such construction as "An historic." It's "*A* historic."

Only because the consultation-day was just starting out did I join this battle. And you know what? Nobody in the room was even mildly interested in what the books—or I—had to say about this construction.

Trying to save the day with a little humor, I quipped, "I guess everyone had 'their' say on that point."

Blank. So what? We've stumbled so far down the grammatical ladder that singulars and plurals line up together like salt and sugar in the same bowl. "Those kind" didn't move them either.

So I scrapped grammar as a topic of discussion and went on to safer lands, such as omission of size in product description.

Okay, I stamp "borderline literate" on a bunch of foreheads. But are they wrong in ignoring the venerable rules of grammar?

Partly. Only partly.

What We Got Here Is . . .

I've given up on "have got." I was there when "impact" and "access" became transsexual, switching from nouns to verbs. I no longer cringe openly when 39-year-old teen-agers use "party" as a verb.

It isn't that my own standards lie flat on the ground. I'm not Edwin Newman; I'm not Strunk & White, the Harbrace Handbook, or the Associated Press Stylebook. I'm just another guy, toiling in the weedy fields of professional copywriting.

And because our job is to *communicate,* not *educate*—with the gap between those two words getting wider by the hour—I offer *THE RULE OF EFFECTIVE COMMUNICATION:*

> **The target-reader's comfort is the paramount consideration in word-choice.**

This isn't Miss Norwalk's second grade English class. She'd never let her charges end a sentence with a preposition. I not only don't mind this minor gaffe; I embrace it, because of a great big overriding Factor, crazy-glued to the underbelly of The Rule of Effective Communication:

> That's the way people talk.

As communicators, we *should* write the way people talk. In my opinion this isn't inconsistent with basic literacy.

So we writers walk a tightrope. Sure, we have so much latitude the tightrope is the size of the Queen Mary's hawser, and, sure, it's only a few feet above ground. But it's there, that rope, giving us an uneasy footing above the grammatical abyss; when we lose awareness of it we cease to be professional writers at all.

Let's Use the Flaw-Seeking Loupe on Ourselves

I'm bothered that catalogs can be award-winners from one point of view and totally unacceptable from another.

What's unacceptable? Consistently poor grammar, for one thing. The same cataloger who suffers for hours over product positioning on a page doesn't seem to give a hoot that the headline on that same page strings two sentences together, tied by a comma.

I'm looking at a winner of a major catalog awards competition, judged by a panel of experts. It's as gorgeous a catalog as modern European production techniques can make it. But here's a typical headline:

> Each skin type has specific herbal needs, that's why Active Care is such an effective skin care program.

It doesn't matter, you say? It won't hurt response? I'm afraid you're right...and our profession is in trouble. The word "writer" always has had class and dignity, even with the soul-soiling prefix "copy" attached to its front end.

If we're spawning a generation of catalog writers who neither know nor care about learning rules of communication because they concern themselves only with what they call the "visual experience" of each page, then *glut* is too easy a word for the catalog world. *Rut* would be more apt.

Maybe We Should Have Our Own Stylebook

If I didn't know as well as you do that we never can get any two people in the catalog business to agree on anything, I'd suggest assembling a "Catalog Stylebook."

This stylebook would differ from the one developed by the New York Times and the one circulated by the Associated Press.

For example, my ideal stylebook *wouldn't* adhere slavishly to the stringent rules of grammar we learned in the third grade. Oh, I'm not backing away from my insistence that any writer with passable literacy should be able to separate two sentences with a period, not a comma. I *am* backing away from the antique notion of never ending a sentence with a preposition.

Heck, if we couldn't end sentences with a preposition we'd have to put on the outside of a mailing envelope the antique and forceless legend *This is the catalog you requested* instead of the twice-as-powerful *This is the catalog you asked for.*

And I'd allow paragraphs to begin with "And," as this one just did. Perfectly acceptable: The King James Bible has lots of paragraphs starting with "And."

But I'd shoot through the sloping forehead the writer who uses *for* when he, she, or it means *because.* Why? It's a pomposity born of insecurity, that's why. And I'd handcuff to the next atomic bomb-test a writer who in any seriousness uses *etc.*

A Broad Boulevard, Not a Tightrope

If your reaction is, "This guy has us walking a tightrope," my answer is: "It's a broad boulevard, not a tightrope. Catalog writers are supposed to be communicators, and all we have to do is follow the easiest, least-stringent, and most logical rule of force-communication— *THE "WHOSE MESSAGE IS IT ANYWAY?" RULE* already mentioned in this text. Just in case you've forgotten:

> Your message should operate within the experiential background of the message-recipient, not within your own experiential background.

Does the typical reader of your catalog use the word *for*...or the word *because?* Does that reader ever use (as some order forms do) the phrase *referenced items?* Does that reader use *impact* and *access* as verbs?

The last question gives away the game: The world of computers does use *impact* and *access* as verbs. (I do draw the line at *window* as a verb.) If you're writing for this group, within their experiential background, they won't be cowed or outraged or puzzled by the terminology.

Can you write a whole 48-page catalog of computer accessories and peripherals without once using *impact* or *access* as verbs? You bet. This gives hope to the broadly-educated writer who doesn't have mastery of in-terms but does know how to communicate.

Poets Beware

Poets revel in inside-out descriptions, in "conceits" tying two unlike thoughts together, and in abstruse literary references.

So unless they can switch off their afterburners, poets aren't good catalog copywriters. Still, sometimes a benevolent or desperate cataloger hires a poet, who stays in practice by peppering catalog copy with inside-out descriptions, conceits, and abstruse literary references.

I assume it was an unsuccessful poet who wrote:

> DRINK TO ME
> ONLY WITH THINE EYES...
> ...and I'll drink in, with my own orbs, your romantically elegant and relevant knit. Crumple? Perhaps in rhapsody, never in the midst of revel. At witching hour, this Fairyland Black comes into its own, but Cinderella needs only glass slippers to claim her prince.

Like one of those puzzle contests in which 20,000 winners get a new set of puzzles, this copy leads into itself. Let's see: Ben Jonson wrote "Drink to me only with thine eyes," but so what? He's been hit and run over by the rest of this copy. Cinderella—ah, there's a recognizable name. At midnight, did she turn into a pumpkin? No, that isn't right. Let's start somewhere else: "Witching hour" is midnight. The knit dress is black. Whee! Solved one. But "Fairyland" wouldn't have witches, would it? It wouldn't be black, would it? And why the capitalization? Is "Fairyland Black" a name, like Morgan Fairchild?

Let's look at this copy through less-jaundiced eyes. We realize that high-fashion copy can invent its own set of rules. Depending on the ambience—Bloomingdale's catalog, for example—the reader *expects* unconventional copy.

A quick look at a Bloomie's catalog gives us evidence. Some headings for fashion-descriptions:

- Your message to the world: Keep an eye on this body
- Reversing or traversing
- The statement is you, pure and simple
- Carole Little explores the color/shape equation
- An undemanding delivery
- Gloria Vanderbilt's weekend joys

(To a male who stumbles onto this catalog, that last one is brutally uninviting.)

But that's Bloomingdale's. Their catalogs are of a piece. Consistency overrides the Clarity Commandment, especially since, after the headings, copy settles down to hard-boiled, Windex-clear descriptions.

(With an occasional exception: Copy for a blazer refers to "creamy black suede with tuxedo-like lapels of ostrich lamb." No one I know can identify "ostrich lamb," and if it's supposed to mean "ostrich-*grained* lamb*skin*" the young woman who called this copy to my attention would appreciate the clarification.)

Why Not Have An Outsider Read It?

Let's not get too inbred. Inbreeding brought hemophilia to the royal houses of Europe. Inbreeding weakens the bloodlines of racehorses. Inbreeding of humans is outlawed in most states.

So why not bring in outsiders—fresh genes—to proofread catalog copy?

If you really want to avoid the witching hour at Fairyland, go a little overboard in your instructions to the proofreader. Ask for red stars next to copy carrying the seeds of obscurity. Then, after the outside proofreader has gone back to Conehead Corners for the night, make dispassionate executive decisions. (You want a detective, not an ombudsman, and proofreaders are guides, not gods.)

Don't just get anybody to read proofs. Look for a demographic/psychographic match. The closer an outsider parallels your target-group, the more likely your copy will follow The Whose Message Is It Anyway? Rule. Matching message to recipient won't win a prize for poetry, but it's a good way to stay in business.

Aw, What's the Big Deal?

My plea: Don't plant more weeds in our grammatical garden. Let those other guys debase the language. We'll be there as aerial observers, and when their linguistic atrocities become slang and then general usage we'll alertly adapt.

But let's not lead the way to perdition by following the lead of whoever wrote, in an upscale fashion catalog:

> A richer, heavier silk is styled with fully stitched
> front pleats that always lay flat . . .

Now, let's suppose your reaction is, "So what? Who knows or cares that the word is *lie,* not *lay?* What's the big deal?"

The big deal parallels finding a tiny rivulet of blood trickling down your face. Where did it come from? Are you quietly bleeding to death?

Nothing so dramatic. But writers—even copywriters—still carry a reflected glory, a patina rubbed off from Shakespeare and Aldous Huxley. Over the last five years or so, we've seen The Invasion of the Grammar Snatchers, and Brasso has replaced silver polish.

Too obscure? A handful of specifics, then:

Let's Not Use These Terms

If your own grammar is a little shaky, how about this:

Between now and one month from today use this Starter Kit of minor errors in English. Just avoid *these.* Then, every month, add one or two more.

> DON'T SAY The pearl necklace *compliments* the worsted suit.
> INSTEAD, SAY The pearl necklace *complements* the worsted suit.

DON'T SAY You'll feel *badly* if . . .
INSTEAD, SAY You'll feel *bad* if . . .

DON'T SAY *Irregardless* of what you've used before . . .
INSTEAD, SAY *Regardless* of what you've used before . . .

DON'T SAY It's *different than* any other high-density disk.
INSTEAD, SAY It's *different from* any other high-density disk.
(Anglican countries: *different to.*)

DON'T SAY We *might of* used a looser weave.
INSTEAD, SAY We *might have* used a looser weave.

DON'T SAY We'll *try and* get your order out the same day.
INSTEAD, SAY We'll *try to* get your order out the same day.

DON'T SAY We'll *appraise* you of the shipping date.
INSTEAD, SAY We'll *apprise* you of the shipping date.

DON'T SAY This *luxuriant* set of furniture . . .
INSTEAD, SAY This *luxurious* set of furniture . . .

DON'T SAY The cassettes will *learn* you to speak French.
INSTEAD, SAY The cassettes will *teach* you to speak French.

DON'T SAY You'll know where *it's at.*
INSTEAD, SAY You'll know where *it is.*

If you're unconvinced that grammar and effective catalog copywriting are related, I'm not chagrined. Compiling this minilist won't have affected (not *effected*) you, but it makes me feel better!

**VACUUM DESIGNED
FOR PET GROOMING**

Used by trainers and breeders, our new *Pet Vac*® is specifically designed and engineered for your loving pet. This cordless electric grooming device actually draws your pets loosened hair through its brush quickly and easily. Its 6-volt vacuum removes dirt and fleas off your pet so quietly that they may actually look forward to the next grooming. Operates on 4 "C" batteries (not included). Measures 13" x 3 1/2". Weighs 1 lb. 90 day warranty.
■ Pet Vac VI#21 $34.95 (4.95)

Figure 7-1

This description says the Pet Vac "actually draws your pets loosened hair through its brush. . ." Oh, we might attack the word *actually,* a "Golly, Gee Whiz!" word which doesn't help comprehension because the name of this item is "Vacuum." But let's focus our wrath instead on *pets loosened hair.* Without the apostrophe, *pet's,* we have to go back for a comprehension pit-stop. And once we've built up a head of steam, let's blast whoever wrote ". . . removes dirt and fleas off your pet so quietly they may actually look forward. . ." This "actually"-happy writer actually should go back to school to study actual agreement between matching components. I mean, actually, *pet* takes the singular *he, she* or *it,* doesn't it, actually?

C. THE TOMCAT FOLDING KNIFE
The TOMCAT by SOG Specialty Knives represents the spirit of the Fighter Pilot-Bold, Strong and Daring. The TOMCAT is unlike any other knife on the market today and serves faithfully as either a survival/utility knife or as a defensive tool. The SOG TOMCAT possesses the following attributes:
—All stain resistant steel construction
—A 3¾" Bowie style blade which features exact grind lines and superior cutting capabilities
—A New negative-draft locking system
—An exclusive "point-positive" Kraton® grip
—A duel-mount nylon sheath
The TOMCAT is equally at home in the field as in close-quarters. The bold syling provides an extremely visual blade that is distinct from any other production or custom folder today.
Q72-155 The TOMCAT Knife $79.95

Figure 7-2

The hyphen between "Pilot" and "Bold" may not be the copywriter's fault. (See the difference between *Pilot-Bold*. . . and *Pilot—Bold*. . .? What? You don't? You're reading the wrong book. Back to "Run, Dick, Run.") But somebody—copywriter or proofreader—should have seen "duel." Dueling is illegal in this country, so open advertising of a *duel-mount nylon sheath* might appeal only to Alexander Hamilton and Aaron Burr. Let's hope it was the typesetter who misspelled "dual."

Figure 7-3

The subhead under the picture: "Don't Bake in Your Birth!" You mean this writer doesn't know the difference between *birth* and *berth?* (Yeah, one sometimes stems from the other, but not in copywriting.) Doesn't your opinion of *what's being described* sink? We readers scramble into a single blob whatever is being described and the way it's described, like the white and yolk of an egg.

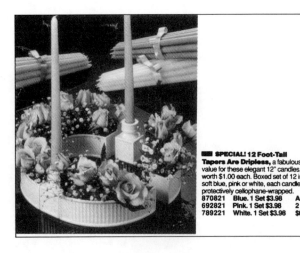

Figure 7-4

118

Figure 7-4

Where was the proofreader? Did you ever see a 12 foot-tall candle? Maybe in the Guinness Book of Records. As the body copy correctly points out, these candles are 12 *inches* tall. Somebody should have seen it before the presses rolled. ("A dozen" instead of "12" would have prevented this puzzle from happening.) A suggestion to catalogers who have either a) the time or b) access to college English instructors and/or students: Pay them by the page to proof-read. Have them put a pencil-dot above every word, then sign the page. Count the number of typos and obvious grammatical errors they find. *Then* decide about the value of this extra checkup.

CHAPTER 8

Why Not Tell 'Em What It's For?

FIRST, *YOU* **TRY IT!**

Your assignment: You're teaching Catalog Writing 101. A student hands in this description of an automobile seat-cover:

> RICH, THICK LAMB'S WOOL SEAT COVER gives you high style and high comfort. Fits every domestic and imported car (specify make and model).

"Nope," you say. "You've left out the key ingredient."

"What's that?" your student asks. So you tell your student what *you'd* have included, which is . . .

Take 30 seconds. No longer than that.

Okay, what did you change or add? Right! Your student didn't realize that many catalog readers don't know why they should install a lamb's wool seat cover. Telling them what it *is* and what it *does* interests the seller; telling them what it will do *for them* interests the readers.

So you add, "You'll be cooler in summer, warmer in winter." As a parallel, you add, "You won't need to run your air conditioner as much." You add, "Genuine lamb's wool seat cover helps circulation of your blood by equalizing weight-distribution." You add, "It protects the upholstery."

Lord knows *what* you add. But as a professional copywriter you know the difference between what the vendor cares about—what it is—and what I as buyer care about—what it will do for me.

Phrases with a Promise

What do these phrases have in common?

- This will enable you to . . .
- Now you can . . .
- Ideal for . . .
- For the first time you'll . . .
- Wear it to the . . .
- This not only will . . .
- When you need . . .

It doesn't require a heavyweight guess to give us the answer. Each of these is a promise: The copy that follows will tell us what it's for.

What Could Be Easier?

A primitive function of the copywriter is to swap places with the reader. The copywriter, in the reader's position, asks, "What's it for?"—and then answers the question.

Sometimes we forget: The reader's experiential background doesn't parallel ours. We assume a knowledge-base that doesn't exist.

(I wonder how many millions of sales-dollars are lost in computer software, peripherals, and supplies because the writer doesn't swap places with the reader. The writer blithely uses initials and in-terms the digit-heads know but the typical user doesn't know. Unwittingly the catalog aims itself at a coterie instead of the broadest base of potential buyers.)

What could be easier than telling us what it's for? Sure, a hammer doesn't need a ton of use-description—unless it differs from standard hammers. But how about a knife? Haven't you seen copy glorifying by *label* the type of steel and the type of handle, with no space allocated to *use?*

A key benefit of telling the reader what it's for: You help justify the price.

What brought this to mind is a copy-block I saw in a catalog I much admire. The first sentence is useless. The second sentence specifies uses, within a narrow range outside my fields of interest. Once the copy gets into gear do I as reader begin to salivate? By the time the writer completes the description, has he or she diddled my imagination so the relatively high price justifies itself?

It's the copywriter's call, because space is adequate and plenty of information exists. The description:

> Here's everything you ever wanted in a pocketknife—and more! [*That's the useless sentence.*] Ideal for hunting or fishing, with 29 implements it's also the perfect general purpose knife. [*That's the weak "covering" sentence.*] Features include: large blade, small blade, corkscrew, can opener with small screwdriver, cap lifter with screwdriver and wire stripper, reamer/awl with sewing eye, scissors, Phillips screwdriver, magnifying glass, wood saw, fish scaler with hook disgorger and ruler (cm & inches), nailfile with metal file/metal saw and nail cleaner, fine screwdriver, keyring, tweezers,

toothpick, chisel, pliers with wire cutter, mini-
screwdriver, ballpoint pen. Crafted in Switzerland of first quality stainless steel by
Victorinox. 3¹/₂″ closed. Weighs just 6.5 oz.
2691T Swiss Champ Knife............$72.00

All right, you're the copy chief and this crosses your desk. What's your comment?

Obviously the copy chief for this company said, "Okay, get started on the next item." Would you have made a few suggestions to broaden the appeal-base? For example:

> 1. We say, "Ideal for hunting and fishing" and sug-
> gest no other uses. Are these all the possibilities?
> How are all those screwdrivers pertinent to hunting
> and fishing? Mightn't we say, "A whole tool-chest in
> your pocket, no matter where you are. Ideal for hunt-
> ing and fishing"? We no longer exclude logical
> buyers.

> 2. How about that ball-point pen? When has any-
> body seen a knife with a built-in pen? Can't we make
> something of this?

> 3. The laundry-list of features seems to be copied
> off the manufacturer's spec-sheet. Why not combine
> the screwdrivers ("Five different screwdrivers!") and
> list the blades by use-groups?

I'm beating this about the head and shoulders unnecessarily, because except for that first sentence we have a completely acceptable
piece of copy. What we don't have is recognition of the total marketplace: a) I don't hunt and I don't fish. b) This isn't an outdoor sports
catalog. c) What's in this knife for me?

A Couple of Words Will Do It

Take a look at this copy-block and imagine how much weaker it
would be if the words "without using a stove" weren't there:

> Imagine being able to have a *hot meal* in your
> car, office, dorm and even in bed *without using a*
> *stove!* Our soft, vinyl pouch container with its
> automatic thermostat that's set at 170°, will
> steadily warm and hold any cooked food put in-

> side! It safely heats unopened canned goods, thaws and warms frozen dinners or boil-in-bag entrees. Keeps them *piping hot for up to 10 hours,* without loss of taste, texture or quality . . . ready to eat when you are. Plug it into standard household current or into cigarette lighter of your car, boat, or recreational vehicle! (adapter included). Interior is insulated, so the pouch always stays cool to the touch. Measures $9'' \times 12'' \times 1^{1}/_{2}''$. UL listed. Brown. P.S. It's great for shut-ins!

Even without the *stove* reference, it's a superior piece of descriptive copy, because it tells the reader what it's for, three different ways. The *stove* reference adds another evaluation-level—a touchstone. We know going in, this isn't just warm; it's really hot.

And When They Obviously Know What It's For...

We knew when we started this chapter what those lamb's wool automobile seat covers were for: They cover the car seats.

But now we know a little more. We know we should look at those seat covers and that knife and *everything* we sell and ask: Is that really what they're for?

Covering the car seats is what seat covers *do,* not what they're for. To unearth their purpose we dig into the magical world of *benefit.* If you expound on benefit you implicitly tell the reader what it's for.

That's how we answered our 30-second question about lamb's wool seat covers. Are they for covering the car seats?

No.

They're for a whole bunch of benefits—physical, aesthetic, financial, status. When you describe benefits, you tell the reader what it's for.

A Modest Proposal

Knives, meal heaters, lamb's wool seat covers—these are easy and obvious examples.

When you're writing copy for men's or women's fashions, for luxury accessories, for flowers, for exotic foods, for office supplies—that's when you should hurl down the gauntlet at your copy.

Ask yourself, "Have I told 'em what it's for?" If you haven't, delete some of the puffery, some of the surplus adjectives such as "beautiful" and "attractive" (for that matter, deep-six the word "useful" unexplained), and even some of the historical base if it takes up space you need for reader-benefit.

Use the space you've picked up to increase the pulling-power of your description by telling the reader what it's for.

Figure 8-1

How simple . . . and how elegant! What if this copywriter had limited the description to what bungs, buttons, and dowels *are,* instead of telling the reader what they're for? Do you think the company would have sold as many assortments? Nobody wants 1100 pieces of wood; every craftsman wants his jobs to have a finished, professional look.

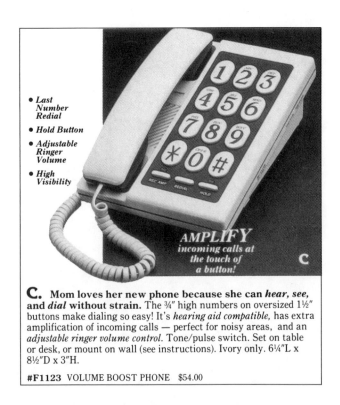
Figure 8-2

Figure 8-2

A phone with big numbers and amplification is *what it is*. Will the reader add the missing component? Maybe. Maybe not. So this writer wisely emphasizes not what it is, but *what it's for.* That's the difference between a salesperson and a sales clerk.

KITCHEN GARDEN

Ruta graveolens 'Jackman's Blue', Phlomis italica

BEE SKEP

The skep has been used in kitchen gardens as a bee hive since the Middle Ages. We have found some made in the traditional way, hand-coiled of rice grass and bound with rattan. The Bee Skep encourages a revitalized focus on herb and culinary gardens. And in case it crossed your mind, you needn't worry about becoming an unwilling host to a hive; this skep purposely lacks an entry. 15" across, 16½" high.

#2511   **$21**

Figure 8-3

Okay, so it's a bee skep. Gee. What's it for? How's that? You say "it encourages a revitalized focus on herb and culinary gardens"? That's very helpful. As soon as I figure out why I should have one (because you never do tell me), you'll hear from me. But don't wait by the phone.

CHAPTER 9

Give Them a Reason

FIRST, *YOU* TRY IT!

Your assignment: You're selling a high-style salt and pepper mill which grinds rock salt and peppercorns without mixing the two. You want to stop the casual page-flipper who ignores anything that doesn't grab and shake the imagination. What headline would you put on a description of this item?

Take 30 seconds. No longer than that.

Okay, what do you have? "Grind Your Own Salt and Pepper Right at the Formal Dinner Table"? Good for you. You've written a better headline than whoever wrote the flip, nondescript heading in an upscale catalog—Fig. 9-1.

Not As Obvious as It Seems

Let's suppose I have a retail store.

I also run newspaper ads, in both the main news section and the classified section.

And I mail catalogs four or six times a year.

Quick, now: In which marketing media should I most carefully consider giving my prospective customers a *reason* to buy what I'm displaying—whether that display is an array of the actual merchandise or a word-display describing the merchandise.

If you answer quickly, "All of them," in my opinion you've knee-jerked an automatic response based on the differential between a salesperson and a sales clerk, without considering the buyer's state of mind as he or she enters the arena.

Aware? Or Unaware?

In two of the four instances, the buyer enters the arena *aware.* When a customer walks into my store, unless that guy is a "mall-browser" he knows what I sell. The desire to upgrade awareness to buying impulse depends on whether my merchandise is well-displayed, whether my price and ambience match the buying mood, and (for impulse-buys) whether I'm able to generate instant excitement.

Only that last area—a big one, I'll admit—suggests a point-of-sale piece, a striking mannequin, or an actual demonstration to create a reason to buy. Why? Because the customer has come to me. I'm the host. Our encounter isn't accidental.

Even clearer-cut is my advertising in the classified section. Classified ads *aren't* (or at least shouldn't be) parallel to display ads, because the marketplace isn't the same. Once again, the prospective buyer plowing through the classified ads is *aware*. That individual may not have sought *me* out, but she's sought out my category.

So my classified ad should be competitive with what I expect the reader to find in the ads atop and beneath mine. I don't have to emphasize a *generic* reason to buy; I have to emphasize a reason to buy *from me*.

Now consider r.o.p. newspaper ads, magazine ads, and the catalogs I mail.

In these instances I catch the reader *unaware*. The generic desire to buy may pre-exist in embryo or dormant form, but it hasn't been triggered. That's my job. I have to give the reader a reason to buy.

So the half-trained clerk in my retail store may not damage the sale by limiting his pitch to a naked description. The counter clerk at the newspaper may not ruin my ad's chances by writing a bare-bones classified ad whose copy limits itself to an announcement of product for sale.

Sure, my cup runneth over if either of those individuals has some knowledge of salesmanship; but the significance of their words isn't as critical as the descriptions in my catalog.

So Why Doesn't Everybody Do This?

Why doesn't every copy-block in every catalog include a reason to buy?

Four possibilities: 1) The catalog-writer or instigator doesn't agree with the concept. 2) The catalog is from a source so well-known, so thoroughly established, and/or so dominant that the catalog itself *becomes* a reason to buy. 3) Space is too tight. 4) The writer doesn't think in terms of buyer-benefit.

I yield graciously to the second reason, and I sadly acknowledge the third, warning that in many cases it's an argumentative ploy. To those who subscribe to the first and fourth reasons, I'll point out that the "hot" catalogs of the last five years almost universally pitch "reason to buy" in their copy, sometimes allocating this facet of the marketing mix double the space allocated to "what it is."

We might add a fifth reason: "We're doing very well, thank you." No argument, except: How about testing copy with a "reason to buy" thrust?

An example: The catalog which has this description of a group of travel accessory-cases could very well claim, "We're doing very well, thank you." Yes, they are, but the pages of this book offer us a laboratory setting. Random selection of this copy doesn't mean it's defective, but rather that it's typical:

> *Personalized Packs* are trimmed in tan genuine leather—handsome in textured black vinyl with 22K Gold initials, smart snap-flap closings. Toiletry pack hangs 15³/₄" long on brass-plated ring for easy access to 3 nylon zip sections—one 9¹/₂×5¹/₂×2¹/₂" deep for bulky essentials. Super-slim tie pack holds up to 8 neat and crease-free on sturdy brass-plated rods.

Description is satisfactory. But I, as a casual page-flipper, read a few words and keep flipping. Unless I've been looking for a "Personalized Pack" (is this the best grabber-description?) I'm left outside the copy. The writer hasn't given me a reason to buy.

Leaning on the Everlasting Crutch

From the first day I sank my fangs into the neck of this so-called profession I've heard the weary cliché, "We don't have enough space." No, we never do, and I used to lean on that crutch myself.

The reason I now attack where I once sympathized isn't because the statement is flawed; no, it's universally true. It parallels somebody saying, "The reason I'm ugly is because I have two ears," or, "The reason I'm slow is because I only have two legs." Hey, there—*everybody* has two ears and two legs. Find a more logical excuse. *Everybody* has too little descriptive space, even those fellows who use two solid pages to describe an exercise machine.

An excellent catalog, one from which invariably I buy something I didn't think I wanted when I picked up the catalog (ah, what a triumph for the copywriter!), invariably packs reason-to-buy into tiny copy blocks.

An example, in a block 1¹/₄" wide × 1¹/₂" high (I'm ignoring the heading, because that's grist for another chapter):

> Here's a cutting board that isn't hard on finely-sharpened knives, won't absorb food flavors, and won't harbor bacteria. What's more, it won't develop low spots over the years. It's made of a space age thermoplastic, easy to clean, and perfect for rolling pastry with just the lightest dusting of flour. It's huge—24" by 17³/₄" by ¹/₂"!

What could be more pedestrian than a description of a cutting board? But look at the motivators crammed into that little copy block! Why they used one of my least-favorite phrases ("What's more") I'll never know, but I forgive them because they loaded the copy with reasons to buy.

Think for a moment:

The product manager gives you a sample cutting board and asks you to write a quick description of the item. Misled by the word "description" you do describe. Unless the product manager spoon-feeds you some reasons to buy, you don't emphasize reasons to buy.

Opinion: Your catalog writing is 30 years out of date. What's your opinion of this description?

> LEATHER BRASS ACCESSORY CASE from Spain
> has brass fittings for an exquisite look that is
> perfect for any man or woman.
> velvet lined 8" × 6¹/₂" × 4."

"...for an exquisite look that is perfect for any man or woman" is awkward, but that isn't the major problem. Rather, it's the *substitution* of this cumbersome phrase for a reason to buy. Professional catalog copywriters should know how to mask puffery within the reason-to-buy cloak. "An exquisite look" smacks of desperation, not inspiration.

Wordsmithy in Business-to-Business Catalogs

It's my opinion that writers of business-to-business catalog copy are more likely to think automatically of benefit, and this is strange.

It's strange because the catalog itself is more likely to parallel a classified ad than a consumer product description. Business-to-business catalogs implicitly are aimed at a "vertical" marketplace where seller says to buyer: "What's in these pages matches what you use and/or need."

Answering the Question, "Why?"

The reader knows we want to make a sale. As long as we're pitching, why don't we carry our sales argument to a logical conclusion?

We say to the reader, "Buy this."

The reader says, "Why?"

If we can answer, "Because..." we enter the kingdom of heaven by adding the magic password—a reason to buy.

Figure 9-1

"New!" is safe, but it's about as inventive as "Dinner is served." That isn't a copywriting problem. Failing to specify a reason to buy *is* a problem. "Finally there's a Salt and Pepper Mill that looks good on your table, works great in the kitchen" has *zero* specificity and selling power. This writer has another problem you'll never have: He or she doesn't know, as you do, you always have a stronger way to start a selling argument than "there is . . ." or "there are . . . ."

Figure 9-2

See what this company is selling here? A *non*-product. And see how they're selling it? Not as a fake alarm system but as "99% of the deterrence power for a fraction of the price." Only after grabbing and shaking us with buyer-benefit does this excellent piece of copy (despite the word "deterrence") go to nuts and bolts. Then it recapitulates what? A reason we should buy it, of course.

G. TALBOTS WHITE COTTON SHIRT WITH COVERED BUTTONS AT COLLAR, FRONT AND CUFFS. ONE BREAST POCKET. MACHINE WASH. IMPORTED. WHITE (80). $42.00
G 2931. SIZES 4-18
Ga 2931. PETITE SIZES 2-14

H. COMFORTABLE CORDUROY PANTS FROM DAVID BROOKS HAVE ELASTICIZED SIDES AND TWO FRONT PLEATS. FRONT ZIPPER, TAB WAIST, TWO QUARTER TOP POCKETS. ONE BUTTONED FLAP BACK POCKET. COTTON/POLYESTER. MACHINE WASH OR DRY CLEAN. MADE IN U.S.A. TAN (61), NAVY (8), OLIVE (14), BERRY (27), EGGPLANT (48). $52.00
H 2931. SIZES 6-20
Ha 2931. PETITE SIZES 2-14

Figure 9-3

Why buy this shirt? Why buy these pants? If you can think of a reason, apply for a copywriting job with this company. Setting the type all caps doesn't do much for clarity, but that may be outside the copywriter's sphere of influence. (If it's within *your* sphere of influence, insist on caps and lower case.)

Figure 9-4

Every copy block on this page is "run-in" bullet-style. That means using bullets but not lining them up vertically. You can see the pro and the con: The pro is the ability of a page to hold six competing microwaves without having any one of them become so dominant it destroys the others. The con is the extra burden on the headline, which has to cover all the sell. Here, the most expensive microwave has the smallest copy-block and the thinnest sales rationale. "Full Size! Full Power!" has all the excitement of "Fresh Fish." The less-expensive model below it is marked "Top Rated," but neither the headline—a puzzler—nor any bullet explains *why* this one is top rated. (And *who* says it's top rated?)

CHAPTER 10

Lovely? Useful? Unique? Prove It!

FIRST, *YOU* TRY IT!

Your assignment: You've written a description of a golf instruction videotape. This is your copy:

> "Arnie's Army of Tips" is as useful as it is practical. Packed with great and important golf tips, this is the ultimate golfer's video."

Your copy chief hands it back to you, commenting, "You haven't said anything."

"Yes, I have. I've called it useful, practical, packed with great and important tips, and the ultimate."

"I know. You haven't said anything. Do it over."

Take 30 seconds. No longer than that.

Okay, did you replace all those non-specifics with specifics? Did you write a line similar to, "Watch Arnold Palmer in slow-motion show you how to cock your wrists on the backswing and get an extra 40 yards on your drive"? Did you write, "When (if ever) should you use a 2-wood? How far apart should your feet be when you putt with a flat-bladed putter? How about a knob-headed putter?" Did you insert some *guts* in your description? Getting rid of *useful, great, important,* and *ultimate* is a wonderful way to start beefing up your copy. (Want to read some golf videotape copy? Look at Fig. 10-1.)

You Call Yourself a Writer?

Let's sit in the boss's chair. Now it's *our* turn to squat on our perch atop Mount Olympus and throw thunderbolts at those other guys whose catalog copy wasn't as inspirational-motivational as ours.

See this catalog? The writer describes a dress and doesn't even use the word "lovely." What kind of writer is she, leaving out that word? We use it all the time.

And how about this one? This guy writes about a silver-plating solution and doesn't even use the word "different." He ought to be drummed out of the corps for leaving out that word. We use it all the time.

Here's a floating flashlight. The photograph shows a hand pulling it out of the water, but copy just tells us it's waterproof and doesn't even give us the word "useful." What kind of catalog writing is that, leaving out the favorite word we use all the time?

The Era of Generalized Encomiums

Sometimes, reading product descriptions—especially in consumer catalogs—I get the feeling copy was written by the same person who writes boiler-plate eulogies.

You know what I mean if you've ever been to a funeral and heard a clergyman, who never met the fellow in life, lauding the dearly departed. Dignity in death demands a degree of extolment and verbal tribute, but lack of familiarity limits the encomium to generalities.

What might the clergyman say? "He led a useful life"? Gee, that man of the cloth might be just the person to write our next catalog.

This is the era of generalized encomiums (encomia?). We take the low road. The clergyman sees an address and a fur-clad widow and is safe in using the word "useful" to describe a life. We see a tool with a bunch of gadgets and are safe in using the word "useful" to describe what we're selling.

In neither case do we cut through the gauzy separator between message-sender and message-recipient. In both cases we step off the word-trail before we've reached and opened the psychological gate.

Watch for These Words

Generic words, used as substitutes for specifics, create copy which marks time. It runs in place.

Example: "feature-packed." This term is okay as a space-filler, *provided* the writer follows up with a solid description of what some of the features are.

But if you've been thinking of complaining you don't have enough space to mount a valid description, take a look at a hunk of your copy before marching into the boss's office. Has your own copy degenerated into a group of generalized encomiums (encomia?)?

Here are some words to look for. Hit the "search" key and see how many of these you find:

- add a special dimension
- beautiful
- the best
- decorative
- easy to use

- effortless
- feature-packed
- great
- important
- incredible (a ruined word)
- a must
- oh-so-wearable
- practical
- pretty
- revolutionary
- sensational
- special
- timeless
- ultimate (a ruined word)
- useful

Understand, please: These words deserve attack when they substitute for specifics. When they're a prelude to specifics, they're safe, protected by The Live Encomium Rule.

The Live Encomium Rule

The Live Encomium Rule is the protector of those who use generalized encomiums (encomia?) as the alpha of an alpha-to-omega—or at least alpha to gamma—sales argument.

Sure, they'll call a traveler's first aid kit useful, but then they'll explain *why* it's useful. Sure, they'll call fashion timeless, but then they'll give us a comparison explaining *how* it's timeless.

THE LIVE ENCOMIUM RULE:

> **A generic description becomes dead puffery unless ongoing copy justifies it.**

(We're talking about psychological justification, not typesetting.)

Some words are exempt from the Rule. "Heavy duty" and "classic," for example, lift themselves out of the morass of generalization by drawing a word-image for the reader.

Careful, now! Don't lean on these exempt words too hard. Remember what happened to words such as *quality* and *value*. They went to that Great Lexicon in the Sky, killed off by overuse. Should we hold a service for them, larded with encomiums (encomia?)?

Other words, such as *stylish, luxurious, exclusive,* and *deluxe,* are borderliners. They *almost* draw a word-image.

I mentioned *incredible* and *ultimate* as ruined words. Here we have once-powerful words which, mildly tarnished, were downgraded to respectable. Now, beaten about the head and shoulders by thoughtless wordsmiths, they've become spongy, of such dubious worth that most copy is more successful when a sad but realistic editor blue-lines them.

Are these thoughts of caution making you gun-shy of your keyboard? One golden ray: If catalog copywriting didn't involve word-selection discipline, we couldn't justify what we do as a profession, could we? And we couldn't get, from all the readers we inspire, such encomiums (encomia?).

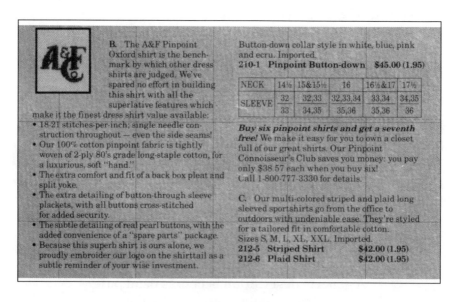

Figure 10-1

The first sentence worries us: "The A&F Pinpoint Oxford shirt is the benchmark by which other dress shirts are judged." It's a generalized encomium. But then the copywriter switches into overdrive, smacking us with specific after specific. This is good copy because it doesn't just applaud the shirt; it gives *us* a reason to applaude the shirt.

146

Figure 10-2

Did the writer actually see the videotape of "Slammin' Sam's Secrets"? What *specifics* might the writer have injected into this generic—ergo, flat—copy if he or she had? Compare it with the specifics-loaded description of the 1988 Masters Tournament videotape.

E. Autumn's splurge takes flight in Andrew Marc's bomber jacket—an indulgence you deserve. In softest nappa lambskin, it's buttery to the touch, burnishing beautifully with age. Comfortably shaped to be classic yet moderne, and fully lined with zip front. Imported in black for S(4-6), M(8-10), L(12-14), #40941 SPECIAL PURCHASE **399.98**

Figure 10-3

Here's an interesting play on words. "Autumn's splurge takes flight" doesn't make much sense, even tied to the bomber jacket. Tied to "an indulgence you deserve," it becomes mildly poetic. Poetry flowers in the next sentence, a triumph of imagery. How many writers can equal "In softest nappa lambskin, it's buttery to the touch, burnishing beautifully with age"?

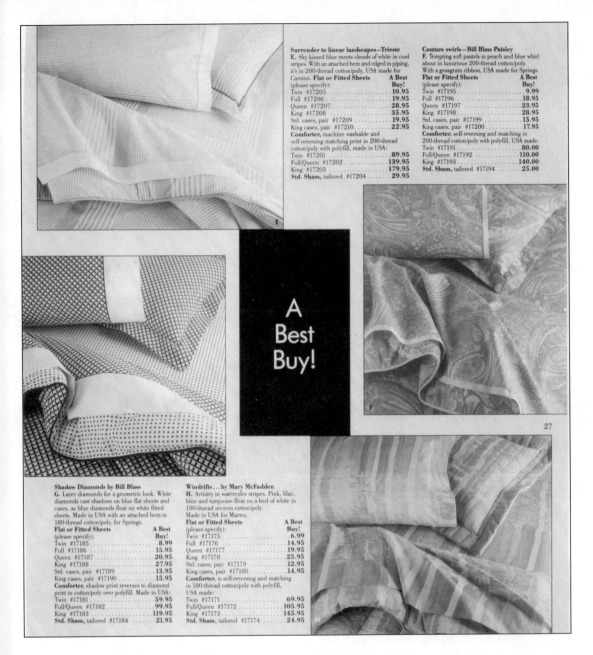

Surrender to linear landscapes—Trieste

E. Sky kissed blue meets clouds of white in cool stripes. With an attached hem and edged in piping, it's in 200-thread cotton/poly, USA made for Cannon.

Flat or Fitted Sheets (please specify):	A Best Buy!
Twin #17205	10.95
Full #17206	19.95
Queen #17207	28.95
King #17208	35.95
Std. cases, pair #17209	19.95
King cases, pair #17210	22.95

Comforter, machine washable and self-reversing matching print in 200-thread cotton/poly with polyfill, made in USA:

Twin #17201	89.95
Full/Queen #17202	139.95
King #17203	179.95
Std. Sham, tailored #17204	29.95

Couture swirls – Bill Blass Paisley

F. Tempting soft pastels in peach and blue whirl about in luxurious 200-thread cotton/poly. With a grosgrain ribbon, USA made for Springs.

Flat or Fitted Sheets (please specify):	A Best Buy!
Twin #17195	9.99
Full #17196	18.95
Queen #17197	23.95
King #17198	28.95
Std. cases, pair #17199	15.95
King cases, pair #17200	17.95

Comforter, self-reversing and matching in 200-thread cotton/poly with polyfill. USA made:

Twin #17191	80.00
Full/Queen #17192	110.00
King #17193	140.00
Std. Sham, tailored #17194	25.00

A Best Buy!

27

Shadow Diamonds by Bill Blass

G. Layer diamonds for a geometric look. White diamonds cast shadows on blue flat sheets and cases, as blue diamonds float on white fitted sheets. Made in USA with an attached hem in 180-thread cotton/poly, for Springs.

Flat or Fitted Sheets (please specify):	A Best Buy!
Twin #17185	8.99
Full #17186	15.95
Queen #17187	20.95
King #17188	27.95
Std. cases, pair #17189	13.95
King cases, pair #17190	15.95

Comforter, shadow print reverses to diamond print in cotton/poly over polyfill. Made in USA:

Twin #17181	59.95
Full/Queen #17182	99.95
King #17183	119.95
Std. Sham, tailored #17184	21.95

Windrifts . . . by Mary McFadden

H. Artistry in watercolor stripes. Pink, lilac, blue and turquoise float on a bed of white in 180-thread no-iron cotton/poly. Made in USA for Martex.

Flat or Fitted Sheets (please specify):	A Best Buy!
Twin #17175	6.99
Full #17176	14.95
Queen #17177	19.95
King #17178	25.95
Std. cases, pair #17179	12.95
King cases, pair #17180	14.95

Comforter, is self-reversing and matching in 180-thread cotton/poly with polyfill, USA made:

Twin #17171	69.95
Full/Queen #17172	105.95
King #17173	145.95
Std. Sham, tailored #17174	24.95

Figure 10-4

See that huge reverse, "A Best Buy!" in the middle of the page? Two questions: 1) Can all 40 items on this page be a best buy? If so, shouldn't the wording be the plural, "Best Buys!"? 2) With all that space, couldn't we have even one little comparative with a previous price or a mini-explanation of the "Best Buy!" claim?

149

Figure 10-5

The idea is sound, but can you squeeze any excitement out of the copy-stack on the left? Copy like this is why the Live Encomium Rule exists as a control. While we're at it, the word *executed* is loaded with danger.

b. Donegal Sport Coat. Classic brown and grey Donegal tweed updated with a colorful windowpane check. Tailored in U.S.A. of pure wool. Soft shoulder, center vent. Fully lined. 38 to 46 Regular; 38 to 42 Short; 40 to 46 Long. U3766 $375

c. 'Weymouth' Repp Stripe Tie. Traditional stripes take new direction from this unusual, yet versatile, color combination. Handmade in U.S.A. of pure silk woven in England. U1688 $45

d. 'Kilkenny' Cable Crewneck. Traditional Aran character, yet it's a comfortable mid-weight. Handfashioned in Ireland of soft, natural wool. Sizes S, M, L, XL. U2446 $135

e. 'Moritz' Print Shirt, made for fun, capturing the colors and charm of 19th Century botanical prints. Made in Switzerland of finest Swiss cotton twill. Sizes M, L, XL. U2330 $115

f. 'Layton' Suede Oxford by Bruno Magli. A truly sophisticated shoe, handcrafted in Italy in plush brown suede. Full leather sole, leather/rubber heel. Medium width: 6½ to 12, 13. U7802 $245

151

CHAPTER 11

The Ultimate Explosive... and Other Overused Oddities

> **FIRST, *YOU* TRY IT!**
> Your assignment: You've written a catalog description of a tele-
> phone headset. Your copy begins with this headline:
>
> > *The ultimate executive*
> > *headset—works like*
> > *a handset!*
>
> You realize you've used the word *ultimate* in headlines for other
> descriptions. This becomes one time too many. Looking through
> the product sheet, you see benefits: Lifting it activates it; putting
> it down hangs up the phone. It weighs ½ ounce and has an ad-
> justable volume control.
> Change the headline to get rid of *ultimate,* replacing the word
> with a descriptive term.
>
> **Take 30 seconds. No longer than that.**
>
> What's your solution? "The half-ounce headset that thinks it's
> a full-size phone"? Not bad. "At last! The headset you can hang
> up like a regular phone"? Not bad, but not as good—because
> "hang up" without a prior reference has too many peripheral
> meanings. "The best handset phone...in one super-comfortable
> feather-light headset"? Pretty good except that it isn't true, be-
> cause the best handset phone has a lot of buttons you won't find
> on a headset.
> (The original description—and it's pretty good, except for the
> heading—is Fig. 11-1.)
> Whatever your solution, replacing nondescriptive hyperbole
> with selling fact is a step forward.

Loose Superlatives Don't Hack It

The Good Book says: "Wisdom crieth aloud in the streets," or something like that.

No, no, I'm not the Guy who wakes up just before dawn each morning, says, "Let there be light," and confidently settles back under a
blanket of golden clouds. I'm just a catalog-reader who wonders,
month after month, why copywriters think they've perfected a product
description by plastering the same nondescriptive superlatives onto
one product description after another.

Thoughtless Underscoring

You've seen this argumentative ploy before:

The person who's losing an argument—or worse, an audience—gets shrill. The way to grab attention is to shout, not to caress or convince. So here goes that inevitable lapse into nondescriptive shouting adjectives.

This is thoughtless underscoring, the "Wow! Gee Whiz!" effect. The writer's brain is out of gear and, idling at high speed, it spits out words to keep the flow going until the reader turns the page.

If you're an inveterate catalog reader you know two of the words catalog writers use and abuse as scarecrows: *important* and *ultimate*. Damn these writers anyway. They've made me so gun-shy of those two once-proud words I've begun to use them less frequently than they deserve, in my own copy.

Some New Candidates

I've been reading through a catalog I usually admire, and now I have some new candidates. Leading the pack is the once-explosive word *explosive*.

The inside cover of this catalog explodes with the headline:

Explosive CD Automation

Are we supposed to ignore the obvious mismatch between those two words, concentrating instead on what must have been the writer's intent—to stop and grab the reader? Okay with me, but WARNING: *Explosive* is a far more mnemonic word than *ultimate*. You've used it. Keep it in your hip-pocket for the rest of the catalog.

Not this writer. The secondary headline begins:

Your stereo system's sound will explode with
life. And, you'll thrill to the ultimate in CD automation.

If the word *ultimate* weren't in there and if the statement made some sense, the doubled use of *explode* would be within the bounds of logical copywriting. (Hold that word "thrill" for a moment.) But in the very first paragraph of body copy we read:

...this new...multi-disc CD player will explode any perception of sound quality...

We still aren't done, because on this same page we have, as a sub-head in the copy:

> UNLEASH EXPLOSIVE AUTOMATION
> RISK FREE

Not only is this too many explosions, but I as reader still am uncon-vinced the words make sense. Instead, I get the feeling the writer is in love with the word—a dangerous rhetorical game.

Let's add some more words to this arsenal of terms. Overused, they're blanks in the communication-gun.

First, we have "thrill." We've already seen it once, and, like "explo-sive," it's a word we can't keep popping away with, as we might with "a," "an," or "the." But here's what we find, on this same page:

> You'll thrill to a signal-to-noise ratio of 96db...
> And, you'll thrill to every musical nuance in a stunning new way...

The next candidate for overuse becomes the runaway leader in this catalog: *incredible.*

> Before we explore the incredible sound you'll hear...
> Because of the incredibly low price of this awe-some 6-CD changer...

We're in a word game, where one clue leads to another. *Incredible* leads to *awesome.* Before we struggle out of this page we stumble over:

> From the awesome digital sound...
> AWESOME AUTOMATION (a subhead)...

And we bring back an explosion to make the description incredibly awesome:

> I wish I could be there to see the expression on your face the first time you hear the awesome CD sound explode around you.

These words still aren't burned up. A few pages down the line we have a radar detector: "X and K band sounds explode into action"; on page 5 we have an "automated" cassette deck: "...you'll have the in-credible vibrance of 105db dynamic range." (*Vibrancy,* isn't it?)

For a software program: " . . . an incredibly sophisticated integrated word processing and graphics program."

Next page, same item: "This program is incredibly powerful . . ." and "Make your ideas explode in front of your readers." (Huh?) Last sentence on the page: "And oh, it's so incredibly easy to use."

You get the idea. Within seven lines of each other we encounter "these incredible systems" and "you get an incredible deal." Page 11 brings the words even closer together: "This typewriter represents an incredible value for your investment and an incredible savings of typing time."

Champion is the page which has—

— an incredible breakthrough price;
— an incredible wail for help;
— They're incredibly rugged;
— this incredible safety/entertainment device;
— this incredible system;
— just count the incredible number of entertainment and emergency features . . .

We aren't finished with "explode" either. The copy block for a jet printer begins, "Let your ideas explode in front of your readers." At that point I put the catalog down, convinced that if I wanted to wander through more pages of this golden realm I'd enjoy additional incredible explosions. They'd be thrilling and awesome, I knew, because those words kept popping up too.

The Rule of Word Re-use

Sometimes it does pay to re-use a word. Just in case you aren't sure whether your next try does or doesn't fit the mold, here's a working example:

> You may think you own a great CB. But I'm talking about a *really* great CB.

That's *THE RULE OF WORD RE-USE:*

> If you have to re-use a word, emphasize the key word before its second use to show the reader the repeat is intentional.

This Rule won't do much for your writing finesse. (In fact, if your descriptive power is limited to the word "great" you have big problems in this profession.) The Rule does have the potential of adding pep to flat copy. And, oh, yes, another benefit: You tell cynical readers like me: I *meant* to re-use that word or phrase.

A couple of computer programs, "Grammatik" and RightWriter, have the capability of counting the number of times you've used the same word in one piece of copy. If you're plagued by the falling-in-love-with-a-word affliction, one of those programs might be an eye-opener—and a salvation—for you.

Does all this nonsense thrill you? It should. It's incredibly explosive.

The ultimate executive headset—works like a handset!

Try it once—you'll never want to give it up. OmniSet gives you the best features of both a handset and a headset. Like a headset, your hands are free—without straining your neck and shoulders. But like a handset, you pick it up and put it down with each call. No need to unplug each time you leave your desk.

How does it work? Lightweight OmniSet perches in your ear. It weighs just ½ ounce, so you'll barely even notice it's there. Adjustable volume control and a selection of nine different earpieces ensures comfortable fit. A superior quality microphone transmits your voice clearly.

OmniSet is compatible with virtually any phone: model 2084 is for carbon transmitter phones; 2085 for electronic transmitter phones. Not sure which type your phone is? See the compatibility chart on page 10, or call us at 1-800-444-3556. Order today—and remember that you found it at Hello Direct because when your co-workers see it they'll all want one too.

No-hands freedom in an innovative headset.

OmniSet (Compatibility Chart on page 10.)

ITEM #	DESCRIPTION	1-2	3-4	5+
2084	For Carbon Transmitter Phones	$165.	$160.	$156.
2085	For Electronic Transmitter Phones	$199.	$194.	$189.

Modular to PABX Adapter

ITEM #	1-2	3-4	5+
1023	$12.95	$12.60	$12.25

For 2-prong handset jacks, use with OmniSet #2084.

Figure 11-1

Suppose you're a customer in the store. You ask the sales clerk: "What's different about this headset?" The clerk answers, "It's the ultimate headset." You ask, "Because what?" The clerk explains patiently, "Because it works like a handset." Wouldn't you say, "Oh," and ease out of the store? A catalog headline has to kill with one blow. This one is too nonspecific to even maim. *How* is the headset like a handset? The answer to this question has to result in a superior headline. (Otherwise, the description is well-written.)

Figure 11-2

Ignore "The Kwik Way." It's there to show you exactly how close together the two "ultimates" are. The ultimate chess opponent lets me play chess wherever I travel. Sorry, that's not ultimate. Ultimate word power will handle my daily spelling/writing situations (ghastly copy even without *ultimate*, which it isn't). At least these aren't awesome.

b. The Bobby Jones Golf Shirt. The ultimate in comfort, generously cut for extra ease on or off the course. Made in Italy of very soft, fine two-ply mercerized cotton lisle, with pearl buttons. Green, white, light blue, pink, yellow, navy or red as shown, and black. Sizes M, L, XL, XXL. U2343 $65

Figure 11-3

Does being "generously cut" qualify this shirt to be "the ultimate in comfort"? How about being made in Italy? Well then, wouldn't you give the "ultimate" title to mercerized cotton lisle, with pearl buttons? Sorry, shirt, you aren't the ultimate in comfort. But don't cry: My custom-tailored shirt isn't either.

Explosive CD Automation

Your stereo system's sound will explode with life. And, you'll thrill to the ultimate in CD automation. Now you can automatically play 6 of your favorite CDs in any order you choose, or even randomly, for hours of uninterrupted listening pleasure. And now, it's yours at DAK's $199 sound barrier-breaking price.

By Drew Kaplan

It's shocking. From the awesome digital sound delivered by its 3-beam laser system, to its 6-disc capability, this new 16-bit, 2X oversampling CD changer will explode any perception of sound quality and musical automation you've ever had.

Before we explore the incredible sound you'll hear (and with this CD Changer's 20hz to 20,000hz frequency response, 96db signal-to-noise ratio and 92db dynamic range, the sound is fantastic), let's look at the automation that you'll command.

AWESOME AUTOMATION

First, it plays 6 discs automatically. You can program up to 32 choices (including entire discs) to play in any order you like.

You can choose different selections from all 6 discs and create your own 'playlist'. Now you can enjoy your favorite songs, from 6 different discs, in any order you like.

Now you decide which song should follow which song. Plus, you'll still have complete control of the programmed songs.

You'll also have total programmability for recording, too. Now you can easily make custom cassettes of your favorite music for use in your car or personal stereo.

Plus, when you're recording, you can have this amazing Changer automatically pause at the end of each side of your cassette.

It's easy. Just tell the Changer to pause at

You'll thrill to fingertip control of Play, Program, Shuffle and more from the remote.

the end of the cassette by pressing auto-pause' when you program the last song.

Now you can fade out the music before the end of the tape. And you'll never 'chop off' a song at the end of a cassette again.

And, just wait till you hear how your cassettes, recorded direct-from-CD, will sound.

REMOTE HEAVEN

This Changer's front control panel is a joy to use. You'll control every function by just touching the electronic direct-action buttons. Or, sit back, relax and use the powerful remote.

You can remotely select any of the 6 discs. You can randomly select tracks. You can program up to 32 tracks from any or all of the 6 discs. Or, you can let the Changer decide what song comes next by touching 'Shuffle'.

It's great. You'll never hear songs in the same order twice. Want to hear a favorite song again? Just touch 'Repeat'. Now, you can enjoy your favorite music uninterrupted for hours on end. It's very romantic.

You can repeat one song. You can repeat all programmed songs. Or, repeat one disc or all six discs. Plus, you'll remotely control Play, Pause, Stop, Manual Search, Track Search and more right from the remote.

In fact, virtually every function I've ever seen on an expensive CD player or changer is at your fingertips.

BUT IT'S THE SOUND

You'll thrill to a signal-to-noise ratio of 96db. That means you won't hear even a hint of hiss, a single scratch or best of all, any surface noise whatsoever.

Conventional records and tapes have a dynamic range of perhaps 50db. Dynamic range is simply the difference in sound level (volume) between the softest and loudest recorded sounds on a record or tape.

But, this CD Changer gives you a 92db dynamic range. That's roughly equivalent to the difference between absolute silence and standing next to a jet engine.

Imagine listening to music with a frequency response from 20hz to 20,000hz +0.5db - 1db. Imagine sound so pure that harmonic distortion is an amazing less than 0.009%. And, if you're into zeros, flutter and wow is 'unmeasurable'.

Don't be fooled by DAK's price. This changer isn't expensive. But, no expense was spared in its superb design, engineering and manufacturing.

The specs are so far beyond human hear-

With a 6-disc magazine, 32-track programmability and random play, you'll enjoy your favorite songs, uninterrupted for an hour, an evening or forever.

ing that the sound will knock your socks off.

But, what's really astonishing, is its ability to automatically manipulate 6 discs in any order you like. You'll enjoy everything from Bach to rock exactly the way you want.

Because of the incredibly low price of this awesome 6-CD Changer, I can't advertise the manufacturer's name.

But, it's manufactured in Japan and backed by an ironclad standard limited warranty.

UNLEASH EXPLOSIVE AUTOMATION RISK FREE

I wish I could be there to see the look on your face the first time you hear the awesome CD sound explode around you.

And, if you make as many tapes as I do for your car and personal stereo, you'll love the programmable track selection. And, 'end of cassette auto-pause' is a joy.

If you're not 100% thrilled and astounded, simply return it in its original box to DAK within 30 days for a courteous refund.

To order your Automated 6-CD Changer with 32-Track Programming, 3-Beam Laser System, 16-Bit, 2X Oversampling, Sophisticated Digital Filtering, Shuffle Play, Auto-Pause, Repeat, Skip, Oversize Display, Full Function Remote with Manual Search, Track Search, Headphone Jack and 6-Disc Magazine with your credit card, call toll-free or send your check for DAK's sound-barrier breaking price of just **$199** ($12 P&H). Order No. 5330. CA res add tax.

Extra 6 CD magazines that pop in and out are just **$19⁹⁰** ($2 P&H). Order No. 5418.

You'll be astounded by the ease-of-use automation. And, you'll thrill to every musical nuance in a stunning new way.

Figure 11-4

If you're a fan of this catalog, which uses *thrill* (or *thrilling*), *awesome, amazing,* and *explosive* repeatedly on almost every page, you'll like this description. On an evening when you've finished the crossword puzzle too quickly, count the number of times versions of the word *explode, thrill, awesome,* and *amazing* appear in this copy. I've ordered from this catalog—because of the thoroughness of the descriptions and despite the copywriting.

CHAPTER 12

"Why Should I Pay You That Much?"

FIRST, *YOU* TRY IT!
Your assignment: You're editing copy for a small appliance catalog. This crosses your desk:

> **The Waring Professional Toaster**
> If you're tired of "semi-pro" results from your
> old toaster, move up to the Waring Professional.
> 4 large slots, a button for heating just two slices,
> pull-out crumb tray, automatic switch-off timer.
> $275.00

You hand the copy back to the writer with this comment: "You've left out something." What was it the writer left out? Think about it.

Take 30 seconds. No longer than that.

Actually, you shouldn't have needed more than ten seconds if you read the title of this chapter. The writer left out a *reason* for charging $275. Assuming the typical toaster costs $25 to $45, what makes this one worth so much more?

So you probably added phrases such as "heavy duty" or "the last toaster you'll ever have to buy" or "stainless steel" or "at last, perfect toasting every time" or "the only toaster guaranteed for five full years." Whatever you did, you justified the cost—an apparently extravagant amount without the justification.

(The original description for the toaster is Fig. 12-1. The line "Originally designed for hotels and restaurants" helps save it, but this copy too could use a more powerful justification.)

Ask—Because the Reader Will Ask

How much is a pair of tennis shoes?

The question isn't as blind as, "How much is a house?" Typically, tennis shoes cost $20 to $50 a pair. Occasionally you'll see them on sale for less and occasionally you'll see a super-featured shoe for more.

I ask the question because, reading a product description in a current catalog, I wondered: Why do these tennis shoes cost so much?

Here's the complete product description:

> A. *For Tennis..* A man's performance tennis shoe
> that combines lightweight comfort with extraor-

> dinary support. Leather saddle over special ure-
> thane sole. Made in the U.S.A. *$60.00*

Okay, suppose you're in the market for tennis shoes. You see ad after ad in your local newspaper. Every pair these days says it combines lightweight comfort with extraordinary support. For a tennis shoe manufacturer that's like saying, "Good morning." Leather saddle and urethane sole? Standard. So what makes these shoes worth sixty bucks?

Fish for the Answer. . . THEN Write the Copy

I didn't call this catalog house to ask. First of all, whoever answers the 800 number presumably doesn't have any more information than the ad imparts and probably would say to a fellow operator, "I have some nut on the phone. He's burning up our 800 toll charges to find out why the shoe costs $60.00."

Second, if the 800 operator *does* know, then something is grotesquely awry within this company's internal lines of communication. How can the operator know and the copywriter *not* know?

It can't be the brand name or the catalog's upscale intention. A couple of pages away is "the favorite loafer, classic in every detail," for $54.00—considerably less than I'd expect to pay.

What happened, I think, is that the copywriter was hypnotized by a stack of shoe-descriptions. He/she went at the stack doggedly, whittling it down by extruding workmanlike descriptions, neither adding nor subtracting any psychological impellers.

But somebody should have yelled, "Hold it! The description doesn't justify the price."

What if the copywriter had asked the buyer: "Hey, why are these tennis shoes so expensive? I can buy Adidas and Nikes and Pumas and Reeboks up the gazoo for $30 to $40, and every one of them has all the features we've named here."

The buyer then would *have to* open some hidden box of facts and give the writer what this product-description needs: ammunition.

What Fact (or Non-Fact) Justifies Price?

1. A name-brand justifies price.

So if this were a "designer" shoe, *any* price becomes logical. Sure, we've all prostituted the word "designer" so it has about 30 percent of the impact it had ten years ago. But 30 percent is way, way above zero.

"A genuine Bartolizzi design..." would have done it. Any shoe designer worth ten cents has an Italian name, doesn't he?

Not any shoe designer. Calvin Klein, for example. A simple deck shoe costs $59.00—considerably more than comparable shoes—but it has the name-brand justification:

> Calvin Klein Sport designs a classic deck shoe of softest suede or napa leather with rust-toned rubber sole. Imported. White suede or coffee cream leather.
> Whole and half sizes. N 7½–9. M 5½–10.
> *8279A Calvin Klein Sport Shoes $59.00*

2. Strangely, a price reduction justifies price.

A lot of people care less about the actual cost of an item than they do about what the price was reduced from. Another catalog shows an ordinary-looking woman's low-heeled shoe with an ordinary description...plus the magic words, "Made to sell for $169.95. Special price $99.95." The reduction justifies the price.

Consider, too: This reduction is *artificial,* but it still works. "Made to sell for..." isn't a statement of fact; it's a statement of puffery. If this were a college course in logic, it would fade under the genuine sunlight of, "Listed at $169.95 in our last catalog. Special price $99.95." Now the touchstone is factual. But so what? Casual catalog-readers aren't that analytical.

3. Scarcity justifies price.

This is a tough concept for shoes, but the "limited edition" notion works almost anywhere, so I suppose a limited edition shoe isn't that outlandish an idea. Even if it is, we can justify scarcity by pointing out that these are handmade (or "handcrafted," a more generalized and less-assailable term), one pair at a time.

4. Publicity justifies price.

If these are the shoes Boris Becker wears (not the same pair he just wore for that five-set match; the same *brand*), some might think the magic of the arm might bleed off into every wearer of the shoe. If a celebrity wears these shoes they're lifted out of the gray milieu of sameness.

How about Just Words?

Words? Words can justify price if the words aren't transparent rhetoric with puffery substituting for fact.

But I suggest to catalog-buyers who expect the copywriter to turn lead into gold: At least supply the makin's.

Let's form two tiny rules—two of the thousands hovering in the heavens—to guide us as we try to justify the last item in any description, the price. We'll call the first one *THE EVIDENTIAL SUPERIORITY PRINCIPLE:*

Declaration isn't as convincing as evidence.

This means a *statement* of bargain...superiority...scarcity...no matter how well-written, isn't as powerful as *evidence* of bargain, superiority, or scarcity.

While we're at it, let's tack on the second rule. We'll call this one *THE ANTI-B.S. PROCEDURE,* because it explains why heavy production, full bleed, printing in six colors, and sending 40 people to Baluchistan to shoot photographs aren't, combined, as effective as an explanation of superiority:

It's more logical to throw selling facts at the reader than to mask lack of facts with lavish production.

The Anti-B.S. Procedure in Action

The Anti-B.S. Procedure apparently was unknown to one of the giant producers of collectibles...and was very much in the mind of a catalog house which gave us a classic comparison.

B.S. *isn't* parallel to seasoning. Separating the two is one criterion of catalog copywriting professionalism. It parallels adding monosodium glutamate for just a touch of taste-bud vibration.

A cook sprinkles some Accent on a nondescript-tasting dish, and taste-buds respond with delight.

A catalog copywriter has the same opportunity...but not always the same inclination. Sometimes the writer ignores the challenge to galvanize the reader's salivary glands into action.

Sometimes the writer pours a whole can of rhetorical Accent onto the copy, smothering description with puffery.

Sometimes the writer (usually a beginner who just has to be related to the owner or he/she wouldn't get away with such unprofessional writing) *replaces* description with puffery. Ugh.

Ah, but sometimes the writer realizes the need for romance and yet has the discipline, tempering that inclination to drown information in a sea of romance. The wonderful balance should be award-winning—and would be, if awards weren't canted toward the cosmetic aspects of catalog production.

Enough allegory.

King Tut and Friends

Occasionally we see the same item advertised by several vendors. This gives us the opportunity to compare apples with apples.

In the sample I'm looking at, it gives us the opportunity to compare pharaohs with pharaohs. It's a framed depiction of King Tutankhamen, prepared by (so help me) the Papyrus Institute in Cairo.

(An irreverent thought: Can you imagine a parent's reaction if a high school graduate said, "Dad, I want to continue my studies at the Papyrus Institute"?)

One version is a full page, with a restrained heading:

> Until now, only museums owned original art like this.

Body copy gives us minimal information:

> THE PAPYRUS INSTITUTE IN CAIRO
> REDISCOVERS A LOST ART FORM.
>
> You have a rare opportunity to own a museum masterpiece created with the same painstaking techniques developed by the ancient Egyptians. Portraying the fabled boy king Tutankhamun and his lovely queen.
>   Rich symbolism. Timeless art. Glowing with gold and copper. Hand-painted on authentic Egyptian papyrus, hand-made by an art which has endured for 5,000 years. Preserved in a Far Eastern frame of black lacquered hardwood and gleaming brass. $275.

And that's it, except for a coupon which has its own problems. I'll come to that in a couple of paragraphs.

No, this wasn't in a catalog, and that's exactly why it's a good example—because a better description *was* in a catalog.

I'm considerably less annoyed by partial sentences than I used to be, but I don't think I'll ever be able to take "Portraying the fabled boy king Tutankhamun and his lovely queen" as an acceptable noun-less, verb-less sentence. While I'm carping, who says the queen was lovely? From the art, she looks hydrocephalic.

(While we're in the neighborhood, if the art has been "rediscovered" it couldn't have "endured," could it?)

Now to the coupon:

What do the words "I wish to commission the Tutankhamun Papyrus" mean to you? Don't they mean the piece is made to order? Clever copy, perhaps—unless someone looks at a catalog.

(Which you can do. The space ad is Fig. 12-2. The catalog description is Fig. 12-3.)

Same Item, Different Pitch

A catalog shows this same art reproduction. It's one of five items on page 11. The frame doesn't have brass corners, but the price is $75 less.

That isn't our concern as catalog copywriters. Compare the copy:

> *Tutankhamun*
> *Papyrus*
>
> (left) The splendor of ancient Egypt casts its timeless spell. Glowing in rich oils and goldleaf paint, this masterpiece depicts the young King Tutankhamun and his wife, Queen Ankhesenamun, in a ritual hunting scene. Discovered in the tomb of "King Tut" in 1922. This faithful reproduction was painted on authentic Egyptian papyrus, handmade by 5000-year-old techniques at the Papyrus Institute in Cairo. It comes with a certificate detailing the making of a papyrus, and a full explanation of the scene. To show it to best effect, we offer a 24"h × 29.5"w black beveled frame with the papyrus suspended between see-through perfex. You will own an artwork of majestic beauty.

No ball game here. The catalog, which devotes about 18 square inches of space to this art reproduction, gives us ten times the reason to buy we have from the full page ad, which in 70 square inches transmits almost no specifics.

Can "Rich symbolism. Timeless art. Glowing with gold and copper." compete with "Glowing in rich oils and goldleaf paint, this masterpiece depicts the young King Tutankhamun and his wife, Queen Ankhesenamun, in a ritual hunting scene."? For that matter, can the nonsense-phrase "his lovely queen" compete with the queen's actual name?

The very inclusion in this catalog—might it be in other catalogs as well?—explodes the "I wish to commission . . ." myth: Obviously if the same art is in a catalog, the work already has been commissioned by a third commercial source.

What's the Point?

The point of this harangue is the combination of two rules of force-communication:

1. *THE PUFFERY-DEFEAT INEVITABILITY:*

> **No amount of puffery or self-applause can sell as effectively as a listing of specific benefits.**

2. *THE RULE OF IMPLIED IMPORTANCE:*

> **Importance should relate to the state of mind of the reader, not the writer.**

That second rule comes clear when we read "Rich symbolism," unexplained; "Timeless art," unexplained; "Far Eastern frame," not only unexplained but out of key (the typical reader thinks at once of bamboo).

Did the writer of the space ad have access to the same information available to the catalog writer? Probably. Why didn't the space ad writer use that information? Again, because the writer either didn't know or ignored two other rules of force-communication:

1. *THE RULE OF IMPORTANCE DETERMINATION:*

> If you claim importance, prove it.

2. *THE FIRST RULE OF WEASELING:*

> An effective weaseled claim is written so the reader slides past the weasel without realizing it.

Usually, a comparison of expensive space-ad copy and catalog copy leaves the catalog writer in the dust. What a pleasure it is to be on the winning side!

And That's the Sermon for Chapter 12

Much as we writers like to claim importance for our craft, we're firing blanks in a marketplace in which the target-individual has some sense of values, unless whoever hires us gives us some bullets for our word-guns.

Pass the .44 Magnum, please. It's catalog-writing time!

A gourmand's best friend...
Cuisinart® Little Pro™
A. Here's the latest addition to our favorite family of food processors. A handy compact marvel for small culinary jobs, it features a powerful motor. A chopping blade is used with the removable 3 cup Lexan® bowl—and slicing and shredding discs are used with the continuous feed chute. Pulse and continuous speeds, 12½"H" #17717 **89.95 ★**

The consummate answer to preparing meals—Cuisinart® Mini-Mate™
B. It's compact but mighty, and exceptionally versatile. Just watch how its powerful 2-speed motor and reversible blade handles your every project with ease—from mincing parsley and grating cheese, to blending sauces and grinding coffee beans. 9-oz. Lexan® bowl, #17716 **40.00 ★**

For toast to sandwiches
C. Rowenta's Cool Touch toaster has a slimline profile and textured exterior. And it features a long adjustable slot that toasts everything from bagels to muffins...and more. #17707 **40.00 ★**
Bun warmer attachment #17708 **10.00 ★**
Sandwich maker attachment #17709 **15.00 ★**

52

The Waring Professional Toaster
D. Originally designed for hotels and restaurants, it's in stainless steel—with 4 large slots and a button for heating just two slices. With pull-out crumb tray, automatic switch off timer, it keeps bread warm without over toasting. 14½ x 9 x 8½" #17706 **275.00 ★**

A heavy duty pro—the Waring blender
E. Concoct mouth-watering drinks and delicate sauces. Dependable and efficient, its 2-pc. lid doubles as a measuring cup. A glass jar with removable blades, and heavy chrome base, #17712 **100.00 ★**

And the Livin' is Easy

A touch tells all, from Salton
F. A fabulous design for modern kitchens. Salton's toaster has a cool touch exterior—to keep heat inside, not out. Extra wide and long slot automatically adjusts to brown bagels, muffins—even thick homemade bread. Crumb catcher and safety features #17710 **45.00 ★**

The world's first espresso, cappuccino and drip coffee maker—all-in-one
G. Salton's Three for All brews 4 cups of espresso, steams milk for cappuccino and makes up to eight cups of coffee simultaneously or separately #17715 **99.95 ★**

Salton's Perfetto Cappuccino
H. The only machine that draws up to a gallon of milk, steams it, then dispenses it into awaiting mugs. Makes up to 10 cups of rich espresso, two at a time #17711 **200.00 ★**
★ For warranty information see order form

ORDER TOLL-FREE

Figure 12-1

On the same page of this catalog we have the handsome looking Rowenta Cool Touch toaster—for $40, and the Waring Professional toaster—for $275. Does the phrase "Originally designed for hotels and restaurants" plus a few extra bits of gimcrackery justify a $235 difference in price, especially when the Rowenta has an adjustable slot and the Waring apparently doesn't? Not to me...and if you're a professional copywriter determined to squeeze the last ounce of selling power into every description, I hope not to you. A parenthetical thought: The word *originally* not only doesn't help this copy; it hurts it.

175

Figure 12-2

When form becomes paramount to substance, invariably the amount of information transmitted from writer to reader decreases. Whoever wrote this almost factless description can only hope the reader won't a) ask what the Papyrus Institute is, b) won't look at the illustration to explode the inferior "lovely queen" reference, c) won't ask *how* the art shows "rich symbolism," d) won't wonder why an Egyptian work of art is in a "Far Eastern frame," and e) won't wonder why it's necessary to "commission" this papyrus when it's available outright elsewhere.

**Tutankhamun
Papyrus** ◄

(left) The splendor of ancient Egypt casts its timeless spell. Glowing in rich oils and goldleaf paint, this masterpiece depicts the young King Tutankhamun and his wife, Queen Ankhesenamun, in a ritual hunting scene. Discovered in the tomb of "King Tut" in 1922. This faithful reproduction was painted on authentic Egyptian papyrus, handmade by 5000-year-old techniques at the Papyrus Institute in Cairo. It comes with a certificate detailing the making of papyrus, and a full explanation of the scene. To show it to best effect, we offer a 24"h x 29.5"w black beveled frame with the papyrus suspended between see-through perfex. You will own an artwork of majestic beauty. ■#2173. King Tut Papyrus $89.95. ■#2174. Framed King Tut Papyrus $199.95.

Figure 12-3

How is it the catalog writer knows the queen's name and the space ad writer (Fig. 12-2) doesn't? How is it the catalog offer includes a certificate and the space ad offer, which suggests exclusivity, doesn't? Suggestion to the company running the space ad: Hire whoever wrote the catalog copy.

Available in three widths to size 15

E All-leather Bally® Meteor Shoes for men outclass other sport shoes. Performance standards show how: balanced dual-density soles, front and rear stabilizers, padded footbeds, shaped rear tendon protectors, cotton terry lining and speed lacing. Color: White. Sizes Narrow (B) 8-12, 13, 14, 15; Medium (D) and Wide (EE) 7-12, 13, 14, 15. **#1056Y Bally Meteor Sport Shoes $92.00**

Figure 12-4

These are nice-looking tennis shoes. Despite what the description says, they obviously aren't *all*-leather. Can you imagine leather soles on a tennis shoe? All right, they have "balanced dual-density soles." Is that good? Copy doesn't tell us. They have front and rear stabilizers. The photograph just shows a pair of tennis shoes. If the stabilizers are inside the shoe, what do they do? Padded footbeds, shaped rear tendon protectors, cotton terry lining, and speed lacing? If "speed lacing" means grommets in the lace-holes, most shoes have all these.

The copywriter didn't even help us with boiler-plate copy such as, "These are the very best tennis shoes we carry." So how do we justify either the one hundred percent puff statement "outclass other sport shoes" or the $92 price? I guess we don't.

Bally's 'Meteor' Running Shoe. Expertly designed with a multi-density, all-court sole. Shaped Achilles tendon protector and padded ankle guard for safety and comfort. White leather with black and red detailing. Narrow: 8 to 12, 13, 14, 15: Medium and Wide: 6 to 12, 13, 14, 15. U7709 $85

Figure 12-5

Here's the same shoe we saw in Fig. 12-4. This description doesn't refer to "balanced dual-density soles," whatever those are. Instead it mentions an "all-court sole," although the heading calls it a *running* shoe. Terry lining is omitted, as are padded footbeds; but we do have a padded ankle guard. And it's seven dollars less.

F NEW! Get set for action with K-Swiss™ Athletic Shoes, for men and women. Comfortable leather upper with convenient D-ring lacing; removable EVA padded insoles with cushioning heel pads. Herringbone soles. Color: White.

Sizes: Men's Medium (D) 7-10, 11, 12.
#7097Y Men's K-Swiss Athletic Shoes $50.00
Sizes: Women's Medium (B) 5-10.
#7117Y Women's K-Swiss Athletic Shoes $50.00

Figure 12-6

The same company selling the Bally Meteor shoe for $92 has this K-Swiss for $50. It seems to have goodies the more expensive shoe doesn't. Was that why the writer copped out with the useless opening, "Get set for action"?

f. Child's White Wicker Rocker will make young recipients feel very grown up indeed. The small scale, sturdy rocker is trimmed with laminated fabric and bows. 19½" high; 17½" wide. (Sorry, it is too large for a gift box.) #AC18F. $160. [15.00]

B. For your little ones, our child-sized white wicker chair with wooden rockers is sturdily built. 11½" x 10" seat, 18" deep with a 21" tall back. #NTF423 75.00 value **SPECIAL 39.99** *(9.35)*

Figure 12-7

The rocker on the left is $160. The one on the right is $39.99. That means we can buy four of the ones on the right for the price of the one on the left. Does the description justify the cost? No, for two reasons: First, "...will make young recipients feel very grown up indeed" isn't exclusivity-motivational. Second, the word "sturdy" isn't an apt descriptive word for an expensive rocker. Even the cheaper chair is "sturdily built."

CHAPTER *13*

Positioning: A Key to Higher Response

FIRST, *YOU* TRY IT!

Your assignment: You've written this headline and first sentence of copy for a luggage cart:

> STURDY LUGGAGE CART WITH 2 RETRACT-
> ABLE BACK WHEELS
> Holds up to 175 pounds, folds compactly for
> storage.

The head of the company shakes his head. "No, no, we can't just describe. We have to *position* this cart. Everything we sell has to be unique. Make this the cart that holds more weight than any other."

"But others sell a cart that holds twice as much," you protest.

"That's their problem. Our job is to sell this one. Write me a headline and first line of copy proving our superiority."

Take 30 seconds. No longer than that.

What did you write? The headline is easy: Just add the word "The." The definite article is a *positioning* article. (Want proof? If I'd said, "The definite article is *the* positioning article," you'd interpret the statement to mean no other positioning article exists.)

The first sentence isn't so easy. You have to make a comparison, and—whether you or I agree with this sleazy philosophy or not—your boss demands it. So you probably wrote, "This Hercules-tough cart holds 175 pounds, far more than most others."

Expect your boss to scratch the word "most." If you want to see the copy that actually ran, look at Fig. 13-1.

Making a Deal with the Devil

Discussing current results with catalogers, one begins to understand Dickens: "It was the best of times, it was the worst of times."

Gee, how I'd love to relate the pulling-power of a catalog to the copywriter's talent. But that not only would be self-serving; it wouldn't reflect a professional attitude.

Oh, sure, good copy can boost—maybe even double—response. But mediocre copy won't kill an item if the other two elements—photograph and raw product description—are passably adequate.

Now, what if the copywriter goes one step beyond exciting description, into the precarious word-world of extravagant claims? It gives a synthetic boost to response. Do we pay a price? Have we made a deal with the devil?

Cataloger, Position Thyself

Some of the murk clouding those catalogs which offer similar products and use similar themes seem to be clearing. Catalogs with "personality" are beginning to separate themselves from catalogs adhering to the traditional "Here's what it is. . ." approach.

The key: *positioning.*

A statement of position makes a catalog super-competitive, *even if no competitor exists.* The reader actually believes, "This is the only place I can get this," even though it's a standard catalog item.

An example of this is a catalog which in almost every product description includes a flat statement of superiority. One simple trick is use of the word "the"—"The Hands-Free Personal Headlights"; The Automatic Home Bread Maker"; "The Personal Bedside Television."

Visualize these headings without the definite article: "Programmable Electric Bathroom Heater" instead of "The Programmable Electric Bathroom Heater." See the difference? Without "the," implicitly we suggest the existence of competing electric bathroom heaters. The definite article suppresses them.

A Dangerous Precedent?

The same catalog takes an editorial position by an Olympian labeling system (see "I Am the Greatest" copy, chapter one):

— "The Best Pants Presser";
— "The Best Cordless Phone";
— "The Only Travel Scale";
— "The Smallest Folding Guest Bed."

Is this the best pants presser? Is this the best cordless phone? Might we find, on this planet, another travel scale? If we looked hard enough, could we find a smaller folding guest bed? (Or is it the guest who folds?)

At the moment, the answer is inconsequential because a reader who asks these questions isn't convinceable anyway.

184

What makes this a dangerous game is the possibility of abuse. The company's stated evidence parallels surveys taken of co-religionists, then crowing, "Preferred by four out of five people surveyed."

I should clarify: I have to admire this procedure, because this company knows *THE RULE OF PRE-ESTABLISHED ATTITUDE,* a tenet of primitive psychology:

> **A product is what it is, plus what the buyer thinks it is.**

So a user *thinks* he/she is buying the best cordless phone. That this one transmits signals 900 feet and others transmit signals 1500 feet is inconsequential. This one has been declared "best."

Underlining Superiority

The same catalog uses another technique well-known to anyone who ever wrote copy for computer software. It's the magic of four little words:

Unlike other models which...

I use software as an example because as a veteran of these intramural wars, in which the difference between spreadsheets or word processing programs isn't always clear...and the superiority of what we're selling isn't absolute...we know a sophisticated copywriting practice, *THE LAW OF COMPETITIVE SELECTIVITY:*

> **Select only the vulnerable targets, and attack.**

So copy which reads, "Unlike other models with one or two channels, it has 10 FCC approved channels to eliminate interference from other cordless phones," suggests *all* other models have one or two channels. But read it again. No, no, that isn't what it says. It's just what the writer wants us to think it says.

185

Therein lies the brightness of the writer—and the danger of the game. Catalog copy has been curiously exempt from this pre-flavoring.

We balance the benefit of cleverly-constructed claims of superiority against the detriment of having others bring hopeless confusion into the marketplace by establishing their own "Institutes." We see uncontrolled private, arrogant, coldly unscientific testing designed to prove a preconceived copy-point. And we see—what?

Not pretty, is it?

A Happy Middle Ground

Is this the only way to claim superiority? I'm unconvinced.

What gives me hope for the future of copywriting which isn't so baldly self-serving is copy such as the description of a pair of insulated gloves (Fig. 13-3). Headline:

> It's Not Just a Glove
> —It's a System

Copy glorifies the gloves, as it should. The reader concludes there just ain't no gloves like these, as the reader should. The effect is there without the danger. What if this heading had been "The Only 'System' Gloves" or "The Best Waterproof Lightweight Insulated Gloves"? Would that sell more gloves?

I hope you're thumping the table and saying, "Whether an 'I Am the Greatest' headline pulls better or not isn't the question."

No, it isn't. The question is subtly double-faced.

The obverse face: Are catalogs, in the struggle for survival through positioning, beginning to build a dependence on cunning?

The reverse face: Isn't it logical for the copywriter to use every ounce of ingenuity to keep the catalog's bottom-line healthy?

As a catalog-lover with a predetermined viewpoint—part of my income depends on them—I lean, emotionally, toward survival at any legal price. As curmudgeon-in-residence I lean, intellectually, toward exhausting our brainpower in a more responsible direction before balancing on the long incline toward duplicity . . . or, just as bad for the world of catalogs, the accusation of duplicity.

That's probably the Kingdom of Heaven, and I suspect few of us, with our cynicism and hard-boiled business attitudes, ever will get a set of keys to that Kingdom. But we'll enjoy the battle of wits before we disappear into limbo, won't we?

THE BEST JOG-AND-WALK PEDOMETER. In comparison tests conducted by the Hammacher Schlemmer Institute, this pedometer was rated best for its superior accuracy and ease of use for both walking and jogging. Unlike other pedometers that have incremental stride settings, this unit has a patented variable stride adjuster (between two to five feet) and measures strides that would normally fall between incremental settings. Its spring-balanced mechanical pendulum senses even subtle strides and records up to 99.9 miles. ABS plastic housing. Height: 1⅝ inches. Width: 1¾ inches. Depth: 1 inch. Weight: 1 ounce.
33816T . . . . $29.95 Postpaid and Unconditionally Guaranteed

Walking Tapes. The tempo of these four 90-minute musical cassette tapes helps you maintain a consistent walking pace and lets you progress from beginner (20-minute-per-mile walk) to advanced (15-minute-per-mile walk). Each plays over 35 popular songs.
37427T . . . . $24.50 Postpaid and Unconditionally Guaranteed

THE BEST TRAVEL WORLD BAND RADIO. In comparison tests conducted by the Hammacher Schlemmer Institute, this lightweight and compact travel world band radio was rated best for its fine tuning ability, 36 preset station buttons and two quartz clocks that set at two different time zones. Unlike other world band radios that offer fewer than ten preset station buttons, this unit can be programmed to provide automatic tuning for up to 36 stations. Its LCD bar graph signal strength meter and manual fine-tuning dial allow you to accurately receive frequencies in any given area, and its quartz phase-locked loop synthesizer system automatically tracks fluctuations on AM and FM bands to ensure optimum reception. Two quartz digital clocks provide times for zones anywhere in the world. Operates on six AA batteries (included). Includes earplug and SW external antenna. Length 7¾ inches. Width: 4⅝ inches. Depth: 1¼ inches. Weight: 1.78 pounds.
35216T . . . . $319.50 Postpaid and Unconditionally Guaranteed

THE FLIGHT ATTENDANT'S LUGGAGE CART. Recommended by the Hammacher Schlemmer Institute, this luggage cart holds up to 175 pounds, 3½ times more than other models, and folds down compactly for storage. Its two retractable back-support wheels enable the cart to be pulled on four wheels. Its step-slide bar provides easy access over stairs and curbs. The patented aluminum handle telescopes from 19½ to 41½ inches and locks into place. Elastic cords hold luggage in place. Rubber rimmed wheels. Steel platform; Lexan® handles. Width (platform): 11¼ inches. Depth (folded): 6½ inches. Weight: 9 pounds.
23044T . . . . $89.95 Postpaid and Unconditionally Guaranteed

THE TRAVEL-CHARTING WORLD MAP. Used by travel agencies, business executives and international travelers, this laminated Rand McNally world map includes a charting kit to help you plan future trips, record past travels and chart business territories. The 1:600-scale Mercator projection map has a 10-mil. thick Poly-Mylar™ film surface that accepts water-soluble pens and can be easily wiped off with a damp cloth, allowing you to redraw and update travel routes and comments. Reproduced in eight colors, the 52 x 34-inch map clearly shows major cities and towns, national boundaries and major bodies of water. It also displays the world's 24 time zones and air-mile distances. The charting kit includes 100 location pins, a land ruler for determining distances and a medium-point red marking pen. Gold anodized aluminum frame. Height: 34 inches. Width: 52 inches. Weight: 8 pounds.
37641T . . . . $96.50 Postpaid and Unconditionally Guaranteed

United States Laminated Charting Map. Same as above, except shows the fifty states on a 1:75 scale.
37642T . . . . $96.50 Postpaid and Unconditionally Guaranteed

The Best Travel World Band Radio

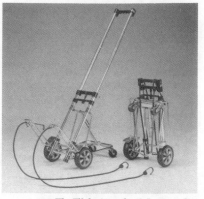

The Flight Attendant's Luggage Cart

The Travel-Charting World Map

Figure 13-1

Just what is the "Hammacher Schlemmer Institute"? Is it parallel to Underwriters Laboratory? Or is it a promotional ploy? A small copy block at the bottom of page 3 says, ". . . an associated, but independent Hammacher Schlemmer Institute has been established which makes direct comparisons between products on the market. Whenever an item in this supplement catalog is characterized as being 'the best' or 'the only one' to perform in a particular way, this is, of course, unless qualified, only by comparison with all other products known either to the store or to The Institute...."

How many readers of this catalog will penetrate this disclaimer? How many, buying a luggage cart which holds up to 175 pounds, know of another cart, *costing $37.00 less,* which holds 350 pounds—and doesn't claim to hold "more than other models" (see Fig. 13-2)? The copywriter, attacked by a case of ethics, has a choice: Write copy within the corporate philosophy or get a job elsewhere. How frequently does this kind of problem arise? Fortunately, not often.

A. Mighty Mini® Heavy Duty Compact Carrier

Our rugged, folding luggage cart is guaranteed to hold up to 350 lbs. With its unique "step slider" feature, the cart glides smoothly up and down steps on sturdy 6" ball bearing wheels. Tough enough to check through as luggage at the airport, the unit comes with a ten-year warranty. Fully assembled. Includes 6' stretchcord.
Cart ....MMC 2501 $52.95
Back Pack/
Carry Bag......MMP 2502 $19.95
$69.95 for both

Figure 13-2

Compare this bare-bones description with Fig. 13-1. This cart holds twice as much, has a 10-year guarantee, and costs $37 less. Would it outsell the other cart? As a guess, no, unless the two were shown side by side. Even then, some catalog readers would respond to flat statements of superiority head-to-head with less dynamic statements of fact.

Men's Portage Pacs Are Waterproof AND Warm in Five Insulated Styles

A All Portage Pacs are not created equal: many styles you find are not insulated, but still carry a price comparable to ours. These Portage Pacs for men combine waterproofed leather and rubber with Thinsulate® insulation to keep your feet dry and warm. We offer five styles, including the 8-Eyelet Pac, which we are bringing back in response to your many requests.

Portage Pacs insulate your feet from cold ground with a layer of Thinsulate insulation built into the rubber bottoms. Thinsulate gives incredible warmth for its weight, and keeps its loft and effectiveness even when wet.

Uppers are oil-treated, chrome-tanned leather to defy mud and rain. These are multiple stitched to the vulcanized gum rubber bottoms. "Chain-link" tread rubber soles provide traction. Your feet rest comfortably on a removable contoured foam insole, lined with soft acrylic pile.

Our 5- and 8-Eyelet Pacs have full leather gussets that discourage seepage. Ankle-high Slip-Ons and over-the-ankle Pull-Ons are favored by boaters for their easy removal. The 3-Eyelet Pacs have a padded scree collar. Colors: Tan or Navy rubber bottoms w/Brown leather uppers. Sizes Medium (D) 7-13 (half-sizes, order next size up).
#3402Y 5-Eyelet Pacs $49.00
■ #3404Y 8-Eyelet Pacs $60.00
#3403Y Pull-On Pacs $50.00
■ #3400Y Slip-On Pacs $42.00
#3401Y 3-Eyelet Pacs $47.00

■ CATALOG ONLY

Charge by phone toll-free
1-800-426-8020
We welcome
Eddie Bauer Preferred Charge,
MasterCard, VISA and
American Express

Figure 13-3

This copy grabs and convinces without artificial superlatives. It accomplishes one of the most difficult jobs in catalog copywriting—establishing a solid desire to buy, without establishing an artificially competitive position and without lapsing into artificial superlatives. Comparative references are to "many styles you find," not the duplicitous "unlike others." Good copywriting!

C. Our peerless croquet sets, made *exclusively* for us, add a new dimension to backyard croquet. Experience the "click" and heft of solid hardwood mallets, and the durability and playing quality of premium components. The American Croquet set (pictured) features nine steel wickets, exotic hardwood mallets, balls, stakes, clips and rule book, all packed in a handy Cordura™ carrying bag. A cut above: our Estate set, with magnificent leather-gripped Brazilian hardwood mallets, composition balls, wickets, stakes, clips and rules, all in a handsome pine storage case. The ultimate: our Ultimate 6-Wicket set features championship lignum vitae wood mallets, Jacques "Eclipse" balls, 6 lb. iron wickets, and championship-grade accessories, all in a stunning brass-trimmed wood case.

826-1 **American Croquet**
          $225.00 (15.95)*
826-2 **Estate Croquet**
          $725.00 (24.95)*
826-3 **Ultimate Croquet**
          $1650. (34.95)*

Figure 13-4

Does calling a croquet set "peerless" shift copy into an unethical posture? No. "Peerless" is harmless puffery, and we welcome any description which avoids "ultimate." In fact, ethics are the rule here. Why? Because the illustration shows the *least* expensive of the three croquet sets. Most catalogers would show the most expensive set, which has to be the most visually attractive and have the most gimcrackery. This description does a good job of positioning all three sets: The customer ordering "American" doesn't feel he's getting a bottom-end set.

Figure 13-5

You'll seldom see a better piece of comparative copy than this one. No puffery here. Instead, the writer backs up each claim with a solid example. Some $40 jeans don't have no-rust rivets. The low price of these is backed up by the claim that this company doesn't charge for TV ads, high rent mall locations, "and other things you *can't* wear." The statement is mildly laughable, but it's as empathy-engendering as any catalog copy could be. Note the callouts (those little descriptions with a line pointing to the appropriate place) on the jeans themselves. Callouts, excellent reinforcements for verisimilitude, are underused by catalogers.

CHAPTER *14*

Turning on the Reader's Toggle-Switch

FIRST, *YOU* TRY IT!

Your assignment: Visualize how you'd describe a sterling silver art nouveau rectangular pin with artistic cut-outs and a leaf-and-berry effect at two corners. It's an eye-catching accent for a tailored outfit but too understated to compete with a floral print. Re-read the assignment twice more before you start...No excuses that you aren't a fashion writer, because a professional writer can handle *any* description.

Take 30 seconds. No longer than that.

Did you ignore "an eye-catching accent for a tailored outfit but too understated to compete with a floral print"? I'd have ignored it too, not only because it's too abstruse a concept to transmit in brief catalog copy but also because it's reasonable to assume the illustration will make this point.

Did you build romance around the art nouveau aspect rather than the sterling silver? That's what I'd have done, because it's the only unique handle to grab.

Whatever you wrote, I guarantee it's superior to the copy which actually ran. I've buried it in the text to enhance the possibility of your reading this chapter.

Keeping Our Heads Clear

Anyone reading these words isn't a typical catalog recipient. We're in the business—probably competing with the catalog we're reading tonight—and our reactions are analytical rather than emotional.

No problem. That's how we keep our heads clear.

But when our *target-readers* slowly transmute their attitudes from emotional to analytical, we've lost that bronze word—*neutrality*—or, worse, that silver word—*interest*—or, heaven help us, that golden word—*rapport*.

The Seven Stages of HU-Man

The recipient sees your catalog and has one of seven reactions:

1. Disgust.
2. Annoyance.

3. Neutrality.
4. Faint interest.
5. Moderate interest.
6. Strong interest.
7. Rapport.

The seventh "stage" usually is reserved for those who are already multi-buyers. I greet the catalogs from Sporty's and Quill Office Supply as old friends; my wife is so tuned to Gardener's Eden and Lands' End she's begun to point out typos.

But how does a catalog, mailed to a "cold list" name, achieve this magic seventh stage?

Let's accept as a fact of business that X-percent of recipients greet your catalog with annoyance or disgust. If that percentage is higher than, say, 10 percent, it's time to question lists, copy, or both. You have a mismatch: The people you're reaching don't want what you're selling or don't respond to your type of pitch; you're projecting arrogance; your layout screams "Schlock!" while your copy murmurs, "Class"; *something.*

At the very least, go back to chapter one and re-examine the list of approaches. Can you, with your most cold-blooded analytical attitude firmly in place, find a mismatch between what you're writing and who your best prospects are? Might an experiment—not with your whole list but with a segment—lead you into a more profitable marketing avenue?

Recognition that one person's meat is another person's poison sometimes leads catalogers to start up an entirely new catalog with different copy, layout, and even pricing, to appeal to the market the original catalog misses.

Nobody Bats a Thousand, but . . .

Converting the first stage to the third is possible, by a powerful match of product to recipient-psychographics, probably on pages 2–3 of your catalog. (If the cover achieves this match, you probably won't be cast into the first or second stage dungeon to start with.)

Converting the third to the seventh is possible, if your copy generates an "I like these guys" reaction from the reader.

Can you lift a recipient from the first stage all the way to the seventh, in one catalog? Not likely.

Sure, you can attract a first-time buyer with a sweepstakes or a bunch of discount coupons or a wild offer or photograph on the cover;

but you aren't then working up from the first stage. At the very least, you have a fourth-stage running jump for that reader.

Oh, by the way: It's a lot easier to fall quickly *down* those golden stairs than it is to climb them tortuously. That's the potential problem all of us should mount sentries to detect.

For example:

I'm looking at a catalog photograph and description of a garden hose. Copy is certainly adequate, although the name of the hose—Flexogen—suffers from an epidemic of circled-"R" registration notices, which destroys the reading-rhythm.

That problem won't transform a seventh-stage reaction all the way down to stage one. But another factor will:

The photograph shows a $3 cash rebate certificate attached to the hose-package. The last words in the copy-block: "Rebate is no longer in effect."

Hold it, fellows. This isn't a case of The Hose giveth and The Hose taketh away. I hadn't even thought about a rebate. *You're* the ones who brought it up. If the rebate is no longer in effect, couldn't you have replaced the illustration?

Or, if the deadline was on your neck, couldn't you have raised the price $3 and then sent the rebate yourselves, explaining that the manufacturer's rebate has expired but *you're* the good guys?

Cast this copy back into the pit of stage one.

On the Other Hand. . .

The very same catalog won my heart with its description of an insect killer which has the wonderful name Big Stinky.

In the description of Big Stinky, we see this parenthetical phrase:

```
(not recommended for inside homes because of
its smell)
```

Huge flaw in the copy—in print, it says "because of *it's* smell," the universal symbol of borderline literacy. I'm violating my own rule of never giving a positive comment to copy misusing *its* and *it's;* in this case sincerity wins out over education.

Here's the actual copy from the "First You Try It" exercise which began this chapter. Would you buy from this actual catalog description which downgrades interest from stage five to stage two with a too-lean description of the silver pin?

Compare your copy with this, the total description which appeared in the catalog (and which undoubtedly ate up considerably more than 30 seconds of copywriting time):

> Our new 2″ sterling silver pin is a proper finish-
> ing touch to so many outfits (164Z) $56

We're back to the old saw, the Specifics Superiority Principle: *Specifics sell. Generalizations don't sell.* My guess: The writer never saw the pin. Neither did you—but you know better than to fill even minimal space with generic no-motivator copy.

Who Is Reading This?

The catalog writer has a big edge over the writer who creates a solo mailing—a generalized profile-knowledge of customers who have bought before.

Our job, then, isn't to be all things to all men. Our industry has come too far from the good old Sears catalog of the 1930s.

In an era of hyper-specialization, we're supposed to hold prior buyers firm at stage seven. . .lift non-buyers from stage three to at least stage six. . .and hope no misstep on either our part or the list-selector's part will result in any copies lying dead in the cemetery of stages one and two.

The Story of PGA Touring Pro Peter Jacobsen,.....................and the MacKenzie Walker.™

When I got the message that Peter Jacobsen had called from the Doral Country Club, I'll admit to being a little surprised. Although I'd followed his career on the Tour, I'd never met him, and had no reason to believe he had the faintest idea who I was! I knew Peter had wins at the Colonial Invitational, Hartford Open, and Buick Open to his credit. And that he had been a three-time All-American at the University of Oregon. That he'd played on the victorious U.S. Team in the Ryder Cup. Naturally I'd seen his name frequently in *Golf Magazine*, where he serves on the Pro Advisory Staff. And I'd seen him increasingly on T.V. as a network color analyst, most recently on "The Skins Game". But what could Peter Jacobsen want with me, way up here in New Hampshire? So I called him. (Continued next page!)

Getting Back to Basics — Peter had a problem. Often when he needed to practice, he preferred being alone, and there usually were no caddies around anyway. And Peter, like many of us, simply won't use a golf cart. He believes that cart-riding interferes with golf's natural rhythm. *To Peter, walking is a sacred part of the game itself.* Now, have you ever tried walking 18 holes with a huge Staff Bag around your neck (the kind that weighs 15 lbs. *before* you put the clubs in!)? That was Peter's dilemma. Anybody else would have bought a cheap canvas "Sunday" bag and be done with it. But not Peter. He went out and developed his own lightweight Walking Bag. **Peter's Vision** — Being a purist, Peter wanted an all-leather bag. Leather, like persimmon woods and the Masters in April, is as much a part of golf's tradition as St. Andrews. But he wanted a light, *comfortable* bag, as he'd be spending long hours carrying it himself, engaged in solitary practice rounds. And he wanted a *simple* bag devoid of all the paraphenalia and gee gaws that tend to show up on the tour. (I could tell listening to Peter, even before I saw it, that this bag *would not* resemble a walking billboard!).

The MacKenzie Walker — Peter wanted a bag just large enough to carry a full set of 14 clubs without crowding, so he settled on an 8" cowl. He chose the finest, most supple leather available, tanned to look and feel more like a thick golf glove than a stiff suitcase. Just two pockets, one to carry a rain suit, sweater and hat; the other for a towel and *plenty* of balls (Peter explained that he might replay a particularly tough shot a dozen or more times right in the middle of a practice round). To stand up to the rigors of the Tour, Peter designed the bag for durability, with a thickly padded leather handle joined to the bag with 8 (count 'em!) rivets. And a channelled shoulder strap attached with a nickel-plated, pivoting lanyard. He even put suede on the strap so it wouldn't slip off his shoulder. As a tribute to golf's birthplace, Scotland, Peter named his creation "The MacKenzie Walker".

The Herrington Connection — Peter had created a 3 lb. marvel of functional simplicity. When he showed it to his friends on the tour, the reaction was overwhelming (Palmer had to have one!). So Peter decided to set up his own small company in Oregon to craft his MacKenzie Bag. Not being certain who, other than fellow pros, might appreciate his bag's utter simplicity, quality, and light weight, he called to ask my opinion. (It turns out he's been a good customer of ours for years, although no one told me!) Did I think the Enthusiasts who receive our catalog would have a need for a bag that in many ways was a throwback to a simpler time — when golfers *walked* the course (and before bags looked like motor homes!). After evaluating the sample Peter sent to me, I assured him The MacKenzie Walker was *made* for the serious Enthusiast, and that the aroma and feel of the fine leather alone was worth the price!

Peter Jacobsen's MacKenzie Walker — $250.00   **#G284 St. Andrews Brown**
#G285 Baltusrol Black   #G286 Muirfield Gray   #G287 Augusta Blue

Figure 14-1

   We're supposed to believe that Peter Jacobsen (have you ever heard of him?) phoned the head of this catalog company to ask him his opinion of a 3-pound golf bag. Whether we believe this narrative or not, do you think the prelude to what's being sold is too long? Do you believe it isn't particularly interesting, and the writer might have had a more *reader-involving* way to introduce this golf bag? I do.

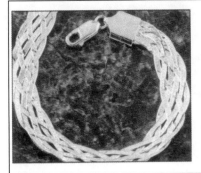
Figure 14-2

How many pieces do you see in the photograph? Me too. One. We don't quite see all of this piece, which looks like one end of a bicycle chain. Copy says "Pair" in both heading and subhead. Should we blame the writer? No, the person to blame is whoever separated the pair. The writer probably didn't even need to see the photograph. With either a fact sheet or a sample at hand, how could the writer anticipate copy being at odds with illustration?

Figure 14-3

Before looking at the photograph, close your eyes and imagine the sound of a British bulldog barking. Don't you get the feeling of a gruffer, deeper, growlier sound, tinged with slow humor? Now look at the picture. German shepherd? Rottweiler? Whatever that dog is, it isn't an English bulldog. What's puzzling isn't the mismatch of dog and copy. It's why the writer specified "British bulldog" at all. "Mastiff" or "attack dog" would have been more in keeping with the security-image.

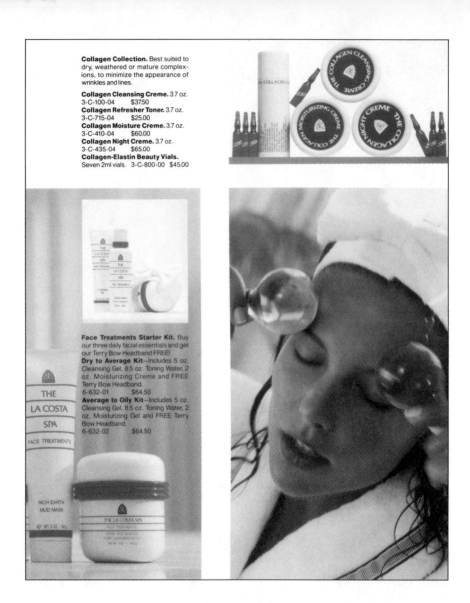

Figure 14-4

All right, what's going on in the photograph at lower right? How does it relate to anything being sold on this page? Are those Christmas tree ornaments, light bulbs, or electrodes? Nothing on this page gives us a clue. Probably the layout artist took pride in a pseudo-avant-garde effect of undescribed picture; don't you do it, or your readers will be as disgusted as we are, hunting for a non-existent explanation of what's causing this girl's sensual reaction.

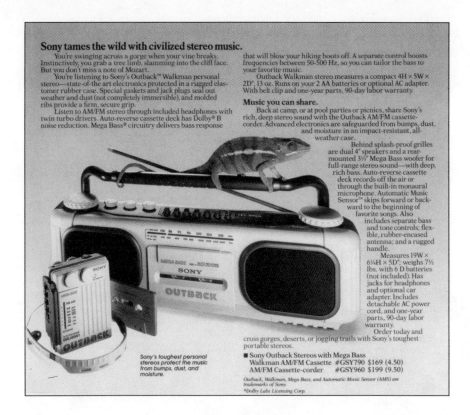

Figure 14-5

Why have the lizard perched on this radio? If we didn't have the "tames the wild" headline, it would be just another acolyte at the "That-which-is-different-equals-that-which-is-better" shrine. With the headline, it's a clever and harmless eye-catcher. The lizard serves another purpose, too: It gives us a thin clue to the size. If *you* were writing this copy, what graphic effect would you have used to make your point about this radio's impact, weather, and dust resistant case? An outback hat? Some water droplets and sand? Communication between writer and graphics designer results in copy/picture matchup.

CHAPTER 15

Describing the Complicated Item... Explaining the Deception Perception... and Other Matters

FIRST, *YOU* TRY IT!

Your assignment: Your overseas buyer hands you a sheaf of descriptive information on a "Digital Diary." He tells you, "I want a headline telling our buyers of electronic gadgets what this is. For example, 'Latest business success team: You and "The Boss"'."

You ask, " 'The Boss'?"

"Sure. Boss. B.O.S.S. Business Organizer Scheduling System. Oh, and tell them it has double the memory."

"Of what?"

But he's gone.

You look at the photograph. It appears to be a tiny computer the size of a large wallet. It has a keyboard and an LCD screen, and it has "64K Super Memory" emblazoned on its face. A fact sheet tells you it can store thousands of phone numbers and notes, up to 384 characters each. "B.O.S.S.?" you muse. "Double the memory?" You decide to write your own headline. What is it?

Take 30 seconds. No longer than that.

Is your headline, "Carry this powerful computer . . . in your suit pocket"? Not bad. Is it, "An electronic secretary with more than 64,000 bytes of memory—in your purse?" Pretty good.

Believe it or not, one of the world's best known marketers of electronic gadgets used this unappealing headline:

> *Latest business success team: You and "The Boss."*
> Top-of-the-line Digital Diary has double the memory. And more.

The actual copy, which commanded the catalog's entire inside cover, is Fig. 15-1. Whatever headline you wrote, I'll bet it was more communicative than the one which appeared in the catalog.

The Rule of Absolute Communication-Connection

One of the stiffest tests of catalog writer professionalism is the ability to describe a complicated item to readers whose technical knowledge is—or may be—nonexistent.

Note the hedge: The difference between *is* and *may be* in my opinion doesn't exist. If it's *may be,* it's *is.* I justify this appeal for primitivism in descriptive copy with solid fact, *THE RULE OF ABSOLUTE COMMUNICATION-CONNECTION:*

> **Simplifying the description won't alienate those who have the same background you do; showing off your product knowledge with terminology and "Level II" description positively does alienate those who don't have the same background you do.**

What a universe of difference in reader-reaction between "The writer is telling me something I didn't know before" and "The writer is telling me he knows something I don't." Want to have the opportunity to sell whatever it is to *all* your catalog readers? Swallow your arrogance.

So I admire whoever wrote this description of "Nike's Training Monitor":

> *NIKE'S training monitor coaches your workout—in English*
> You simply strap on the NIKE Monitor and take off on your run, walk or hike. It automatically keeps track of your speed, pace, mileage and heart rate and reports them to you on command—with its digitized voice—so you can custom-tailor your workout.

Note the use of words. It "keeps track of," not "registers." It "reports them to you," not "discloses" or "apprises." You can "custom-tailor" your workout, not "adapt" or "modify."

Deeper in the copy, the writer unlooses *Doppler Effect ultrasound,* but by then we're buddies.

And that's one of the keys to effective catalog copywriting, whether consumer or business: Don't lead off with a display of encyclopedic terminology. Save it for later. Bury the castor oil in a chocolate soda.

Another example—a painting on Egyptian papyrus (not the same one we saw in chapter 12). The undisciplined writer would pick up a pedantic description of papyrus and regurgitate it onto the copy-sheet.

This writer gets off to a rocky start with the standoffish word "rendition" and a meaningless "rare"-puffery reference; but overall the copy succeeds because the writer wasn't afraid to communicate on the reader's level:

> *King Tut's legacy lives on.*
> As bold as the Pharaoh himself and unlike any other rendition, *The Funeral Mask of King Tut*, an Egyptian painting on *papyrus*, is a rare—and valuable—find. The bright colors you see in this picture are paints made from the natural pigments of plants, rocks, and vegetables. Pressing the papyrus paper is an art in itself—stemming from a 3000-year-old process. Stocks of the papyrus plant are cut, pressed and woven by hand . . .

"Sensational" and All Those Nondescriptions

In earlier chapters I've registered a reader-objection to overuse of key words. Remember the cataloger who uses "explodes" or "explosive" a dozen times in each catalog?

That's his option, assuming he's aware of his infatuation with the word. But when a major catalog hits us with an unbacked "sensational," it's time to pound the "delete" key.

Copy says:

> Vaneli pairs comfort and style in these sensational new leather sandals. They're made in Italy with open toed, woven strapped fronts, closed backs, and side buckles. Allow four to six weeks for delivery.

Okay, what about this description makes the shoes sensational? Made in Italy? Every pair of shoes my wife owns comes from Italy. Open toed, woven strapped fronts? A pair of huaraches qualifies.

I'm not attacking the worth of the shoes. I'm attacking the laziness that excreted the word "sensational" without justification. (For that matter, *any* use of "sensational" in catalog copy is suspect.)

I'll tell you what else bothers me: carelessness.

So I was surprised to see, in a catalog I admire enough to be a customer, the same illustration used for two different products. One was on page 6. The other was on page 30.

Let's suppose the two are allied. The one on page 5 is to cover fever blisters cosmetically; the other is to control those blisters. A professional way to handle this is to have one illustration serve both masters, with copy blocks adjacent. Using the photographs twice *seems* to be a mistake even if it isn't a mistake—because the person interested in one implicitly is interested in the other.

The Deception Perception

Catalogs traditionally have been free of an occasional ailment afflicting some solo mailings. I call this ailment *THE DECEPTION PERCEPTION:*

> When a reader penetrates a statement whose intention is to mislead, getting an order drops to a likelihood of near-zero or less.

So we have two options:

> 1. Don't give the reader any ammunition to strengthen preconceived skepticism.
>
> 2. Couch misleading wording so cleverly or positively that the reader doesn't penetrate the rhetoric.

Does this copy, from a "membership"-type catalog, qualify for either option?

> *No Risk Membership!*
> Cancel at any time and the balance of your membership dues will be refunded.

Sorry, buddy, I don't regard a refund for the "balance of my membership" as a no risk membership. *No* risk doesn't mean *some* risk. If I sign up and decide after seeing one or two copies of your Insider's Hotline it isn't for me, I still owe you for those issues. I'm at risk. Why not borrow a page from subscription promotions and actually make it *no* risk? That way, you won't have to hedge. (The whole copy-block for this offer is Fig. 15-3.)

Can Tight Description Still Sell?

Some catalog writers complain about the space-restraint: "I don't have enough space to describe *and* sell. The only solution is to describe."

Right, if it's that tight. But we've all seen tight descriptive copy that still sizzles.

"Sizzle," in fact, is the key word in a description which lifts itself above the pile of standardized fashion copy. Total sell – copy = four words in a group and one word within the copy. But look at the way it brings a pedestrian description to life—and visualize the flatness of copy if those four words weren't there:

> Sizzle . . . this dress does. Cut high on top and short on the bottom with contrasting/contouring white taping and front zipper completing the sultry appearance. Acid-washed blue cotton denim with polyester/cotton trim. Machine wash. Made in U.S.A.

Without those first four words and the wonderfully descriptive *sultry,* it's just another piece of journeyman copy. Here, somebody was thinking: How do I add *sell* without larding up the copy with a bunch of synonyms for "beautiful"?

Do YOU Love It or Hate It?

When you hit the "Enter" key, if you're a professional writer you're always a little dissatisfied . . . but your dissatisfaction is vague, not specific. You don't *know* you've oozed out a bunch of words instead of grabbing and shaking the reader. Why? Simple: If you do know, and you don't rewrite, you aren't a professional writer.

Figure 15-1

Do you regard this headline and subhead as inviting? In my opinion, to those who aren't previously acquainted with this type of item it suggests we've wandered accidentally into the wrong catalog. The body copy is loaded with benefits. The headline is empty of them. And the phrase "And more" is hasty semi-pro, not worthy of this catalog.

Figure 15-2

Compare this description to Fig. 15-1. The item is similar but not identical. The headline is no world-beater, but it doesn't turn off the reader; and the descriptive copy is specific, clear, and bright.

Figure 15-3

(Last paragraph) You say you guarantee my complete satisfaction? Welllll... Not quite, friends. If I'm unhappy, "the balance" of my membership dues will be refunded. Why risk reader-annoyance and antipathy by weaseling this way? Any competent writer can create copy describing the offer in non-weasel terms, in two minutes. And this writer *is* competent, because even though the copy is seldom specific, it still is dynamic and exciting...with one exception, in the very paragraph we're dissecting. Did you spot it? "The balance of your membership dues will be refunded" is passive and standoffish. Much better: "We'll refund the balance of your membership dues."

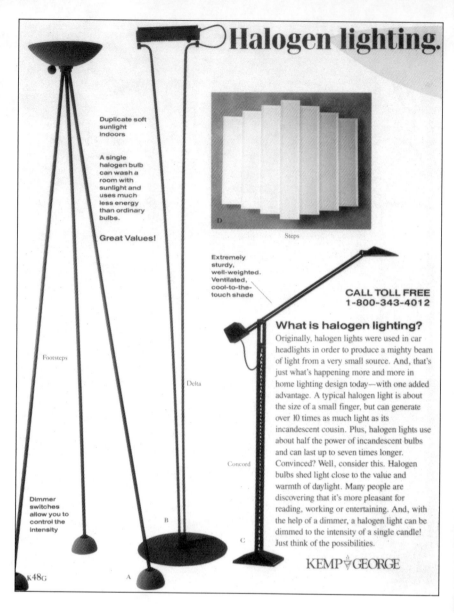

Figure 15-4

This thoughtful two-page spread includes a clear, positive, benefit-
laden description of halogen lighting. Would a reader be as likely to
see the superiority of these lamps if the explanation weren't included?

.. a bright idea!

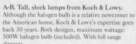

A-B. Tall, sleek lamps from Koch & Lowy. Although the halogen bulb is a relative newcomer to the American home, Koch & Lowy's expertise goes back 30 years. Both designs, maximum wattage: 500W halogen bulb (included). With full range dimmer.

A. Footsteps. An off-beat, leggy design with a very special appeal. The 11" reflector dish enables its 500W halogen bulb to flood any room with light. Or use its mood setter (the ball-shaped dimmer switch at the left) to adjust the light's intensity. 74"H.
Black. #72018 . . . .**Just $198!**
Brass shade/black legs (not shown).
#72019 . . . .**Just $238!**
Black shade/yellow legs (not shown).
#72020 . . . .**Just $198!**

B. Delta. This torchiere can be used in practically any room. It stands 74"H and measures 8¾" × 2½". Shade can be pivoted 45°. Available in a scratch-resistant, suede-like finish or white enamel.
Black, #72021 or White. #72022 . . . . . .**Just $175!**
Matching wall light available on page 52.

C. Concord. This ingenious design from Artup employs the use of a counterweight-balance system so you can have light exactly where you want it. 50W halogen bulb included. High-low switch.
Black, #72009 or White. #72050 . . . . . .**Just $198!**

D. Steps mirror. Seven mirrored strips with ½" beveled edges. 17½" × 27½". #63008 . .**Just $110!**

E. Orion floor lamp. Light up an entire room or use its dimmer floor switch to set whatever mood you like. Available in a black or white finish; with a frosted white glass shade. 70"H × 13"W. One 250W halogen bulb included.
Black. #72023 or White. #72024 . . . . . .**Just $198!**

F. Comet torchiere. An extremely versatile floor lamp in almond, black, white or gunmetal. Built-in dimmer. 500W halogen bulb included. 72"H × 15"W. Please specify color.
#72025 . . . .**Just $148!**

G. Illusions. A simple, yet elegant torchiere topped with a triple-tiered crystal glass shade for dramatic lighting. In white or black. 71"H. 250W halogen bulb included.
White. #72029 or Black. #72030 . . . . . .**Just $150!**

H. Ventura. Its 6 frosted rectangular shades provide the perfect counterpoint to its sleek black finish. Full-range dimmer. 74"H.
500W halogen bulb included. #72028. . .**Just $260!**

J. Meridian. This incandescent torchiere's light flows upward, yet filters out through the frosted glass shade for a soft, warm glow. Three-way switch. 69"H × 10"W.
Polished brass. #72027 . . . .**Just $110!**
Black (not shown). #72026 . . . .**Just $110!**

Orion

E

Comet

Illusions

Ventura

Meridian

K49

CHAPTER 16

The More You Know... the More You Can Say

FIRST, *YOU* TRY IT!

Your assignment: You're writing copy for an office products catalog. Copy blocks are small—about seven or eight lines of about 40 characters.

Here's a box of ten hanging folders in assorted colors. Oops! What can you say that will fill even seven or eight lines? After all, they're just hanging folders. Think of a "grabber" first sentence to eat up a couple of lines without wasting them.

Take 30 seconds. No longer than that.

Did you use those first couple of lines to tell the reader a benefit or two of hanging files? Then you're a real pro. You can compare your copy with the copy which actually ran, in Fig. 16-1.

The Catalog Writer's Hair-Shirt

The relationship between underdescribed copy and merchandise returned because of buyer-dissatisfaction is one of the more obvious hair-shirts catalogers wear.

More subtle, statistically, is the number of sales lost because a writer *over*described an item, introducing fact/puff/trivia weakeners more damaging than helpful.

And a third reaction-level is why copywriters exist at all: Total generation of buying impulse by the raw power of copy.

If You Don't Tell Us, We Can't Tell Them

I'm looking at a copy-block for a home pinball machine. As I read it, I'm reminded of Tom Wolfe. Adrenalin starts to flow. Rhetorical pheromones beckon. I don't want a home pinball machine, but I'm tempted—not because of the item but because of the writer. A sampler:

> *Slam!* You flip the ball up and it crashes into a kick-out crater, setting off an explosion of sounds and spinning scoring drums. *Whoosh.* The ball shoots out of the crater, and your perfectly timed flip blasts it up the hyperspace channel, where it disappears into a black hole.
>
> Now, the whole galaxy erupts . . .

219

You get the idea.

What this copy says to me is: The writer actually played this pinball machine. The writer wrote from experience, not a fact sheet. The writer had an advantage over most of us, who get a photograph and description and who can't match the vivid "You are there!" quality of this description.

Compare this with a description of Picasso prints:

> Pablo Picasso's overwhelming creativity, versatility and energy place him among the greatest masters of all time. By special arrangement, we are able to bring you these limited edition prints *Femme au Chapeau* . . .

My conclusion: The catalog writer has little idea who Picasso was, why his paintings "place him among the greatest masters of all time" (ugh), or, really, what's being sold here. And please, don't think I'm suggesting we have an art teacher write this copy. I'm suggesting copy which both creates and *justifies* a desire to buy.

As catalogs evolve from the general to the specific and from the specific to the *hyper*-specific, successful descriptive copy will lean more and more on writer-experience.

I'll point out a danger in this: specialization.

Writers who want to sell anything to anybody have to communicate on the experiential level of the message-recipient, not themselves. That's why an art teacher, describing a Picasso print, probably would communicate on the wrong level with casual catalog browsers. Even in business-to-business catalogs aimed at vertical interest-groups, we have to be careful not to overuse private terminology.

Don't Duck the Negatives

Fear of killing the sale causes catalog copy to slide off-center and go awry.

Sometimes it's as simple as tiptoeing over negatives such as "requires assembly" or "batteries not included." The unwary buyer—who may be 85 years old and arthritic—gets the exercise bike in what seems to be a thousand pieces. The single line, "Some assembly required," might have killed off the order but also would have prevented an automatic return. ("A child can assemble this in 12 minutes" might get the order without generating the return.)

Sometimes the copywriter doesn't have enough information to euphemize around a negative—or, for that matter, to include it. Negatives have, literally, a "negative value" as preventives: The phrase "Not for use in..." has prevented not just returns, but lawsuits.

Attention-Getting, but...

Let's suppose you sell lingerie with a secret compartment designed to hold a passport or credit cards. How would you describe it and how would you show it?

I'm looking at a catalog which shows a striking female model (un)dressed in a camisole. The illustration carries our eye far past the passport pouch, down her shapely legs to spike-heel shoes which don't quite fit. As attractive as she is, *she* isn't what they're selling. Product ends at the hips; the rest is for dramatic effect. Ancient curmudgeon that I am, even as I admire the ma'am's gams I wonder if this isn't a scam—the cataloger preventing me from turning the page by the most venerable of attractions.

Okay, he wins. I do stop and read the copy (Fig. 16-4). But this item is one hundred percent female, and the suggestion is more seductive than salesworthy. Did it justify the space? I've learned not to ask this question without having a bodyguard at my side.

Use Product Knowledge to Sell

Magalogs—catalogs masquerading as magazines, in magazine format—have sold merchandise where straightforward, descriptive catalogs haven't. Description of what something *does,* not tightly tied to a bunch of selling adjectives, often cracks the apathy-barrier, justifying the dedication of page-space.

I once had the happy experience of including a four-step diagram of how to tie a bow tie, adjacent to a group of bow ties. The cataloger actually had letters of thanks from people whose old bow ties had been stuck deep in a closet for want of tying know-how. That's no way to keep score; we aren't altruists in this business. *But* most of those letters accompanied an order for bow ties, and inch for inch, this segment was successful.

Think of one article in your catalog whose use, installation, or variations might—just might—not be clear to every reader. In an adjacent tint-block, describe what may be obvious to you but not to the reader. You might attract buyers who otherwise think, "That isn't for me," or, "What would I do with it?"

Polished copywriting suggests transmitting enough product knowledge, easily and simply enough, to attract moths who may not have seen the flame before, or even recognized it as a flame.

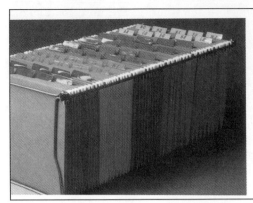

Figure 16-1

The first 3½ lines don't sell these hanging folders; they sell the whole idea of hanging folders. A perfect combination: The headline grabs both those already looking for hanging folders and those just browsing; the first lines pitch superiority and benefit, and then the writer piles on the specifics. Imagine how flat and ordinary this copy would be without those first 3½ lines. . . which most writers wouldn't have thought of.

Weber Patio Fireplace

C We are delighted with this portable fireplace — it extends outdoor evenings by several hours and provides a cozy hearth as well. The specially designed cover radiates heat to warm the air around it, and provides a safe way to extinguish the fire. The black enameled heavy gauge steel fireplace holds enough wood to last for hours. Sturdy and lightweight, you can move it to any spot in the yard. Complete instructions included. (Not for use on wooden decks.) 28″ diam., 30½″ high. #16-265983 $112.00

Figure 16-2

When you read those six words in parentheses, at the end of the copy, is your reaction, "Of course I wouldn't use a portable fireplace on a wooden deck"? I'll bet it's a prohibition you wouldn't have considered if the writer didn't bring it up. Now, suppose the writer had been afraid this thought would reduce sales. Without these words, the buyer faces two possibilities: 1) Finding the admonition in the instructions with the fireplace, which can lead to a return; or 2) accidentally starting a deck fire, which can lead to a lawsuit. Opinion: When issues such as this exist, total disclosure is mandatory.

9-D

**Prints by
Pablo Picasso**

(left) Pablo Picasso's
overwhelming creativity,
versatility and energy place
him among the greatest masters
of all time. By special arrangement, we
are able to bring you these limited edition
prints *Femme au Chapeau* : #9-D, *Tete de
Bleu (Head of a Woman with A Blue Hat)*, and #4-B, *Fillette au
Bateau (Little Girl with a Boat)*. Only 200 each of these fine poster
prints have been reserved by Haverhills. As is customary in quality
printing of poster art, the silk screen used to create them will be
destroyed as soon as the edition is completed. They are available
unframed, or in a matted black frame. This is a rare opportunity to
acquire reproductions of highly imaginative works by a man whose
very name is now synonymous with modern art. They will add an
esthetic note to any room. ■#4653. 9-D Picasso Print $99.95.
■#4654. 9-D Framed Picasso Print $199.95. ■#4655. 4-B Picasso
Print $99.95. ■#4656. 4-B Framed Picasso Print $199.95.

4-B

Figure 16-3

By the time the writer gets to the multi-phrased sentence, "This is a
rare opportunity to acquire reproductions of highly imaginative works
by a man whose very name is now synonymous with modern art," the
reader is long gone. Opinion: Lead off with this sentence instead of the
weak mélange of nondescriptive words that now start the copy-block
in super-low gear.

Figure 16-4

Now that I have your attention, a question: Is getting attention the alpha and omega of catalog-sell? This company obviously thinks so, because the Lady in Red doesn't just dominate this page; she *is* this page. Do they need the legs to sell the theft-preventing lingerie? Another question: How badly does the electronic wallet, upper left, suffer from upstaging?

STRANGER IN TOWN?

What nasty little strangers are lurking beneath the surface of water? The H$_2$OK® Water Filter could be your best friend on the road, or in any emergency. It's portable, lightweight, easy to use with no batteries, no filter changes, no electrical or plumbing hook-ups. With special carbon/silver treatment, water passed through H$_2$OK keeps indefinitely, even unrefrigerated. It processes about a quart per minute. H$_2$OK provides a family of 4 drinking/cooking water for about 3 years. Size 9"H, 3" diam., 10 oz.
H$_2$OK® Water Filter #4076 $29.95 (2.50)

Figure 16-5

If the bright copywriter who created this provocative copy-block had limited the description to information on the fact sheet, the reader wouldn't be drawn into the magical "reason to buy" universe. A selling description requires both writing talent *and* knowledge of product benefit.

When the sun gets hot, take a cooler seat.

"Hey, dude. That's like a really radical chair."

"Yes, bronzed surfer person. It's the Cool Gear™ cooler chair. See, inside is a 10-quart cooler with a movable divider. It holds two six-packs with room left over for food and other supplies. And the included water freezer bottle eliminates the need for ice.

"Close it, and the contoured lid becomes a comfortable seat. And the handle folds back to become an adjustable swivel backrest. I can carry it easily by the handle or the woven nylon shoulder strap. Folded, it measures only 18L × 18W × 7H" and weighs just 8 lbs. The lid locks securely to keep out sand and dust. It's made in America of colorful, high-impact polyethylene and insulated with a layer of pressurized air. It comes with a six-month warranty."

"Wow! I wonder if I could bungee-cord it to my board?"

"I wouldn't recommend that. But you can take it to the beach, pool, camp, boat, ball games, tailgate parties, and barbecues. I even take mine to the annual office picnic."

"Office? Like, what's an office?"

Call today and make your good times outdoors comfortably refreshing.

■ **Cooler Chair #GFU215 $39 (4.50)**

Roomy cooler compartment holds a full day's refreshments.

Figure 16-6

See what happens when the writer's desire to be clever overrides the desire to transmit a salesworthy—but accurate—description? The skimmer-reader assumes the seat is cool. It isn't. Reinterpretation inevitably leads to rejection.

B DRAGON GRASS DOORMAT
Grown in the mountains of southern China, dragon grass is a wonderfully strong, wiry fiber for outdoor or indoor use. In a half-round shape with an intricate arrangement of knots, this handsome doormat resists weather and abrasion. 27" x 16½" x 1" thick. #02-191577 $8.00*

B

Figure 16-7

What a wonderful name, "Dragon Grass"! We all have seen this type of fiber mat in housewares catalogs, but this company gives it a name. The dragon grass mat becomes a proprietary, beyond-comparison product.

Marinated Vegetables: A Garden Of Earthly Delights

Come back with us to old-fashioned kitchens where loving grandmothers spend their days carefully putting up vegetables in mason jars, and then displaying them proudly on open cupboard shelves. Today, we present a most appealing selection of beautiful fresh vegetables "put up" with appropriate fresh herbs in special marinades, then sealed in glass jars so that all may see their perfection. For antipasti, salads, to accompany main course meats. And to eat right out of the jar.

Dried Tomatoes in Olive Oil with Herbs

For generations Sicilians have dried their plum tomatoes on wicker trays in the sun. Then they're packed in earthenware crocks and layered with vinegar, salt and oil, thus preserving them for winter use.

Now Thomas Garraway is proud to present some of the finest dried tomatoes made in America today — dried tomatoes that are distinctively marinated in olive oil seasoned with fresh garlic and oregano. Use them to enliven pasta and chicken salads, and on antipasto platters. We also like a few strips on many of our favourite sandwiches. Try it for yourself.

90256   Dried Tomatoes in Olive Oil with Herbs   7 oz. $7.50

Hot Dilled Green Beans

Crunchy, snappy, whole green beans in a marinade with hot red pepper flakes and charmingly bottled with a whole garlic clove and a sprig of fresh dill. Medium hot.

90369   Villa Brindisi™ Hot Dilled Green Beans   11 oz. $7.50

Marinated Baby Corn

Tiny ears of tender imported corn, like those used in Chinese cooking, dressed in a marinade of vinegar, oil, herbs and spices and garlic. With a good sprinkling of tarragon.

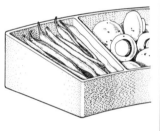

90368   Villa Brindisi™ Marinated Baby Corn   11 oz. $7.50

Marinated Giant Mushrooms

Round and plump, these lovely delicacies are packed in a vinegar and oil blend with garlic, herbs and spices, and plenty of spark.

90367   Villa Brindisi™ Marinated Giant Mushrooms   11 oz. $7.50

Marinated Miniature Artichokes

Not to be confused with artichoke hearts, these are prized perfect whole baby artichokes in a marinade of olive oil, vinegar, garlic, herbs and spices.

90357   Villa Brindisi™ Marinated Miniature Artichokes   11 oz. $7.00

Figure 16-8

If the writer were less knowledgeable, the descriptions would be flat. Here, a historical tie, aided by suggested ways to use the dried, dilled, and marinated vegetables and by colorful words such as *crunchy, snappy,* and *plump,* stimulates the reader's taste-buds as well as her attention.

ELECTRIC ERASER

Don't laugh. This ingenious gizmo is sensationally handy. Has a high-speed rotary-action hard rubber head that lifts errors right off the paper, leaving no telltale smear behind. Lets you correct a single typed letter or tiny pencil line without disturbing adjacent copy or design. Saves you when you fill out forms, keep the books or work on the house plans. And when you're doing none of the above, you can use the attachments to do engraving, smooth chipped glass or manicure your nails!

- Engraving tip and burnishing stone attachments.
- Comes with six extra erasing heads.
- Runs on two AA batteries (not included).

#2-25195-7   Orig. $17   NOW $15   S-14780R-5

HANDSOME REWARDS®
19465 BRENNAN AVE. • PERRIS, CA 92379

Figure 16-9

Whether or not you remember the "Seven Stages of HU-Man" from chapter 14, you'll appreciate the way this writer rockets the reader's attitude up the scale from neutrality to strong interest with two little words: "Don't laugh." On the negative side, the headline doesn't hint at engraving, an equally valuable use for this implement.

CHAPTER 17

The Law of Absolute Confusion

FIRST, *YOU* TRY IT!

Your assignment: You love computers, so when you have the opportunity to describe a new $168.95 computer chess game you don't have to think twice. Your headline: "Powerful 16K Computer Challenges Chess Players on Every Level."

Your copy chief *isn't* a computer nut. She fires the copy back at you with this comment: "Yes, chess players have a more analytical attitude than a lot of other game players, but you've emphasized 'computer' rather than 'game,' and I think this leads to confusion. Try another headline."

You may not agree, but she's the copy chief, so you rewrite the headline, aiming the copy-thrust at chess.

Take 30 seconds. No longer than that.

Did you at last remember the magical word your copy chief didn't mention—"New"? Ah! Was one of the first five words "chess"? Double-ah! I hope you didn't let her cow you out of the computer reference altogether. After all, that's what you're selling. If you added one word, transforming the unemotional word "computer" to the challenging "computer brain," *you* should be the copy chief.

The actual ad is Fig. 17-1. It's no big winner...but somebody paid a professional to write it.

You Have to Kill in Five Words

We know what we meant. But are *those people* out there reading it the way we wrote it?

It may have been a while since you read chapter two. The cornerstone of that chapter, this book, and your career as a communicator, should be *THE CLARITY COMMANDMENT.*

Catalog writers, far more than any direct response communicators, should be slavish worshipers at the shrine of this Commandment:

In force-communication, clarity is paramount. Don't let any other component of the communications mix interfere with it.

The editorial writer has a luxury we don't have—the reader's willingness to accept a subtle or oblique opening shot, reinterpreted as text develops. The creator of a solo mailing has another luxury we don't have—multiplicity of components, so raw product description never stands alone.

THE FIVE WORD NAIL ADMONITION:

> Catalog copy nails the reader within the
> first five words or loses him/her forever.

One exception: The top-end catalog which may allocate a whole page to one item. The reader knows from *format* this isn't a direct, condensed description.

So Why Do They...?

I'm looking at a successful discount catalog. The page has five items, not just one, so it doesn't qualify for the disclaimer.

Two copy-blocks struck me as examples of reader-misdirection. One begins:

> *Listen Carefully*...you can almost hear the
> thunder of the rails and smell the rich aroma of
> gourmet food every time you look at this authen-
> tic replica...

What does this copy describe? A lamp. "Listen Carefully" throws the reader off-track. "If you listen carefully..." might have made the reference less obscure, because it becomes a condition, not a command. Even this change is a band-aid, because the next sense-reference is "smell," which doesn't involve the ears.

The writer is trying to set a mood. It doesn't work because the reader isn't prepared to jump head-first into the mood. Lyrical copy is out of key with most copy in this catalog, but that isn't a major problem; who says catalog copy should be a one-string fiddle? No, the major problem is one of *connection*.

If I were writing this one and an exalted creative director demanded "You are there" copy, I'd have started off:

> Turn on this lamp, an authentic replica from the
> Orient Express. You can almost hear the thun-
> der of the rails and smell the rich aroma...

I'm not suggesting mine is superior copy. No, I'm suggesting it's *digestible* copy because it connects the writer's intention to the reader's awareness.

The second copy block on this same page has as its heading:

> Keep an Eye on Baby
> with the Mobile Monitor

Suppose you read this heading to your spouse. Wouldn't the logical interpretation be, "Oh, a video monitor." That's what "Keep an eye on..." suggests. It isn't; it monitors sounds.

No, these aren't ghastly transgressions. They don't destroy comprehension; they just hinder it a little. So does using them as examples become an unreasonable attack?

I don't know about you, but I don't think so. Copy calling for eyes-closed imagination runs a dangerous course, not because the concept is unsound—in radio copy it's standard operating procedure—but because of the gap-potential between what the writer thinks the reader understands and what the reader actually does understand.

"I Want Shalimar"

A page from an upscale catalog is reproduced at the end of this chapter (Fig. 17-2). No, I haven't asked the publisher to reprint it because of the grammar in the copy-stack at left ("...items that the person never would have thought of for themselves"). Instead, it's a challenge.

See that bottle of Shalimar? In the original, it's in color; the perfumes around it are carefully subdued in shades of shadowy gray.

Okay, where's *any* reference to Shalimar in the copy? (If you're in a hurry, don't bother looking. I already did, and none exists.)

One other question about copy on this page—the 29-line paragraph under the heading, "A Luxurious Gift": Small is 8 ounces; medium is 16 ounces; large is 47 ounces. If the sizes are correct, "large" is the wrong name. Small doubles in size to become medium, but the gap between medium and large is immense.

Now the copywriter gets his turn to create. If the words "small," "medium," and "large" aren't actually printed on the labels, he can name the size of these bottles. "Small" seems inapt because of the price—$50. "Jumbo" seems schlock-filled for a bottle costing $90. So to meet the challenge the writer may (and in my opinion should) abandon generic size words for more salesworthy alternates.

Is Nairobi in Australia?

The catalog description of a man's hat:

> *The Aussie Hat.* A laundered Nairobi™ hat with a
> leather band and poplin lining . . .

I've been to Australia many times and to Nairobi a couple of times. A relationship between the types of hats doesn't exist; and this hat looks like . . . well, like a hat. Check it for yourself—Fig. 17-3.

Let's assume Nairobi, because of the "TM," is a trade name. Do recipients of the catalog know this? Or are they confused by an apparent mismatch? The writer should have known, and heeded, *THE LAW OF ABSOLUTE CONFUSION:*

**Buying interest decreases in exact ratio
to an increase in confusion.**

One more. I'm looking at a catalog of men's wear. Here's a photograph of a typical male model with the fashionable Don Johnson five o'clock shadow. He's wearing a herringbone sportcoat. Just one problem, one we see too often when we relate copy to illustration:

The product description for this picture includes the sportcoat (which I see), the necktie (which I see), and the trousers (which I don't see). Copy is no help, because this is all it says:

> *Bombay Trousers.* #J710 *$59.* Specially priced
> for you! Sophisticated midweight wool allows for
> limitless year 'round wear. U.S. made. Sizes 28–
> 42 (no 35, 37, 39, 41).

Okay, if Nairobi can make an Aussie hat, Bombay trousers can be made in the U.S. Hands, please: How many know what Bombay trousers are? How many know what color these are? Guess, please: Did the copywriter know the photograph didn't show the pants?

Just What DO We Say?

So, so many catalog writers struggle to write poetry, or to *over-*describe, or to mask defects with rhetoric. When their copy does sell, returns are higher than usual because the percentage of buyers who clearly understand what they're ordering is lower than usual.

Fig. 17-4 is a page from a household products catalog. I do admire clarity, and clarity is a long suit here. You and I don't feel cheated by product descriptions in this catalog; we can order any item in it and know in advance exactly what we're getting, how big it is, and what it does.

Better yet: The writer doesn't tell us what it is and stop there. Every headline and even the smallest copy-blocks blend benefit into the description. It's a conscious corporate philosophy, because page after page in this catalog reflects this dedication.

Is the copy brilliant? Better—it's professional.

Your turn:

When you write a product description, do *you* still have unanswered questions in your own mind about what it is and what it does? If you do—and you're the writer—what chance do you have of convincing "those people" out there to order it?

Figure 17-1

If we study this copy-block we *think* we understand what the writer meant: If you turn off the game and walk away, the Astral Electronic Chess player will "remember" where you left the pieces for up to two years. But does that sentence have any relationship with the sentence before it? And do we have any idea how the game works? Does a light flash, does a square vibrate, do the pieces actually move? For $168.95, aren't we entitled to a clearer description?

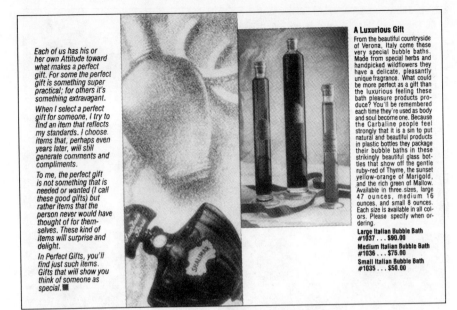

Each of us has his or her own Attitude toward what makes a perfect gift. For some the perfect gift is something super practical; for others it's something extravagant.

When I select a perfect gift for someone, I try to find an item that reflects my standards. I choose items that, perhaps even years later, will still generate comments and compliments.

To me, the perfect gift is not something that is needed or wanted (I call these good gifts) but rather items that the person never would have thought of for themselves. These kind of items will surprise and delight.

In Perfect Gifts, you'll find just such items. Gifts that will show you think of someone as special. ■

A Luxurious Gift

From the beautiful countryside of Verona, Italy come these very special bubble baths. Made from special herbs and handpicked wildflowers they have a delicate, pleasantly unique fragrance. What could be more perfect as a gift than the luxurious feeling these bath pleasure products produce? You'll be remembered each time they're used as body and soul become one. Because the Carbaline people feel strongly that it is a sin to put natural and beautiful products in plastic bottles they package their bubble baths in these strikingly beautiful glass bottles that show off the gentle ruby-red of Thyme, the sunset yellow-orange of Marigold, and the rich green of Mallow. Available in three sizes, large 47 ounces, medium 16 ounces, and small 8 ounces. Each size is available in all colors. Please specify when ordering.

Large Italian Bubble Bath
#1037 . . . $90.00

Medium Italian Bubble Bath
#1036 . . . $75.00

Small Italian Bubble Bath
#1035 . . . $50.00

Figure 17-2

Copy at upper left is nonmotivational because the whole thought is a cliché. But the major problem with this page is the highlighted bottle of Shalimar perfume, which apparently is just a prop, not something the company sells. Adjacent is an art director's notion and a reader's nightmare, a single paragraph running 29 lines. The discrepancy between the number of ounces in the large size and the medium size is disturbing.

D. The Aussie Hat. A laundered Nairobi™ hat with a leather band and poplin lining. Crushable, and best of all, very wearable. From Quaker Marine.
Sizes: S(6⅞-7), M(7⅛-7¼), L(7⅜-7½), X(7⅝).
In Loden-18 and Khaki-05. USA made.
07H2459.................$26.95

H

Figure 17-3

Unless you know what a "laundered" hat is, and unless you have a haberdasher's knowledge of the relationship between "Aussie" and "Nairobi," you'll regard this description as incomplete and confusing. Did the writer regurgitate the merchandise buyer's notes without digestion?

Figure 17-4

Copy on this page proves the writer doesn't have to resort to tricky "how clever I am" copy to inject brightness and benefit. In copyblocks averaging less than an inch, whoever wrote this not only describes items clearly but suggests uses and benefits. Is your copy this intelligible?

Figure 17-5

The cover says it's "A catalog of new traditions." Huh? A near-perfect oxymoron. How can a tradition be new? How about, "A catalog of old innovations"?

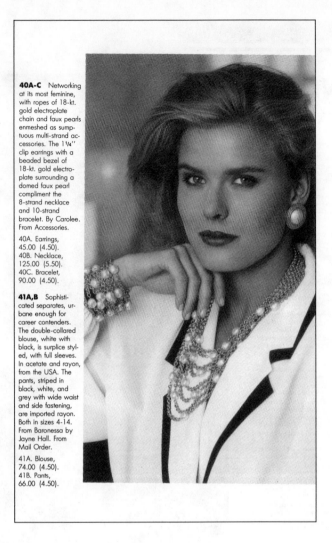

40A-C Networking at its most feminine, with ropes of 18-kt. gold electroplate chain and faux pearls enmeshed as sumptuous multi-strand accessories. The 1¼" clip earrings with a beaded bezel of 18-kt. gold electroplate surrounding a domed faux pearl compliment the 8-strand necklace and 10-strand bracelet. By Carolee. From Accessories.

40A. Earrings, 45.00 (4.50).
40B. Necklace, 125.00 (5.50).
40C. Bracelet, 90.00 (4.50).

41A,B Sophisticated separates, urbane enough for career contenders. The double-collared blouse, white with black, is surplice styled, with full sleeves. In acetate and rayon, from the USA. The pants, striped in black, white, and grey with wide waist and side fastening, are imported rayon. Both in sizes 4-14. From Baronessa by Jayne Hall. From Mail Order.

41A. Blouse, 74.00 (4.50).
41B. Pants, 66.00 (4.50).

Figure 17-6

Words, not ideas: "Networking" is a computer term. So "Networking at its most feminine" is a conceit. It's supposed to describe the interrelationship of the gold-plated chain and faux (do you know what *faux* means? If you don't, I have some pearls to sell you) pearls. For many women, the word *networking* impedes the description rather than enhancing it.

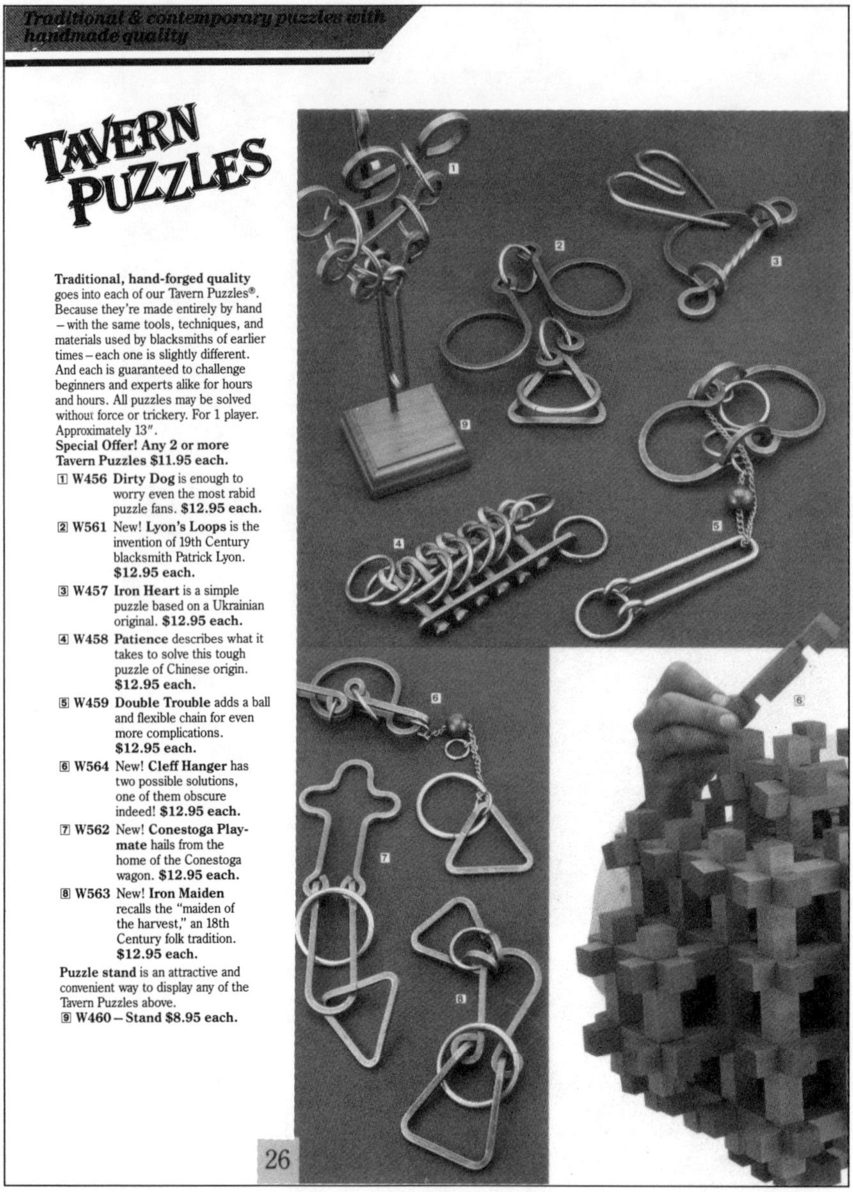

Figure 17-7

Take a look at item 2: It's both new . . . and the invention of 19th century blacksmith Patrick Lyon. Neatest trick of the week!

244

Figure 17-8

Every description gives the reader a reason to buy. Not one of the copy-blocks is longer than two inches. The writer who gripes that the copy he or she excretes would be a lot better if the company weren't so space-stingy should read this and revise the excuse.

CHAPTER *18*

A Little Enthusiasm ...and a Little More Clarity ...Please!

FIRST, *YOU* TRY IT!

Your assignment: As copy chief, you puzzle over this description of an ornate purse-size mirror:

> Exclusively from us, a pretty little purse mirror decorated with tiny mirrors and beading. Each $5^7/8 \times 3''$ mirror comes with a $7 \times 3^1/2''$ silk slip case embellished with antique Zari borders. The slip case could also hold eyeglasses or sunglasses. The mirror, handcrafted in India utilizing the lac technique, is of a specially treated and hardened wax. Six colors, please let us choose for you. From designs by Sudha.

You tell the writer: "I think we ought to make six changes." All right, name three of them. And decide: Are your changes based on lack of enthusiasm in this copy or lack of clarity?

Take 30 seconds. No longer than that.

Probably you concentrated on the phrase "you puzzle over." That would lead you into the more obvious suggested changes:

1. What's an antique Zari border? Tell us.

2. What's the lac technique? Lacquer? What?

3. How can a mirror be made of hardened wax? Obviously the mirror surface isn't wax. Something wrong here, so clarify.

That gives you three out of six. How about the other three? If you didn't see them, read the description again before reading on to see suggested changes 4, 5, and 6. Find them? Right!

4. Telling the reader a mirror is decorated with tiny mirrors is peculiar copy. We need an adjective. "Tiny *diamond-shaped* mirrors"? Or instead of "decorated with," how about "glittering with more tiny mirrors inset into the decorative face and back"? The mirror/mirror reference needs separation.

5. "Is of" is awkward wording. Did you catch this one? If you did, you're a real pro.

6. Does everybody know what Designs by Sudha are?

Did you attack lack of enthusiasm? I don't agree. "Pretty little purse mirror" and "please let us choose for you" give personality to this copy. But clarity? I'm on your side, although apparently the well-known cataloger/retailer who actually ran this description didn't share our puzzlement. The original, with wording exactly as you just read it, is Fig. 18-1.

"What ABOUT This Suit?"

For about one minute, pretend we aren't in the catalog business. We run a retail store, and our image and sales volume both depend on our salespeople.

In comes a woman, shopping for a suit. She inspects the "deep discount" rack and asks your salesperson, "What about this one?"

The salesperson answers, "It's a three-piece navy and white suit with jacket and pull-on straight skirt in an acrylic-cotton-polyester knit. The blouse is polyester. The belt is leather-like."

The customer sniffs. "I can see that much. But what *about* this suit?"

The department manager senses a lost sale and quickly intervenes. "This is a Chanel-inspired classic. The combination of acrylic, polyester, and cotton means it'll keep its shape. And you can see, it's right on target with this season's colors—crisp navy and white."

And the sale is saved.

All right: Back to our real world.

Writers? Or Dull Salespeople?

This is the total copy-block for the suit we just talked about:

3-Piece Navy and White Suit with jacket and pull-on straight skirt in acrylic/cotton/ polyester knit. Polyester blouse. Leather-like belt. Sizes 6–16. #AC47A. Orig. $455. *Now $225.* [6.50]

Percentage of enthusiasm: Zero.

Don't blind yourself to the problem by putting your "see-no-evil" paws over your eyes, covering the lack of enthusiasm by blaming tight space or the suggestion that heavy discounts are their own enthusiasm-generators. If discounts stand alone, who needs a copywriter at all?

Would the copywriter's sweat-glands have drenched the polyester blouse if, recognizing the copywriting *function,* copy had injected a little enthusiasm? . . . Something such as . . .

> *Chanel-Inspired Classic 3-Season Suit*
> Knit, of course. The jacket and pull-on straight skirt combine acrylic, polyester, and cotton for shape-retaining strength. Complete with matching polyester blouse and faux-leather belt. This season's colors—crisp navy and white. Sizes 6–16. #AC47A. Orig. $455. *A steal at $225.* [6.50]

Sure, we've used more words. But sure, the catalog, as typeset, had plenty of open space at the bottom of the copy-stack. Did the writer care about, or even know, *The Rule of Diminishing Enthusiasm?* More to the point: Did the cataloger care about the Rule . . . or, instead, arrogate this assumption: Being in our catalog bestows so much status enthusiasm isn't necessary.

The Rule of Diminishing Enthusiasm

THE RULE OF DIMINISHING ENTHUSIASM justifies our existence as catalog copywriters:

> **Reader enthusiasm is geared to writer enthusiasm.**

Two exceptions to the Rule of Diminishing Enthusiasm:

> **Exception No. 1:** When the catalog wants to project a stratospheric upper-crust image, bubbling enthusiasm parallels putting whipped cream atop a flute of Dom Perignon.

> Exception No. 2: When a catalog has a "Hotlist" of close-out items, heavy enthusiasm is suspect because heavy salesmanship becomes overkill.

Bartlett's UN-Familiar Quotations

Getting tired of my pounding on *THE CLARITY COMMANDMENT?*

> In force-communication, clarity is paramount. Don't let any other component of the communications mix interfere with it.

I guess I'm as familiar with the Creative Desperation Syndrome as anybody in this business. We run out of superlatives. We run out of synonyms for "beautiful." We run out of glorious ways to glorify what we're selling.

If you leave Roget and hop over to Bartlett's, beware! The very act of having to look up an "apt" quotation suggests the reader may not have a working knowledge of that quotation.

A description of cotton separates has this overline:

> " . . . AND I WILL MAKE
> THEE BEDS OF ROSES
> AND A THOUSAND
> FRAGRANT POSIES."
> —Christopher Marlowe—

Okay, what mood does this generate? What, in fact, does it have to do with this descriptive copy?

> The mood is languid, your look romantic . . . in cool cotton separates from Cullinane. The button-front imported sweater has hand-made silk embroidered flowers on the sweetheart neckline . . .

We begin to see what happened. The writer was looking for a touch-stone, seized on the silk embroidered flowers, and searched out a floral quotation. Just one problem: Literary though it is, it's a psychological mismatch for the "languid mood" (isn't this rhetoric a little sluggish?) and a descriptive misfit with the sweater this company is selling.

The Salesperson vs. the Robot Clerk

Once again, transport your imagination to the retail world. Two new-comers start work on the same day. One studies every stock-bin, learns how to wrap packages perfectly, and can quote the printed prod-uct descriptions. The other studies principles of enthusiastic sales-manship.

Twenty years later, who's president of the company? If it's the robot clerk, you can bet this company hasn't achieved any market domi-nance or real corporate growth.

Let's project this same attitudinal disparity into catalogs. We estab-lish the difference between a true marketer and someone who an-nounces product for sale. Those companies with a dramatic growth-pattern over the past ten years are those whose catalogs have *personality*—and personality is the single most necessary ingredient of enthusiasm.

Creative Writing? Or Fact-Regurgitation?

I'm looking at catalog copy for a phone/clock/radio. I just switched over from another catalog, where I read about the same manufactur-er's "Print Phone Facsimile/Copier." The facsimile/copier has timeli-ness going for it in today's marketplace but is described by seven bald bullets, none of which has any enthusiasm and one of which isn't bullet-copy at all: "Built to last."

In this second catalog, the writer's effervescence is contagious, even though the writing is only so-so:

> Do you knock over the alarm clock every time
> you reach for the phone at night? Cobra's
> phone/clock/radio, in a clean, contemporary
> design, may be just what you need to clean up
> bedside clutter . . .

(Why do I say the writing is only so-so? Because the copy-block uses the word "clean" in consecutive lines and because the motivator—knocking over the alarm clock—is far-fetched.)

Enthusiasm has the power to add octane to nondescript copy. Imagine how it can help the fact-regurgitating semi-writers. And imagine how it can add sparkle to copy which, however professionally-written, needs some bubbles.

21U Exclusively from Neiman Marcus, a pretty little purse mirror decorated with tiny mirrors and beading. Each 5⅞ x 3″ mirror comes with a 7 x 3½″ silk slip case embellished with antique Zari borders. The slip case could also hold eyeglasses or sunglasses. The mirror, handcrafted in India utilizing the lac technique, is of a specially treated and hardened wax. Six colors, please let us choose for you. From Designs by Sudha. From Cosmetics.

21U. Purse mirror, SPECIAL VALUE, 15.00 (2.50).

Figure 18-1

Enthusiasm? Just the right amount, because this upscale catalog would suffer from an overabundance of "gushiness." Clarity? In my opinion it's a real problem here, the most grievous example being the implication this mirror is made of wax. "Is of" is clumsy wording which doesn't help.

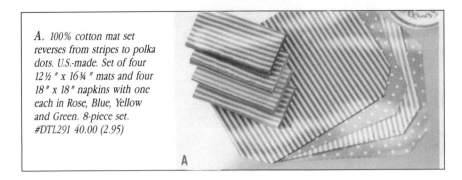

A. 100% cotton mat set reverses from stripes to polka dots. U.S.-made. Set of four 12½ ″ x 16¾ ″ mats and four 18″ x 18″ napkins with one each in Rose, Blue, Yellow and Green. 8-piece set. #DTL291 40.00 (2.95)

Figure 18-2

The company's inventory clerk could have written this copy. How would you, as a professional copywriter, have brought it to life?

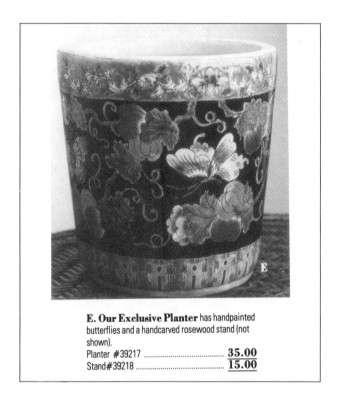

E. Our Exclusive Planter has handpainted butterflies and a handcarved rosewood stand (not shown).
Planter #39217 .... **35.00**
Stand#39218 .... **15.00**

Figure 18-3

Doesn't this planter deserve a description a little more enthusiastic than this bare-bones report? Just adding "Not just a planter—a handpainted conversation piece" would have been a brightener.

CHAPTER *19*

The Negative Rule of Partial Disclosure: Don't Leave Them Hanging There!

FIRST, *YOU* TRY IT!

Your assignment: You're writing copy for an office supply catalog. You know as much about computer peripherals as the typical user, but you make no claims to expertise in this field. Your blood pressure goes up a couple of points when you see you're supposed to describe a "data switch."

Then it drops again when you see the art department already has prepared some line drawings showing the switchbox with a computer and what you assume to be "peripherals"—probably printers. To your relief, you also see the switch comes in two models, depending on whether the connection is 25-pin or 36-pin, so you don't have to explain this aspect. You write this description:

> Two-position switches give one computer two
> choices for peripherals or let two PCs share one
> peripheral for sensible use of expensive equip-
> ment. Use DB25-style connector to connect par-
> allel printers to IBM PC/XT/AT, PS/2. 36-pin
> style for parallel data applications requiring
> centronics style connectors.

Your copy chief reads what you've written and says, "Okay, but you need more explanation of the 'what.' "

"Hey, hold it," you protest. "I'm no expert on computers."

"Maybe not," is your chief's squelch. "But you *are* supposed to be an expert in communications."

"But don't the drawings cover us?"

"Not in my lifetime," says your wise mentor. "Leave your copy-block as is. Don't rewrite what you have, but clarify."

How do you clarify?

Take 30 seconds. No longer than that.

This challenge may have been unfair, because the admonition "Leave your copy-block as is" may seem to contradict the rest of the instruction. Not so.

How? A magical word: *subhead.*

Whenever you (or a critic) might suspect your description isn't adequate, lean on a wonderful helper, these two words:

For example.

The actual description, including illustrations, is Fig. 19-1. (It includes a four-position switch, not part of this exercise.) This is your missing, *clarifying* subhead:

> For example, use one PC with a dot matrix printer and a laser printer; or two PCs with one printer, modem, etc.

Keep the notion of subheads and the words *For example* in your ditty-bag of copywriting tricks. Edicts about format and style may prevent your using subheads, but nothing in any rulebook can ever prevent you from knowing what many less-informed copywriters don't know: the advantage of *For example.*

One of Us Is Inept . . . And It Ain't Me!

Whoever said, "A picture is worth a thousand words," did a horrible disservice to the generation of catalog copywriters pounding their keyboards today.

I say this because we seem to be having an epidemic of copywriters depending on the illustration to say what they themselves don't or can't say. We copywriters throw up a shield against criticism for lack of completeness: Who has the gall to expect a writer to cover the photographer's ineptitude?

But let's reverse the problem. Do we expect the photographer to cover the copywriter's ineptitude?

In most cases, one of the differences between writing a solo mailing and writing catalog copy is *sequence.* The writer of a solo mailing gives the layout artist the proposed words and graphic treatment. The layout artist suggests illustrations. *Then* the job of taking or drawing pictures begins.

Not so in a catalog. The illustration comes with the assignment. The manufacturer or distributor supplies it, or the photo studio makes an extra print or transparency for the writer.

So the catalog writer has less excuse for blind dependence on illustration than the direct mail writer. Evidence is at hand before the first word appears on the word processing screen.

So Why Do They Do This?

I'm looking at a catalog description for a limited edition watch—the "Longines' commemorative watch designed by Charles A. Lindbergh."

At once I'm puzzled. Charles Lindbergh designed a watch? When did he ever demonstrate any talent in that direction?

Three photographs illustrate the copy. One shows the Lone Eagle himself, standing next to his airplane. His hands are in his pockets, so the relationship with the watch is assumptive, not evidentiary.

The second photograph shows a watch. It's a handsome watch with all kinds of numerals and bezel-markings. But it's a watch.

The third illustration, placed too far from the copy block for immediate inclusion in the descriptive mix, is a picture of the backside of the watch, flipped open to show an engraving, in fine script. We can't read it all, but it says, "Longines Hour Angle something, Designed by Col. Charles A. Lindbergh, something Steel Waterresistant, Swiss Made, 989-5215."

Now we're interested. How and when did Lindbergh design this watch? Did he wear it during his 1927 flight? And what's 989-5215? Lindbergh's phone number?

Copy tantalizes but doesn't explain:

> To celebrate the 60th anniversary of Charles A. Lindbergh's historic solo flight across the Atlantic in the Spirit of St. Louis, Longines has produced a limited edition replica of the Hour Angle Watch designed by the renowned aviator. The replica at $4/5$ size has the identical functions and features and is crafted in Switzerland for adventurers aloft and earthbound . . .

The single paragraph of copy runs 39 lines. Instead of answering the "when" and "why," it adds another question: *What?*

This watch is a "$4/5$-size replica"? What does that mean? What's the rationale? Why couldn't it be a full-size replica? Even Mickey Mouse watches are the same size as the 1930s originals. Oh, and by the way: Why didn't the copy block mention it's water-resistant?

The Negative Rule of Partial Disclosure

An easy-to-understand rule of catalog copywriting, *THE NEGATIVE RULE OF PARTIAL DISCLOSURE*, helps explain my personal irritation at the hit-and-run "$4/5$ actual size" reference:

> The reader resents an unexplained variation from the anticipated description.

The Negative Rule of Partial Disclosure also jostles out of any reasonable position my appreciation of the relationship between Lindbergh and this watch. Exotic word-puzzles exist in this copy, such as, "the equation of time, the constantly changing difference between mean and solar time." What do they have to do with Lindbergh? Or with me, for that matter? Explain, please: What is it? *Relate the factual core to the reader* if you want to sell a specialty.

One more carping point—the final sentence of body copy:

> To receive the informational commemorative brochure call LFT 1-800-922-3545.

My question: What's that "LFT" doing there? With the abundance of vanity 800 numbers, the reader is as likely as not to dial LFT. If LFT is the company name, make it "Call LFT *at...*"

...And Other Guilty Parties...

Here's a catalog description of a cable channel converter. This catalog spells it "convertor," but that isn't my principal complaint.

This is every word of descriptive copy:

> Enjoy cable programs on any TV set without additional cable box rental costs. Universal block convertor tunes in 47 cable channels and converts them to UHF. Permits VCR recording on one channel while watching another. Lets you use your current remote control on cable TV. Fine tuning control. FCC approved. UL listed.

Okay, what's missing? This:

> (Of course, you have to be hooked up to a cable system.)

Yes, the line should be in parentheses. Truth in advertising doesn't mean we have to emphasize conditions which aren't part of what we're selling. But copy as written suggests the cable box is the key to cable reception. Without the disclaimer, this company shouldn't be surprised by a high rate of returned merchandise.

The assumption that readers know what you know is both arrogant and foolhardy. Those who have cable know, in general, how it works. Those who don't have it may think this will bring it to them, even if the cable company hasn't yet wired their street.

I had a parallel experience when I ordered a device whose catalog description told me it would bring in cable on every television set in the house. At the time, I had cable on one set but not on five other sets.

What the copy didn't tell me: The gadget requires hard wiring to each TV, and each can pick up only what's being watched on the master set. I sent it back and called the cable company to hook up two more sets. One descriptive line could have avoided my annoyance and the cataloger's shipping and restocking costs.

Here's another, from an office supplies company: We see what appears to be a ream of copy paper and the legend, "Save 61%." The price? $26.88.

Hey, wait a second. If this is $26.88 and I'm saving 61 percent, the regular price must be around $69.00. Can't be, even if this is 100-pound paper. Let's see what kind of paper and how much we get for $26.88.

> Top performing paper for use in both standard
> and high speed plain paper copiers. Also ideal
> for offset reproduction. All sheets are precision
> cut and lint free to assure quality reproduction
> and performance. Letter size, white. (#160966)
> LIST: $69.60.

I'm more confused than I was before. I not only don't know how many sheets I get, I still don't know the weight. It could be 16-pound paper. "All sheets are precision cut"? Does that mean they cut it one sheet at a time? And "lint-free"? I never even considered lint. Does this mean the paper has cotton-content?

How in the world can I—or anyone—order this paper? The Negative Rule of Partial Disclosure haunts response to this copy.

Have You Told Them Enough for a "Comfortable Yes"?

If you market an item that isn't drawing the response you think it should, ask yourself: Have I violated the Negative Rule of Partial Disclosure?

What does the *reader* want to know? Mind-readers don't need catalogs at all. They'll penetrate your brain to get the answers. The rest of us aren't mind-readers, we're just catalog-readers. We aren't so lucky; and when we read your partial disclosures, you won't be lucky either.

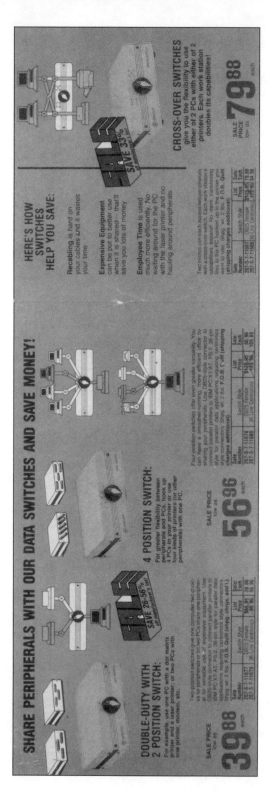

Figure 19-1

Suppose you're an office manager or purchasing agent. A department head sends you a memo: "You have to get us something so we can hook up both PCs in our department to the printer." The subhead under "DOUBLE-DUTY WITH 2 POSITION SWITCH" enables you to say, "This is what he wants." What if that subhead weren't there? Could you be certain, from the description *without* this subhead, you were ordering the right gadget? When writing copy, the words *for example* can clarify as no amount of technical description can.

Figure 19-2

If you're up to a real challenge, read the description of *Senet* and tell us how one plays this game. Really, doesn't the bare-bones, perplexing description *lessen* your desire to own it?

Figure 19-3

What a clever idea! This page in a bicycle catalog uses callouts everywhere. What clarifiers they are. We can almost forgive the writer for the uninspired heading and the production person for running all the type—including the single block of copy at the bottom—on an angle. (Why did the writer capitalize the word *Back* in the copy-block? Probably the three words *Touring is Back!* were supposed to be boldface, which would have made them a mini-headline.)

CHAPTER 20

OVERfamiliarity: Is It the Cause of Your UNDERdescribed "Shadow Copy"?

FIRST, *YOU* TRY IT!

Your assignment: You're one of six writers generating a massive 116-page catalog of audio/video/stereo components. You already have written almost 60 separate descriptions, many of which are for loudspeaker systems. Now, you're stuck. You have three models from the same manufacturer. Model 200SE is $319 a pair; model 250SE is $449 a pair; model 280SE is $529 a pair.

The only problem: All three have the same frequency response, 32 to 20,000 Hz. To audiophiles, frequency response is the bottom line on speakers.

So you've propped up model 200SE with "they let you hear the *power* of the music"; you've covered model 250SE with "if your speakers aren't up to the challenge, you should hear the 250 SE"; you've puffed up model 280SE with "if your system can't capture the true excitement of a rock concert, we've discovered the cure."

Now you're looking over the copy. You're dissatisfied. Why?

Take 30 seconds. No longer than that.

This was an easy one, wasn't it? You're dissatisfied because you underdescribed each speaker, and you think—probably correctly—it's because you're too familiar with speakers.

Why is one more expensive than another? (You can't yet know because you don't have the spec sheets the original writer had; nor do you have what appeared in print, Fig. 20-1.)

Okay, now take off your surrogate mantle. You're a sell*ee,* not a sell*er.* So you look, aggressively, for differences, without using one to damn another; after all, they're in the same catalog.

Ah! Model 200SE has 100 watts of power; 250SE has 125 watts; 280SE has 280 watts. Using the venerable Sears "Good, Better, Best" descriptions, move that element—now buried in tiny "Specifications" sub-descriptions, to the prominent foreground. Then go ahead with your "power" surge for the 200SE; tack on a "Concert hall" overtone for the 250SE; and call the 280SE "Top of the line," which it is.

Your conclusion: Underdescription can stem from overfamiliarity, because the overfamiliar writer buries details the reader needs in order to decide.

What's Missing Here?

Since we're in an analytical posture: You're looking at a photograph of a colorful glass sculpture in limbo, no props included in the picture. What would *you* add to this copy?

Illuminated illusions

Created exclusively for [NAME OF COMPANY] by artist Ross Waldberg, these ingeniously etched glass sculptures exquisitely demonstrate the mystical effect of colors, light, and glass. *Geometry in Motion* portrays an illusion of suspended forms, caused by the concealed neon lights reflecting through four differently shaped etched glass pieces. Each etched section (airbrushed with colors of red, blue, green and amber), when fitted into the lighted parallelogram base, appears to exhibit an apparition of a different dimension. Rearrange or turn the glass and the effect is entirely different.
[DRG751] Geometry in Motion $700.00 (9.75)

For the moment, don't think about word changes. That means you won't attack the evil word "piece," which, following the word "glass," suggests a sharp fragment. You won't suggest replacing it with "panel." You won't question the very questionable phrase, "...appears to exhibit an apparition," because "appears" and "apparition" become a redundancy in this use.

Instead, you take aim at two *omissions* in the copy.

Omission 1: The name of this glass sculpture is "Geometry in Motion." Where's the motion? What moves? Does the lighted parallelogram base swivel? Apparently not, if we have to "rearrange or turn the glass" to generate a different effect. The reader hangs, unable to complete the visual image.

Omission 2: What size is this? The photograph is limbo and propless. Is it a tabletop miniature? A room-size display? What?

Would you as catalog reader *know enough about* this $700 curiosity to order it? OR would you pass, mildly annoyed because you're unable to decode the verbiage?

(The description and illustration are Fig. 20-2.)

Me and My Shadow

"Shadow copy" *almost* tells us enough. Almost...but not quite. Frustration comes from inability to complete an equation: Illustration + copy = What?

The paradox: As often as not, shadow copy results from a writer's *over*familiarity with an item. Overfamiliarity blanks out the *projected curiosity* the writer needs in order to take the posture of a casual catalog-reader.

The claim "Everybody knows what this is" on the corporate level suggests arrogance; but for the catalog copywriter it more likely is the unconscious result of supersaturation with product knowledge.

This writer parallels a computer user who has mastered one word processing program and writes with it every day for a year. Explaining it to a newcomer, the computer user invariably leaves out details—not because of lack of famililarity but because of take-it-for-granted overfamiliarity.

And we get copy such as this:

> *Experiment with Solar from Marklin*
> Marklin, the name synonymous with quality
> electric trains, has introduced a high—quality
> all metal solar construction kit for children. De-
> signed for extended learning playtime, the child
> can spend hours building 5 different working
> models from this 215—piece kit. The child can
> further experiment in a variety of configura-
> tions only limited by his imagination. A com-
> plete series of additional parts, motors, control
> units can be added at anytime.
> *[DMS779] Solar Set $145.00 (6.90)*

Many, many problems here. Grammar suffers from "Designed for extended learning playtime, the child can spend hours..." The reference is absolute and wrong: It tells us it's the *child* who has been designed for extended learning playtime. (Come to think of it, the statement is true for most kids.) But just incidentally, in the context used here, what *is* extended learning playtime?

Then we have the matter of using dashes instead of hyphens. We have "any time" as one word. We have the neutral, nondescript word "quality" repeated within the same sentence.

But okay, okay, this isn't Grammar Day. It's Shadow Copy Day. We want to know the significance of "Marklin, the name synonymous with quality electric trains." We aren't looking at an electric train. (To see what we *are* looking at, see Fig. 20-3.)

The picture suggests it's some sort of construction kit. We see an electric wire stringing away, out of frame. What's *solar* about this kit? Is it the tiny, unexplained square panel at the bottom? Do motors operate the five working models? Models of what? Do they move? Copy doesn't give us a clue.

On the philosophical level, this copy has another problem. Our child can have spent hours and our child can experiment. But how about enjoyment? "Extended learning playtime" parallels taking a piano lesson while the other kids are playing ball.

Do these harsh comments break a butterfly on the rack? I don't think so. This company wants $145 for the all metal solar construction kit, and they haven't told us what it is.

On the Other Hand . . .

All golf clubs are pretty much the same, right?

Or—you have to swing a golf club before you'd ever buy it, right?

Not if you read a high-powered description in a sports equipment catalog.

I'm looking at a catalog *loaded* with golf clubs. It has AccuTech and Ambassador and Yamaha and Spalding and Craig Stadler and Arsenal and Hogan and a bunch of others.

Somehow *this* catalog writer gives each brand a unique selling proposition, so each has a buyer-appeal which doesn't damn the other clubs around it.

AccuTech has "progressive weight placement"—*explained*. Yamaha has "a unique weighting ring around the circumference of the cavity"—*explained*. Craig Stadler clubs have "a wide sole to help you get under the ball from all types of lies, plus a deep cavity back"—*explained*.

The golfer is transported into a rhetorical golf pro shop, where, mentally, he or she swings and samples the various brands. Never does the writer use the word "unique" without telling us why. Never does the writer call any clubs "great" or "wonderful." Comparative benefit is specified . . . and the reader thinks he understands what he's buying.

(An example of this copy is Fig. 20-5.)

The Bullet Copy Solution

The catalog copywriter, sweating under space restraints the free-spirited writer of direct mail packages doesn't have to endure, faces this ongoing problem: In a finite number of words (and sometimes even a finite number of characters) we have to describe well enough to sell.

A second problem: The catalog copywriter races from item to item, making the possibility of hit-and-run underdescription more likely.

Fewer catalogs allow bullet copy these days. We're in an era of high personalization, which means paragraphs instead of bullets. But for the catalog copywriter, bullet copy represents a writing discipline. It demands specifics.

A suggestion, if you re-read your copy and think, "Uh-oh. I've left this out, and I haven't explained that, and I didn't tell the size of the other thing": Make a list of bullets. Draw on that list for your copy, and you surely will see greater specificity in your descriptions. Since specifics outsell generalizations in *any* sales situation, the pulling power of your copy has only one direction to go—up.

Loudspeaker Systems

Cerwin-Vega 200SE [NEW]

There's one reason Cerwin-Vegas are a rock & roll legend: they let you hear the *power* of the music. From the cast aluminum frames of the famous C-V woofers to the self-resetting circuit-breaker protected tweeters, the 200SE is a high-quality system that easily handles the most demanding music. They pound out astoundingly powerful bass for their size. And when you want to crank them up to floor-shaking volume levels, you'll hear your music the way it was meant to be played. Loud and clear.
Specifications: Freq. Response 32-20,000 Hz (±3dB), Max. Power 100 watts, Dim. 22"H x 10½"W x 12¼"D, Black wood-grain vinyl finish, Warranty: 5 years.
Item #050CV200SE List Price: $410
YOUR LOW PRICE: $319 pair

Cerwin-Vega 250SE [NEW]

The digital age has arrived, revolutionizing music enjoyment. If your speakers aren't up to the challenge, you should hear Cerwin-Vega's 250SE. To reveal the spectacular dynamics and full-range sound of today's digital recordings, this 3-way system uses big 10-inch woofers, 6-inch midranges, and 1-inch dome tweeters with an elliptical horn for wider sound dispersion. Self-resetting circuit breakers on the tweeters let you push these Cerwin-Vegas really hard. They just keep on rocking.
Specifications: Freq. Response 32-20,000 Hz (±3dB), Max. Power 125 watts, Dim. 28"H x 12½"W x 11½"D, Black wood-grain vinyl finish, Warranty: 5 years.
Item #050CV250SE List Price: $600
YOUR LOW PRICE: $449 pair

Cerwin-Vega 280SE [NEW]

If your system can't capture the true excitement of a rock concert, we've discovered the cure. Cerwin-Vega's 280SEs are built to be driven to breath-taking sound levels of 117 dB! And they'll handle 155 watts with ease. It takes ultra high-quality speaker components to put up with such rigorous demands: 12-inch woofers with rugged die-cast aluminum frames, 6-inch midranges with high-temperature voice coils, and 1-inch circuit-breaker-protected tweeters. Separate tweeter- and midrange-level controls let you perfectly match the sound to your room. Get ready to crank it up!
Specifications: Freq. Response 32-20,000 Hz (±3dB), Max. Power 155 watts, Dim. 27½"H x 14¼"W x 11½"D, Black wood-grain vinyl finish, Warranty: 5 years.
Item #050CV280SE List Price: $690
YOUR LOW PRICE: $529 pair

Figure 20-1

If the prospective customer reads only the first sentence of each description, he can't sense a difference. Even if he reads all three copy blocks all the way through, only the 280SE shows any superiority. And its superiority is blunted because no basis of comparison exists. What if the writer had paralleled the 280SE's 117 dB sound levels and the 155 watts of power with parallel descriptions for the other models? The reader would have some direction. Power for all three is buried in "Specifications." But even there, we never learn what size the woofers are in model 200SE.

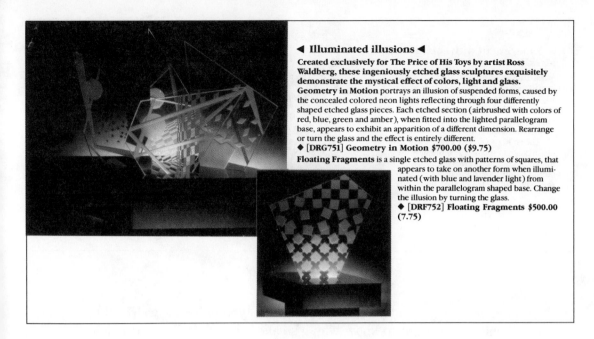

Figure 20-2

Geometry in Motion may "demonstrate the mystical effect of colors,
light and glass"; but the underlit photograph and underdescribed
"shadow copy" is mystical too. How big is this? Where's the motion?
For $700, don't you think we deserve more information about what
we're buying?

Figure 20-3

Suppose you're interested in buying this type of kit for your child. Wouldn't you want to know why it's called the "Solar" construction kit? Wouldn't you want to know the size? Wouldn't you want at least a primitive indication of how it works? Wouldn't you want an indication of how the models work? This copy, larded with generalities, gives us none of this information.

Figure 20-4

Figure 20-4

Suppose *you* began this description with "Tired of multifunction cumbersome phones that don't function?" Mightn't you suggest to the reader *how* they don't function? Or how yours do function? And what do these statements mean: 1) "Simplicity is the essence of these multi-colored single-line phones"; 2) "innovative technology and superior quality controls." This writer either forgot *The Specifics Superiority Principle*—Specifics sell; generalities don't sell—or assumed the reader already knows as much about this phone as the writer is supposed to know.

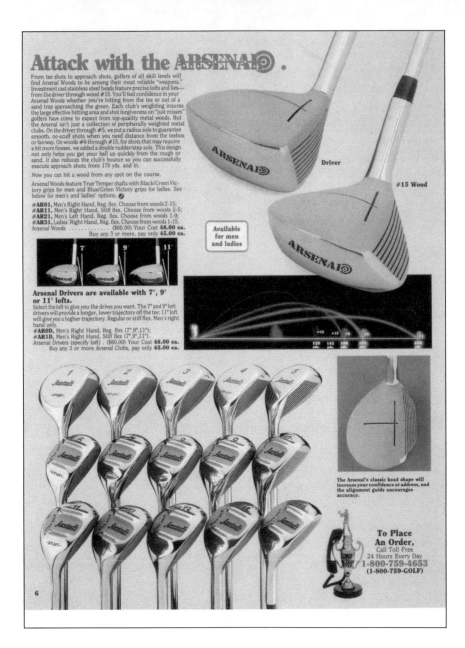

Figure 20-5

This description does more than make a claim; it substantiates each claim with a well-written, well-mixed combination of fact and puffery. Points are reinforced by apparent fact. Who can quarrel with "On the driver through #5, we put a radius sole to guarantee smooth, no-scuff shots when you need distance from the teebox or fairway"? This writer shows constant awareness of what convinces and motivates the reader and never assumes a reader information-base that may not exist.

Cedar Mailbox

D Take a trip to Pebble Beach, California, and you'll see this rustic mailbox in front of almost every cottage or house. Made of cedar, which gradually turns silver-gray as it ages, it blends so well with the wooded landscape of the Monterey Peninsula that it has become the mailbox of choice. The lined weatherproof door has a magnetic closure, and the chimney houses an adjustable flag.

Cedar Mailbox, 22″ x 12″ x 12″ high, weighs 10 lbs. #53-332999 $46.00

USPS Approved Model (not shown) is slightly longer (25″). It's treated with a fire retardant, and has a ribbed interior bottom and a large locking flag. Weighs 12 lbs. #53-333005 $54.00

Figure 20-6

Who would want a mailbox that *isn't* USPS approved? Getting our mail is tough enough without giving the post office another reason for nondelivery. The description is pleasantly professional, until we get to "USPS Approved Model (not shown)." Boy, do we need an explanation here. What about the less-expensive model disqualifies it from approval? It isn't fire retardant? Except for size, that seems to be the only difference of any consequence, but what does fire retardance have to do with post office approval?

LAVENDER
BOTTLE AND HERB
GATHERING TRUG

This charming, old-
fashioned lavender "bottle"
is an inside out bouquet of ever-
fragrant blooms to tuck in your
drawer or display, possibly in this
wooden Herb Gathering Trug.
3/4" deep, 101/4" wide, 14" long,
113/4" high at the handle.
Trug   #6503 $24

Lavender Bottle
#3884 $7

Figure 20-7

Look up *Trug* in the dictionary. If your dictionary is Webster's Colle-
giate, the word isn't there. If you have the big Random House dictionary, whee! *Trug* is a British word for a type of carrying basket. Now,
what if 1) you don't have a Random House dictionary, or 2) try to relate
what you see here to the definition? While we're in the neighborhood,
how long did it take you to figure out the "inside out bouquet" reference? Gee, we'd like to buy this, but our house is already loaded up
with trugs.

CHAPTER *21*

"Hit-and-Run" Copy: Why Not Use Words That Turn the Reader ON?

FIRST, *YOU* TRY IT!

Your assignment: You're a free-lance copywriter, and you want to show the superiority of a telephone answering machine over others on the market. This is your copy:

> NEW! THE WHOLE FAMILY
> CAN TALK AT ONCE!
> This full-featured telephone answering machine
> has everything you could want. Superior
> "pound" key is just the beginning. Desk or wall-
> mountable, it's handy, convenient, and hand-
> some. Remote is beeperless and you have four
> separate function buttons—one for on/off, one
> for "personal memo," one for "save," and one for
> "play messages." 12 one-touch auto-dial keys,
> speakerphone, hold button, and much more.
> $149.95

"What do you think of it?" you ask your client. He shakes his head. "You've missed the boat."

You look at it again...and you figure out why. Okay, why?

Take 30 seconds. No longer than that.

The light-bulb goes on. "Oh, I get it. I shouted 'New!' but didn't prove it. And the features I listed aren't unique at all."

Right. Suppose you go back over that copy. The headline is completely off-target, because you're describing a speakerphone. Even if this answering machine has a built-in speakerphone, you shouldn't lead off with it for two reasons: 1) The speakerphone capability is secondary, and 2) speakerphones themselves are too commonplace.

If answer-phones/speakerphones are unusual, this *is* a point of superiority: "THE FIRST TELEPHONE ANSWERING MA-CHINE WITH HI-FI SPEAKERPHONE AND AUTODIALER BUILT IN." Or you might play up the "Personal memo" key or the "save" feature.

But whatever you do, erase from your memory forever such nondescript openings as "This full-featured telephone answering machine has everything you could want." You'll never build excitement by grinding around in low gear.

What's Wrong with "Award-Winning Product"?

A catalog of gourmet specialties shows an attractive, stylized wine chiller. This is the descriptive copy:

> *B. & C. BYO CHILLER*—When a picnic or party specifies "Bring Your Own," arrive in style with the insulated BYO Chiller. Freeze the BYO's removable chilling compartment and slip it into the carrying case with the wine, beer or soda and they will stay cold. The BYO's handle lifts up and locks the case's lid for traveling. Perfect for those occasions when you bring your own wine to a restaurant. On the table, the BYO sits inside its lid, making an attractive ice bucket. This product's award-winning design is displayed in New York's Museum of Modern Art. Gift-Boxed.

Two questions: 1) Which word in this copy-block is the most jarring? 2) How would you have sequenced the sales argument, using the same informational core?

If your answer to the first question is "BYO" I can't argue...but we have to disqualify the low-class name from this consideration. It may have come from the manufacturer, which overrides any copy objection. My own choice for the most inappropriate word is "product."

Follow my logic (and feel free to disagree with it): Here we have an "award-winning design" (which award?), displayed in the Museum of Modern Art. Does calling it *product* do it justice?

Now the question more directly pertinent to *catalog* copywriting:

The heading is "B. & C. BYO CHILLER." How salesworthy is that? Sure, the copywriter may be struggling inside a rhetorical strait jacket, unable to sway the immovable mind-set of whoever sets policy ("Every headline has to be the product name, damn it!").

But I don't think so, because elsewhere in this same catalog we have "*NEW!* KIR CARAFE" and "FAMOUS BELLINI COCKTAIL SET." Mild as they are, these variations suggest some latitude in headline copy. And anyway, even if an edict from above eliminates the possibility of selling in the headline, how about that deadly, not-quite-clever first sentence of body copy?

What are the strong points here? I see two: the smart design of the wine chiller and the honor of being displayed at the Museum of Modern Art. Is this the only wine chiller on display? Seems likely. Why not lead off with this? (Picture and text are Fig. 21-1.)

Hit-and-Run:
Will They Take Our Word for It?

The catalog description of a punch bowl:

> *HOLLYWOOD PUNCH BOWL*—Entertain in lavish style with this multi-purpose punch bowl set. This breathtaking service set is fully handmade in of finest quality soda-lime glass. Comes complete with 13-quart punch bowl, a dozen 7-ounce glasses, and ladle. A stunning vessel certain to draw raves from your party guests.

Obviously a proofreader should have caught the double preposition—"in of." Too, the heading is "Punch Bowl," yet body copy says it's a whole set and explains, "Comes complete with 13-quart punch bowl, a dozen 7-ounce glasses, and ladle"; so a more logical headline is "Hollywood Punch Bowl *Set.*"

Making those changes doesn't require the professional laying on of hands...or even professional analysis. But in our cold-blooded delight at dissecting somebody else's copy, let's probe a little deeper into the guts of this copy. If you want to read it *in vitro,* look at Fig. 21-2.

Do you see thoughtlessness here? I do, because I see hit-and-run copy. The writer throws out "multi-purpose" and never names another purpose. For that matter, I can't even think of another purpose. It's a punch bowl. If it *does* have other purposes (an apple-bobbing container? a fish bowl?), *name them.* Hit-and-run copy may slide past some readers, but others unconsciously subscribe to the rule of force-communication we discussed in several previous chapters:

> **Specifics sell; generalities don't sell.**

The second problem here is an apparent assumption of familiarity with terminology. To the typical reader, unversed in glass manufacture, "...finest quality soda-lime glass" is as powerful as saying "genuine imitation leatherette." Why not use *crystal* instead of *glass?* And doesn't the word "vessel" make you a little uneasy? Instead, here's a good place to repeat "set."

The Rule of Information Saturation

Every one of us is infuriated when a retail store clerk shows less than perfect familiarity—not with what he or she is selling, but *with what we want to know* about what he or she is selling. As professionals, we shouldn't offer that same basis for criticism in our catalog copy.

Why? Because we have absolute control. If the information isn't complete, we can pick up the missing data before the reader has a chance to call our hand. That is, we can do it if we think the way the reader thinks.

It pains me to propose *THE RULE OF INFORMATION SATURATION:*

> An informational glut can lead the writer to play up details the catalog reader regards as trivial . . . and drop out details the reader needs to form a buying decision.

(I'm pained because in the last decade of the 20th century this Rule should be obsolete, instead of sprouting healthily.)

Really, the Rule is a primitive example of a psychological truism: "Vertical" education leads to loss of viewpoint. Haven't you had conversations with lawyers who were tongue-tied when they weren't talking about law and doctors who were lost when they weren't talking about medicine? What's more deadly than having as a dinner partner a professional, government official, or celebrity whose entire conversational gamut is introspective?

The catalog writer can be seduced or impelled by fear into quiet violations of *THE SELLER/SELLEE EQUIVOCATION EQUATION:*

> The seller's concern = what it is.
> The sellee's concern = what it will do for me.

What do I mean by "impelled by fear"? Too many writers are at the mercy of overriding laws of economics. If they don't regurgitate what

286

the owner or supervisor demands, they're in peril. So, even knowing better, they write what the seller wants to tell—what it is—instead of what the buyer wants to know—what it will do for me.

Verrrrry Interesting...but...

A fascinating novelty idea caught my eye in a well-produced catalog. Total description:

> *Introducing the First Levitating World Globe.™*
> *It Actually Suspends in Mid-Air!*
> How often have you searched high and low for a gift that's truly unique. Well, here's one for the person who has everything. A world globe that actually *levitates!*
> It's simple to use. Just plug it in and the amazing magnetic forces cause the globe to levitate in the air. Go ahead...spin it! There's nothing holding the globe so it spins for the longest time because it's virtually friction-free! Truly an exceptional conversation piece.
> #584500 *$150*

Gadget-junkie that I am, I'd have been interested in this globe—except for a missing description component. Read the copy again if you didn't notice what's missing. (Better yet, inspect Fig. 21-3 and *relate the description to the photograph* so you won't think I'm being arbitrary.)

Precisely! The description starts in low gear but soon achieves a high plateau of lyrical enthusiasm. But the copy itself levitates. It never does come to land. And we never learn what size this globe is.

Will it fit on the desk? Is it toy-size? As so often is true of heavily art-directed illustration, the photograph doesn't even include a human hand to give us a means of judgment.

A Dedicated Picker of Nits

Do we become nit-pickers by demanding the catalog copywriter think "I'm a buyer" instead of "I'm a seller"?

Heck, no. We become effective catalog writing critics, the precursor to becoming effective catalog writers.

If we're always conscious of writing what the reader wants to see, instead of writing what we want to say, who knows? We just might move up to the next level *above* copywriters and become effective salespeople!

Cool Out!

A. CHILLER CARAFE – Here's a creative and decorative way to keep your white or rosé wines constantly chilled without diluting them with ice. Simply place ice in the long chiller compartment which extends into the carafe: the wine will be cooled without coming into contact with the ice. This Italian silverplate and glass, 2-liter carafe is an intelligent way to serve chilled wines – sure to bring admiring comments from your guests. Gift-boxed.
CHILLER CARAFE #828 $39.95 ($3.75)

B. & C. BYO CHILLER – When a picnic or party specifies "Bring Your Own," arrive in style with the insulated BYO Chiller. Freeze the BYO's removable chilling compartment and slip it into the carrying case with wine, beer or soda and they will stay icy cold. The BYO's handle lifts up and locks the case's lid for traveling. Perfect for those occasions when you bring your own wine to a restaurant. On the table, the BYO sits inside its lid, making an attractive ice bucket. This product's award-winning design is displayed in New York's Museum of Modern Art. Gift-boxed.
B. 2 BOTTLE BURGUNDY *(pictured)* **#905 $49.00 ($4.50)**
    2 BOTTLE WHITE #152 $49.00 ($4.50)
C. 4 BOTTLE BURGUNDY #421 $69.00 ($5.50)
    4 BOTTLE WHITE *(pictured)* **#226 $69.00 ($5.50)**

D. CALIFORNIA CHILLER – Working on proven thermo-dynamic principles, the California Chiller is practical, versatile and heavy-duty. Its four separate refreezable cooling elements can take a bottle of wine at room-temperature and chill it within 30 minutes – faster than a refrigerator can. Then, the California Chiller keeps that bottle cool for up to five hours. The removable cooling elements provide flexibility: use all four for rapid chilling, or just two to keep an already chilled wine at perfect serving temperature. No ice, no mess, yet plenty of cooling power in an attractive black and chrome design.
CALIFORNIA CHILLER #721 $24.95 ($3.50)
TWO CALIFORNIA CHILLERS #237 $19.95/ea. ($4.75)

Figure 21-1

Here's an amusing self-test: Assemble the informational and inspirational components describing the "BYO" wine chiller. Then reassemble and reword them to sell the most wine chillers. Would you wind up with this sequence and these pedestrian words? I doubt it.

288

Inside the image:

E. HOLLYWOOD PUNCH BOWL – Entertain in lavish style with this multi-purpose punch bowl set. This breath-taking service set is fully hand-made in of finest quality soda-lime glass. Comes complete with 13-quart punch bowl, a dozen 7-ounce glasses, and ladle. A stunning vessel certain to draw raves from your party guests.
(15⁷/₈" x 15⁷/₈" x 14⁷/₈")

HOLLYWOOD PUNCH BOWL
#117 List $129.00
SALE $99.95 ($8.85)

F. & G. DESIGNER CHILLER – Elegant enough for any table. Simply fill the crescent-shaped compartment with ice, place a bottle or carafe in the circular compartment, and you're set. The highly conductive aluminum alloy ingeniously carries the ice's cooling power throughout the server. Comes with fitted lucite coaster. So effective and beautiful it is used successfully in many hotels and restaurants.
Choose either:
F. POLISHED CHROME #354 $59.50 ($3.75)
G. POLISHED BRASS #331 $59.50 ($3.75)

FEDERAL EXPRESS   SPECIAL RATES See Order Form

THE WINE ENTHUSIAST

Figure 21-2

What's "soda-lime glass"? It may be the most expensive, most delicate mixture used to make the best glass, but to *us,* the reader, it seems dusty and murky. What percentage of readers will respond favorably—unless copy puts the description positively ("made with the very expensive soda-lime formulation used only to create the clearest crystal")? While we're on the attack, copy says the punch bowl set is "multi-purpose." What other purposes can this bowl serve? And doesn't the writer's thesaurus have a less biblical synonym for "vessel"?

Figure 21-3

Don't blame the art director or photographer because we can't determine how big or how small this globe is. Responsibility for transmitting chewable information is the copywriter's. The omission is doubly damning because, reading the copy, we conclude: The writer actually had the opportunity to spin this globe.

NEW! **Hand-Decorated Porcelain Teapot,** an authentic reproduction of an antique from the magnificent Ming Dynasty period. Each side shows 1 symbol of the 8 "immortals" who represent good luck and happiness in Chinese legend. Classic blue underglaze from Guangdong, home of the world's finest porcelains. 5½x6x5", holds 16 oz.—very useful. Dishwasher-safe.
115121   Porcelain Tea Pot $10.98

Figure 21-4

Are you chuckling over "an authentic reproduction"? Do you buy when you laugh at the copy? We wish the writer—who does a totally professional job of tight, informative writing—hadn't used that self-contradictory term.

35A

35A. The comfort of conscious fashion: yours in a
blazer of super 100's wool, in sleek European cut. The
weight is year-round, right for business or pleasure. In
sizes 38-44 and 46 Regular, 38-42 Short, and 40-44 and
46 Long. In navy only. 295.00 (5.10). Man's Store.

Figure 21-5

Just what does "The comfort of conscious fashion" mean? The
phrase suggests *self*-conscious, which certainly isn't what we want to
feel or what the writer meant. Many, many catalog descriptions would
benefit from excision of the first few words, written before the writer
could get fingers into firing position.

Figure 21-6

Prove it, mister. You say, "It's more than 'just another penny loafer.'" Then you describe just another penny loafer. This is what happens when the whole copy platform is based on an impossible premise. Don't attempt to write comparative copy unless you have ammunition for it.

CHAPTER 22

At Last! A "Can't-Miss" Copywriting Instrument: The Benefit/Benefit/Benefit Principle

---

FIRST, *YOU* TRY IT!

What a tough assignment! In a word-processing era, you have to write copy for—a typewriter.

But it's an electronic typewriter, which helps. The manufacturer, whose shrewdness is exemplified by his ability to sell the typewriters to your company, has seen catalogs come and go. He gives you a tip:

"Stress three levels of benefit. You can't miss."

The caption over the product photograph is a strong hint: "The first truly silent typewriter."

That's a statement of superiority, the bottom (first) level of benefit. It should lead to two others. Can you think of *one* benefit to the buyer, based on this "first level" benefit?

Take 30 seconds. No longer than that.

I hope you didn't draw a blank. If you did, take another 30 seconds to think of *how* a silent typewriter benefits the user. That should do it.

What we have here is the only sure-fire catalog copywriting technique I know of—the Benefit/Benefit/Benefit Principle.

Now: How does a silent typewriter benefit the user? By ending office noise. So the "second level" benefit might be:

Office "clatter" is gone forever.

To reach the exalted third level, we have to tell the reader how the second level improves her life. So we might have—

For the first time you can play *soft* music in your
office . . . and actually hear it!

The principle works every time, not only because adherence forces specificity but also because benefit and emotion are closely tied . . . and a sales argument appealing to the emotions outpulls a sales argument appealing to the intellect, every time.

The Height of the Art

The Benefit/Benefit/Benefit Principle, fittingly, is the subject of this, the last chapter.

Until a researcher or master practitioner discovers a more effective procedure, the Benefit/Benefit/Benefit Principle has to be the most powerful weapon catalog copywriters can aim at their targets.

Why? Because it works every time. The specificity, forced by the absolute discipline of this Principle, ties itself tightly to what the reader wants.

Not every writer can master the Benefit/Benefit/Benefit Principle. Huge pots of gold await those who can. And *you* can, because we'll analyze, dissect, and step-by-step it right here and right now.

The Three Stages of Benefit

These are the three stages of *THE BENEFIT/BENEFIT/ BENEFIT PRINCIPLE:*

---

1. Make a statement specifying superiority over others.

2. Relate that superiority to your target-reader.

3. Tell the target-reader how that superiority will bring dramatic improvement to his/her life, career, business, or image.

Here are the qualifiers:

1. The statement of superiority over others has to be within the experiential background of your target-reader. The double admonition: When you compare what you're selling with directly competing products or services, a) DON'T claim superiority without evidence, because this smacks of chest-thumping arrogance, which kills rapport; and b) BE SURE the reader is familiar with your comparison-victim and comprehends immediately what you mean.

That's the first level of benefit. Some business-to-business catalogs survive well, using this level only.

2. When you move up to the second level you see why a statement of superiority ends in limbo if it doesn't connect with the reader's own background: You can't tie the first level to the second level. A simple mechanical trick, forcing out second-level copy: After stating the first-

level benefit, say aloud, "Now you can. . . ." and force yourself to finish the sentence. You'll have a second-level benefit.

If you can conquer the first two levels, you'll be writing copy whose force and effectiveness few other catalog copywriters can match. You're high up the force-communications ladder.

3. Mastery of third-level description is the pinnacle of professionalism. So you'll be pleased to know the single easy road to its door: *practice*. You have *up to* four choices when telling the target-reader how that superiority will bring dramatic improvement. Does it improve lifestyle? Does it enhance career? Does it increase business? Does it build image, professionally or socially, or both? If what you're selling has a single use, you may not have a choice; that's why you have *up to* four choices. But struggling to find all four is always worthwhile, because you're forced into selling avenues you probably haven't considered before.

For example, can a silent typewriter improve lifestyle? Sure: "You won't be a frazzled nervous wreck when you leave the office." Can it enhance career? Sure: "You'll work better and faster. . . and if yours is a large office, the boss will ask who finally turned off the noise." Can it increase business? Sure: "When you're making a business phone call, you can concentrate on what you're saying instead of the mind-numbing racket." Can it build image, professionally or socially? Sure: "The quiet atmosphere is reassuring when a client or customer visits your office"; or "Anyone who calls you will think in executive terms instead of 'another-desk-in-a-noisy-office' terms."

Are some of these stretching? Of course they are. This is an *exercise,* and what we're stretching are our salesmanship-muscles. Unless we have a huge copy-hole to fill, we'd never use them all; we'd pick the most dynamic one.

How about Short Copy-Blocks?

Not every format lends itself to the Benefit/Benefit/Benefit Principle.

Tight little copy-blocks may give you a choice: Exhort or describe. If what you're selling is *competitively functional,* the Principle may have to go out the window. Description comes first.

Can you apply the Principle with bullet copy? Positively. In fact, as this text points out elsewhere, bullet copy is itself a discipline holding the sales argument on its proper rails.

Unquestionably the Benefit/Benefit/Benefit Principle is at its most forceful and most readable when it begins a long hunk of copy. Short copy may limit you to first level plus description or first plus second *or* third level plus description . . . or, once you've gained confidence using this method, second or third level *only* description. But incorporating all three levels into short copy *is* possible. Fig. 22-1 is a tiny piece of copy, but it has all three levels.

Small space tempts the writer to crash directly into the third level. Careful! Leaping directly into the third level may leave the reader out: Overemphasis on third-level benefit, without the background of an earlier level, makes what you're selling secondary. When readers ask, "What is it?" they can be on their way to another page . . . or another catalog.

The Logical Sequence

Should you open with Benefit/Benefit/Benefit copy, stick it in the middle somewhere, or close with it?

In my opinion, if the illustration is at all competent, *open* with it. You're at point-blank range. After you've mortally wounded your target, *then* get down to nuts-and-bolts descriptions.

The easiest way, while you're testing this procedure, is to write a headline of half a dozen words or so. This names the item:

OUR BEST TOASTER-OVEN BROILER

Follow with three subheads, each a higher level of benefit:

- Holds 40% more than most other models!
- One inexpensive toaster-oven does it all—cooks, bakes, broils, defrosts, top-browns, even keeps the whole meal warm!
- At last, gourmet dinners with almost no cleanup!

From this point, copy writes itself: All you have to do is justify the claims you've made, add some manufacturing details, and name the price.

Opening with mechanical details ("The door to this half-cubic-foot model has an 'open/stop' setting . . .") is minor league writing . . . *when you have the Benefit/Benefit/Benefit opportunity.* But (fortunately for the mediocre writers among us) we don't always have that opportunity.

If you're blessed with a catalog whose format enables you to write long, prose-like headings, you have naturally fertile ground on which to plant triple-benefit copy. In my opinion it's best, at the fingertips of an accomplished wordsmith, when wording makes its telling points the way an accomplished debater would.

Can you fill a catalog with triple-benefit copy? Wow! I've never seen one, and I suspect it would parallel serving a dinner with doughnuts as appetizer, heavily-sugared fruit as salad, deeply-frosted cake as main course, and rich ice cream as dessert. Too much! And what a challenge for the writer!

And in Conclusion, Ladies and Gentlemen . . .

Don't hide this book on a shelf somewhere until you've tried the Benefit/Benefit/Benefit Principle for yourself. Try it not just once, but three or four times or more.

You're in for an increasingly warm glow. Your first try will have sweat dripping onto the keyboard. Your second try will correct some of the sequential mistakes you made the first time, such as jumping from first level to third level so you can't ever find ammunition for what you think the third level should be.

Your third attempt will be workmanlike. Your fourth will be printable.

By the time you've written half a dozen triple-benefit descriptions, the technique will come naturally, unforced; and your associates will wonder why your copy is so much stronger than theirs.

Accordian travel tote
expands in size to
accommodate everything you
collect along the way. Starts off
as a 14H x 14½"W shoulder
bag. Unzips to reach an
impressive overall height of 23"
— plenty big enough for all the
goodies you want to bring
home! Made from nylon in
burgundy. Roomy zip pocket,
removable shoulder strap and
four easy-glide casters.
Imported.
6239 Special Value! $29.98

Figure 22-1

Occasionally an unusually alert writer can cram all three levels of
benefit into a small copy-block. Here's an example. Level 1: "...ex-
pands in size to accommodate everything you collect along the way."
Level 2: "Starts off as a 14H × 14½"W shoulder bag. Unzips to reach
an impressive overall height of 23"." Level 3: "...plenty big enough
for all the goodies you want to bring home!" We see a typo here—no "
between 14 and H—but we're too impressed to notice it at first reading.

Figure 22-2 ▶

This well-written catalog regularly heads its copy-blocks with two
levels of benefit. Want to try three-level copy? How about these?
Level 1: Not imitations—GENUINE BRITISH-MADE SHET-
LANDS.
Level 2: Even in London, we've seen Shetlands similar to ours selling
at twice the price.
Level 3: Full-fashioned, top-died impeccable Shetlands are too expensive for much of the world...but not for you!
The phrase "much of the world," which suggests impoverished third
world countries, isn't enchanting copy; but we've tampered enough
with this already-successful copy.

Even with this year's
high exchange rates,
our soft, fluffy

BRITISH-MADE SHETLANDS

are JUST $28.50.

*(And we're talking full fashioning
and top-dyeing too!)*

Much of the world will be doing without the impeccably-made Shetlands of Great Britain this year. Too expensive. (Even in London, we've seen Shetlands similar to ours selling at twice the price.)

But we've managed to make ours of the same fine wool we've always used: lightweight but warm Shetland 100% wool from Australia and New Zealand. Keep every feature we've always had: fully-fashioned shoulders, necks attached the more expensive French loop way, top-dyed fibers. And still sell our Shetlands for $28.50. Pretty amazing.

How did we do it? We bought early. We bought in great quantities. And we sell direct to you. Hand wash or dry clean.

Men's Regular in S 34-36, M 38-40, L 42-44, XL 46-48. 7166C20 **$28.50** *(2 for $53.00)*
Men's Long (2″ longer in body, 1½″ in sleeves) in M, L, XL. 7165C25 **$31.50** *(2 for $58.00)*
Women's in S 33-34, M 35-36, L 38-40, XL 42. 7167C26 **$28.50** *(2 for $53.00)*

Lapis Heather

Natural

Maize

Forest Heather

Purple Heather

Camel Heather

Breton Red Heather

Black Heather

13

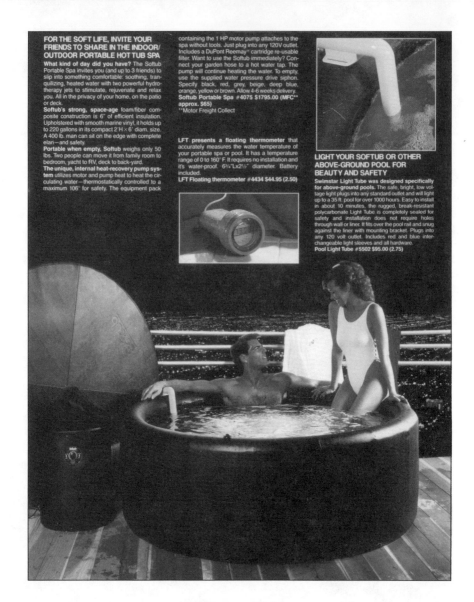

FOR THE SOFT LIFE, INVITE YOUR FRIENDS TO SHARE IN THE INDOOR/OUTDOOR PORTABLE HOT TUB SPA
What kind of day did you have? The Softub Portable Spa invites you (and up to 3 friends) to slip into something comfortable: soothing, tranquilizing, heated water with two powerful hydrotherapy jets to stimulate, rejuvenate and relax you. All in the privacy of your home, on the patio or deck.
Softub's strong, space-age foam/fiber composite construction is 6" of efficient insulation. Upholstered with smooth marine vinyl, it holds up to 220 gallons in its compact 2'H × 6' diam. size. A 400 lb. man can sit on the edge with complete elan—and safety.
Portable when empty, Softub weighs only 50 lbs. Two people can move it from family room to bedroom, yacht to RV, deck to back-yard.
The unique, internal heat-recovery pump system utilizes motor and pump heat to heat the circulating water—thermostatically controlled to a maximum 106° for safety. The equipment pack

containing the 1 HP motor pump attaches to the spa without tools. Just plug into any 120V outlet. Includes a DuPont Reemay® cartridge re-usable filter. Want to use the Softub immediately? Connect your garden hose to a hot water tap. The pump will continue heating the water. To empty, use the supplied water pressure drive siphon. Specify black, red, grey, beige, deep blue, orange, yellow or brown. Allow 4-6 weeks delivery.
Softub Portable Spa #4075 $1795.00 (MFC** approx. $65)
**Motor Freight Collect

LFT presents a **floating thermometer** that accurately measures the water temperature of your portable spa or pool. It has a temperature range of 0 to 160° F. It requires no installation and it's water-proof. 6¾"L x 2½" diameter. Battery included.
LFT Floating thermometer #4434 $44.95 (2.50)

LIGHT YOUR SOFTUB OR OTHER ABOVE-GROUND POOL FOR BEAUTY AND SAFETY
Swimstar Light Tube was designed specifically for above-ground pools. The safe, bright, low voltage light plugs into any standard outlet and will light up to a 35 ft. pool for over 1000 hours. Easy to install in about 10 minutes, the rugged, break-resistant polycarbonate Light Tube is completely sealed for safety and installation does not require holes through wall or liner. It fits over the pool rail and snug against the liner with mounting bracket. Plugs into any 120 volt outlet. Includes red and blue interchangeable light sleeves and all hardware.
Pool Light Tube #5502 $95.00 (2.75)

Figure 22-3

   This description opens with a classic three-level benefit/benefit/benefit. See how inviting the description is, *even before* the writer shifts into mechanical specifics? Benefits outsell features every time, because emotion outsells intellect.

Figure 22-4

Occasionally you can reverse levels of benefit. Here, the first level, the statement of superiority over others—"Ordinary jumper cables don't limit..."—*follows* the second level, used as a headline. No third level here, but we might accept the writer's argument that the opening gun is the third level; "Ordinary jumper cables..." is the first level; and "Start 'n' Charge replaces cables and..." is the second level.

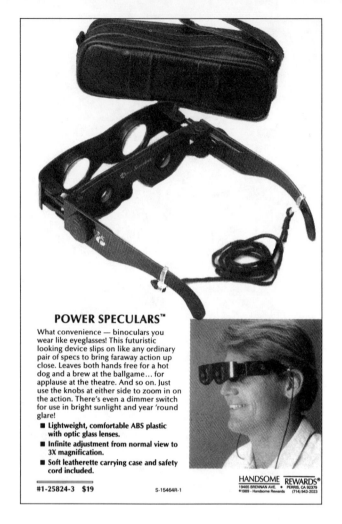

Figure 22-5

Follow the Benefit/Benefit/Benefit Principle through this one-paragraph description:

Level 1: "What convenience—binoculars you wear like eyeglasses!"

Level 2: "This futuristic looking device slips on like any ordinary pair of specs to bring faraway action up close."

Level 3: "Leaves both hands free for a hot dog and a brew at the ballgame."

We're so persuaded we forgive the writer for the otherwise inexcusable "And so on," and for the word *device,* which suggests the binoculars aren't quite right.

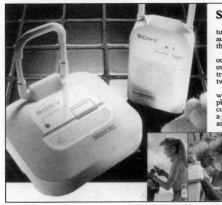

Figure 22-6

Reaching the first two levels results in completely acceptable copy. This description includes a strong first level and second level—in sequence, within the entire first paragraph. If the writer wanted to include a third level, it probably wouldn't be the benefit of being able to hear your baby's voice; this benefit is implicit. More logical third levels: Even when you're taking the baby visiting, carry the two components and relax; or, a *non*-baby use.

A Profitable Game of "20 Questions"

The catalog writer who bangs out "blind" product descriptions, not considering why people buy, is costing the company some money.

Why? Because the three great communications weapons of the 1990s (with no end in sight) are *clarity, benefit,* and *verisimilitude.* No one needs a massive talent to write clearly. But—

Injecting reader-benefit, within the experiential background of the catalog's selected readership, requires some talent in salesmanship. *Validating* benefit, by varnishing the copy with verisimilitude (the appearance of truth), requires at least a seat-of-the-pants talent in human psychology.

Can any journeyman writer superimpose those elements on his or her copy? I say *yes.* How? By playing and winning The Catalog Copywriter's Game of "20 Questions" before casting your product descriptions in bronze.

In my opinion the game should be valid for at least the next ten years, not only because more and more companies are jumping into the swirling catalog-waters, stirring up mud and snakes; but also because the typical recipient gets more and more catalogs, sophisticating the inevitable skepticism attending a competitive situation.

So: Here, for use at least until the year 2001, are the questions to ask as you wearily pound the keyboard:

1. Do you know who reads your catalog?

One quick example: a toy catalog could have three distinct levels of readership: a) Prime buyers—those who look for toys because of a direct parental or grandparental relationship; b) users—children who respond to visuals and described excitement; c) possibles—catalog recipients who have no immediate reason to buy.

Who reads your catalog? Probably all three groups, but not in equal numbers.

2. Is your copy pitched specifically toward the biggest reader-group?

As I said a few paragraphs back, professionalism in catalog copywriting includes a working knowledge of salesmanship. A good salesperson at a store selling expensive toys knows how to sell to the parents without alienating the child. A good catalog copywriter knows how to sell to the biggest reader-group without killing off the less-knowledgeable or less-motivated casual readers.

3. Do you tell the catalog recipients repeatedly why they should buy from you?

Developing a competitive edge is a management decision. The copywriter is only the hired Hessian, the implementer of selling notions handed down from above.

The writer's job is to convince the reader; and if *no* selling notion comes down from above, the writer gets, by default, not only the job of telling the readers why they should buy but also the job of creating the competitive edge in the first place. That's professionalism!

4. What about your product descriptions motivates the reader to buy?

An inventory clerk can describe an item. A supersalesman can make a customer want it. That's why a supersalesman makes more money than an inventory clerk. I suggest catalog copywriters emulate the salesman and not the clerk; you don't need a professional copywriter to repeat a laundry-list.

5. Do you repeatedly use sentences longer than 12 words?

Long sentences slow down the reader's comprehension, especially in narrow copy-blocks. We aren't writing textbooks, and even if we were, we're supposed to be communicators, not picture-puzzlemakers.

An easy way to improve comprehension is to limit the number of words in each descriptive sentence. Don't worry—readers won't think you're a refugee from McGuffey's Reader.

6. Does your description match the illustration?

If you say, "I never see the illustration," I suggest a change in production procedures.

A mismatch, or mutual avoidance by photographer and copywriter, can generate confusion. Worse, when the illustration emphasizes one aspect and the copy emphasizes another, the reader may disbelieve both. That costs you.

7. Does your description cover deficiencies in the illustration such as (if a limbo shot) relative size, (if a black-and-white shot) colors, or (if the product has multiple uses) descriptions of each possible use?

Here's another reason for the copywriter to see the illustration.

Sure, the photographer could have shown the size of that platter by putting a rose on it. But he didn't. Now what? Sure, the two models should have worn different colored sweaters. But they didn't. Sure, that chemical could have been shown working on a motor as well as on a cement floor. But it wasn't. Your job, writer.

8. If you have a "welcome" letter, is it just a bunch of words or is it genuine salesmanship?

Look at the catalogs on your own coffee-table. Inside the front cover of most of them is a "personal" note from the head of the company.

How many of those letters have any sincerity at all? How many climb above the cliché-ridden "We're pleased to serve you" and "Your satisfaction is our dedication"? How many project a genuine personalized image?

You'll find, I fear, that too many waste the one logical use of space allocated to creating an aura of uniqueness.

9. Is your copy peppered with "in-talk" the average reader might find incomprehensible?

Readers resent an in-group of which they aren't part. You can assure this reaction by showing off technical terms and "insider" jargon.

Talking down to the reader and suggesting the reader is a nincompoop because he doesn't share our specialized terminology are short roads to reader rejection. (An easy solution: if you need that terminology, include a short glossary of terms.)

10. Can someone unfamiliar with a new product visualize a reason to buy it, from your description?

You have an elbow-arm that holds a computer monitor. Okay, so what? Why should I spend $95 to move my monitor from its comfortable perch atop my IBM-AT to an uneasy mid-air hammock?

If your copy just tells me what the elbow-arm does, I'm half-sold, unsold, or product-antagonistic. So you don't just tell me what it does; you tell me what it does *for me,* because *benefit* is one of the three golden pedestals supporting powerful catalog copy.

11. Is your order form simplified, easy to fill out?

At the moment of truth, we want no obstacles. The customer should be able to breeze through the order form without a single crease in the forehead.

A good order form does most of the customer's work for him. Does yours? Or do you challenge the customer? (In a duel, you'll lose.)

12. Does the catalog cover excite the reader?

The cover sets the mood. The cover sets the image. The cover sets the reader's state of mind. The cover sets your catalog apart from the competition.

Excitement *doesn't* depend on whether you show merchandise on the cover or not. It does depend on how well you fight your way inside the reader's experiential background. You don't scream at the winds, "This is exciting!" You point at the reader and declare, "This is exciting—to *you!*"

13. Have you cleansed your copy of egomania and megalomania?

Once again, the writer is a practical psychologist. Part of his job is to avoid dislocating the corporate arm from having used it to pat the company on its own back. Another job, which requires a steady hand and uncommon restraint, is creating a climate of acceptance in which the person getting the catalog does the back-slapping for you.

"We have this for you" is better copy than "We have this" because action ostensibly aimed at the reader's welfare has implicit verisimilitude; self-aggrandizement breeds implicit skepticism.

14. Do you pepper your copy with "spot" testimonials, bonus gifts, 800-number reminders, or earlybird discounts?

Excitement doesn't end with the front cover. Any catalog has holes. Fill those holes with inducements; who knows when the urge to order something will strike?

A solid page of testimonials is puffery; a sprinkling of testimonials, here and there, suggests a bandwagon movement.

15. Does your copy stroke the reader by saying, "Only you . . ."?

You can't always answer yes to this question, because some catalogs, especially business-to-business, don't lend themselves to personalization.

Still, exclusivity isn't that hard to suggest. An "issue price" on the cover (which the recipient hasn't paid), some copy about the exclusivity of catalog distribution, a "private club" copy-overtone—these help transmit the flavor of those two lovely rapport-building words, *Only you.* . . .

16. Does your catalog project an image, and does your copy match that image?

Who are you? The cheapest source? The fastest source? The most comprehensive source? The avant-garde source? The snootiest source? The good-folk source? The kindly uncle-and-aunt source? The no-nonsense all-business source?

Whoever you are, your copy should match. Trying to combine two images muddies both those images and damages buyer-confidence. If you do wear two hats, separate your catalog into sections ("This is the *bargain* section"; "Park Avenue Exclusives"; "Billy-Joe's Personal Choices") and you create a magical world in which unlike elements can co-exist.

17. Is your copy timely, tied to the season or period of issue?

Considering seasonality will keep you from heavily art-directed page after page of copy reversed through four colors. Why? Because changing copy becomes a major operation if it's more than a black plate change.

Here's an easy trick to keep copy seasonal: On a separate sheet of paper, list every word you can think of, reflecting the time of year. (Example: for Christmas, *yule, Noel, caroling,* a thousand more; for spring, *crocus, robin, young man's fancy,* a thousand more.) Sprinkle these through the copy. As casual references, they're the "Butter Buds" of catalog copy, adding nuggets of flavor.

18. Do you write in the active rather than passive tense?

If a cynical reader might ask, "By whom?" some of your copy is too quiescently passive.

"These were brought to us..." By whom? "It was decided..." By whom? "Your order will be shipped..." By whom? Take responsibility and assign responsibility and you've written dynamic copy. "We'll ship your order" re-cements the relationship with the customer; "Your order will be shipped" keeps that relationship at arm's length.

19. Are you sure you've selected the key selling point for each item?

To do this, you have to go all the way back to the Second Question. Is your copy pitched directly at the reader?

You may be fascinated by a peculiarity of an item—solid wood buttons, or automatic justification of the right margin, or never add water, or never needs oiling, or one size fits all. But is that what the reader regards as the key selling point? The copywriter's job is to write for the reader, not the writer.

20. Are you positive your catalog has no product descriptions you could have written more vividly if you'd had more time or more information?

If you dismiss the question with, *"Every* catalog has this problem with some items," go to the foot of the class. If you say, "Yes, but..." then okay, you have another chance: your next catalog. Not enough time? Your problem to solve. Not enough information? That's your problem too. Get the time and get the information. Sluggish indolence is for others, not the creative department.

And that's the current list. But please, don't stop here. Make up your own list, based on the deficiencies your steely unflinching eye discovers in the copy you and your associates are grinding out.

Catalog copy, with its impossible deadlines, impossible space limitations, and impossible demands on the writer's prior product knowledge, is a challenge unlike any other facet of professional copywriting. Facing and occasionally conquering that challenge is the most exhilarating aspect of an exhilarating job—*professional* catalog-copywriting.

APPENDIX *B*

Compendium: A Few of the Rules This Book Has Explained

THE RULE OF ABSOLUTE COMMUNICATION-CONNECTION:

> Simplifying the description won't alienate those who have the same background you do; showing off your product knowledge with terminology and "Level II" description positively does alienate those who don't have the same background you do.

THE LAW OF ABSOLUTE CONFUSION:

> Buying interest decreases in exact ratio to an increase in confusion.

THE ANTI-B.S. PROCEDURE:

> It's more logical to throw selling facts at the reader than to mask lack of facts with lavish production.

THE BENEFIT/BENEFIT/BENEFIT PRINCIPLE:

> 1. Make a statement specifying superiority over others.
> 2. Relate that superiority to your target-reader.
> 3. Tell the target-reader how that superiority will bring dramatic improvement to his/her life, career, business, or image.

THE BOILER-PLATE AVOIDANCE PROPOSITION:

> The possibility of depersonalized, interchangeable nondescriptive copy decreases in exact ratio to an increase of usable fact presented to the writer.

THE CATALOG COPYWRITER'S FIRST CHARGE:

> The purpose of catalog copy is to sell the item you're describing. *Every* other facet of creative copywriting is subordinate to this, except maybe the Clarity Commandment, without which copy isn't copy.

THE CLARITY COMMANDMENT:

> In force-communication, clarity is paramount. Don't let any other component of the communications mix interfere with it.

THE LAW OF COMPETITIVE SELECTIVITY:

> Select only the vulnerable targets, and attack.

THE DECEPTION PERCEPTION:

> When a reader penetrates a statement whose intention is to mislead, getting an order drops to a likelihood of near-zero or less.

THE RULE OF DIMINISHING ENTHUSIASM:

> Reader enthusiasm is geared to writer enthusiasm. Two exceptions to this Rule—
>
> *Exception No. 1:* When the catalog wants to project a stratospheric upper-crust image, bubbling enthusiasm parallels putting whipped cream atop a flute of Dom Perignon.
>
> *Exception No. 2:* When a catalog has a "Hotlist" of close-out items, heavy enthusiasm is suspect because heavy salesmanship becomes overkill.

THE RULE OF EFFECTIVE COMMUNICATION:

> The target-reader's comfort is the paramount consideration in word-choice.

THE EVIDENTIAL SUPERIORITY PRINCIPLE:

> Declaration isn't as convincing as evidence.

THE FIVE WORD NAIL ADMONITION:

> Catalog copy nails the reader within the first five words or loses him/her forever.

THE TOP-END CATALOG FIVE WORD NAIL EXEMPTION:

> The top-end catalog which may allocate a whole page to one item is exempt from The Five Word Nail Admonition. The reader knows from *format* this isn't a direct, condensed description.

THE RULE OF IMPLIED IMPORTANCE:

> Importance should relate to the state of mind of the reader, not the writer.

THE RULE OF IMPORTANCE DETERMINATION:

> If you claim importance, prove it.

THE RULE OF INFORMATION SATURATION:

> An informational glut can lead the writer to play up details the catalog reader regards as trivial . . . and drop out details the reader needs to form a buying decision.

THE "ITS/IT'S" LAW:

> Never say anything positive or complimentary about copy which misuses the two words "its" and "it's."

THE LIVE ENCOMIUM RULE:

> A generic description becomes dead puffery unless ongoing copy justifies it.

THE RULE OF PRE-ESTABLISHED ATTITUDE:

> A product is what it is, plus what the buyer thinks it is.

THE NEGATIVE RULE OF PARTIAL DISCLOSURE:

> The reader resents an unexplained variation from the anticipated description.

THE PUFFERY-DEFEAT INEVITABILITY:

> No amount of puffery or self-applause can sell as effectively as a listing of specific benefits.

THE SELLER/SELLEE EQUIVOCATION EQUATION:

> The seller's concern = what it is.
> The sellee's concern = what it will do for me.

THE SPECIFICS SUPERIORITY PRINCIPLE:

> Specifics sell; generalities don't sell.

THE FIRST RULE OF WEASELING:

> An effective weaseled claim is written so the reader slides past the weasel without realizing it.

THE WHOSE MESSAGE IS IT ANYWAY? RULE:

> Your message should operate within the experiential background of the message-recipient, not within your own experiential background.

THE RULE OF WORD RE-USE:

If you have to re-use a word, emphasize the key word before its second use to show the reader the repeat is intentional.

THE YELL-OUT-BARGAIN RULE:

When you're shouting "Bargain!" play up price. The very act of shouting implies a price lower than competitors charge, even when it may not be true.

THE SEVEN STAGES OF HU-MAN:

The recipient sees your catalog and has one of seven reactions:

1. Disgust.
2. Annoyance.
3. Neutrality.
4. Faint interest.
5. Moderate interest.
6. Strong interest.
7. Rapport.

Index

A

ABSOLUTE COMMUNICATION-
    CONNECTION, RULE OF,
    206-7, 317
ABSOLUTE CONFUSION, LAW
    OF, 233-45, 318
Accent, 170
Accessory case example, 136
AccuTech, 272
Active Care example, 110
Active tense, 314-15
Adidas, 168
Adjectival morass, 67-68
Adjectives, use of. *See* Descriptive
    words
Affected v. *effected,* use of, 115
Alden's catalog, 64
All the facts copy, 9-10, 27
Alsto Handy Helper, 48
Amazing, use of, 163
Ambassador, 272
And, use of, 111
Ankesenamun, Queen, 172-73, 177
ANTI-B.S. PROCEDURE, 170, 318
Apprise v. *appraise,* use of, 115
Arsenal, 272
Art nouveau pin
    assignment, 195
    example, 197-98
Art reproduction example, 224
Assignment
    adjective selection, 41
    art nouveau pin copy, 206
    computer chess game copy, 233
    data switch copy, 259-60
    digital diary copy, 206
    electronic typewriter copy, 297
    golf instruction videotape copy,
      143
    hanging folders copy, 219

    headline, 63, 75, 87
    luggage cart copy, 183
    proofreading, 107-8
    purse-size mirror copy, 249-50
    salt and pepper mill copy, 133
    sandals copy, 3
    seat cover rewrite, 123
    speakers copy, 63, 269
    squall jacket headline, 87
    telephone
      answering machine copy, 283
      headset copy, 155
    toaster copy, 167
    vocabulary suppression, 97
Astral Electronic Chess player
    example, 238
Attention getting, 221
Augean Stables, 68
Australian hat example, 236, 240
Awareness, buyer, 133-40
Awesome, use of, 157, 163

B

Baby product example, 307
Bach, 24-25
Bad v. *badly,* use of, 115
Bally Meteor shoes example, 177
Basic
    descriptive heading, 88
    nominative heading, 88-93
Basket example, 67
Battery example, 13, 305
Beatles, 24-25
Becker, Boris, 169
Bee skep example, 129
Benefit, 312
    projection, 50
BENEFIT/BENEFIT/BENEFIT
    PRINCIPLE, 298-307, 318

Berth v. *birth,* use of, 118
"Best Buy!" copy claim, 149. *See also* I am the greatest copy
Bicycle catalog, 266
Big Stinky, 197
Binoculars example, 306
Black-and-white descriptions, 41-43
Black knit example, 112
Blender example, 102
Bloomingdale's catalog, 48, 113
BOILER-PLATE AVOIDANCE PROPOSITION, 47, 318
Boiler-plate copy, 42, 46, 178
Bomber jacket example, 148
Boots example, 80
Bose, 69
Bow ties example, 221
Buckley, William F., 100
Bullet copy, 253, 273, 300
Burr, Aaron, 117
Business-to-business catalog, 46, 136, 220, 298, 313
  example, 37

C

Cable channel converter example, 262
Callouts, 192, 266
Calvin Klein deck shoes, 169
Camcorder example, 14
Camera example, 14
Car seat covers
  assignment, 123
  example, 126
Catalog copywriter
  measurement of, 47-49
  stylebook for, 111
CATALOG COPYWRITER'S FIRST CHARGE, 47, 319
Cat-lovers catalog example, 70
Cinderella, 112-13
Clarity, 64-65, 76-77
CLARITY COMMANDMENT, 43-44, 64, 68, 75-83, 104, 113, 233, 252, 319
Close-out items, 252
Clothes sizing example, 67
Collinear hoe example, 91

Colorful writing, 41-43, 68-69, 98
Commission, misuse of, 172-73, 176
Comparative copy, 293
  example, 191
COMPETITIVE SELECTIVITY, LAW OF, 185, 319
Complements v. *compliments,* use of, 114
Computer chess game
  assignment, 233
  example, 233, 238
Computer software, 158, 185
Computer terminology, 112
Cookware gadgets example, 77
Copy blocks
  to cover illustration deficiencies, 311
  tight, 245, 299-300, 302
Copy/illustration mismatches, 200-3
Copywriting
  purpose of, 47
  sins, 51-52
Cordless phone example, 35, 185
Cotton belt examples, 66
Creative Desperation Syndrome, 252
Creative writing, 253-54
Croquet set example, 190
Cutting board example, 135-36

D

Data switch
  assignment, 259-60
  example, 264
DECEPTION PERCEPTION, 209, 319
Definitions, 98-100
Descriptive copy, 126, 212, 226-27
  example, 212
  heading, 87
Descriptive words, 41-59, 67-68
  example, 54-55
Designer label, 168-69
Designer scarf example, 46
Dickens, 183
Different from v. *different than,* use of, 115
Digital diary assignment, 206
DIMINISHING ENTHUSIASM, RULE OF, 251-52, 320

Discipline, 48-49, 51
Disclosure, 223, 260-66
Dobby pattern, 66
Down home copy, 3, 5, 15
Dress example, 210
Dual v. *duel,* use of, 117

E

Educational copy. *See*
    Informational/educational copy
EFFECTIVE COMMUNICATION
    RULE, 109-10, 320
Egomania, 313
Electrical device example, 30-31
Electronic typewriter assignment,
    297
Encomiums, 144-46
Enthusiasm, 250-54
Equivocation Equation, 286, 323
EVIDENTIAL SUPERIORITY
    PRINCIPLE, 170, 320
Excitement, 313
Explosive, use of, 156-57, 163

F

Fabrics example, 81
Fact regurgitation, 253-54
Fairchild, Morgan, 113
Fairyland Black, 112-13
Family-operated catalog example, 42
Fashion industry, 65-67
Faux pearls example, 243
Ferguson, Robert, 22
Fever blisters illustrations, 208-9
Fiber mat example, 227
Fingerpaint mugs example, 77-78
First person (voice), 5
    copy blocks, 4
FIVE WORD NAIL
    ADMONITION, 234, 321
Force communication, 43-44, 64, 68,
    173-74
Foreign words, phrases, 77
For example, use of, 259-60
Form over substance, 75-76, 81, 176
For v. *because,* use of, 111-12

G

Game example, 265
Garden hose example, 197
Gardener's Eden, 196
Generalities, 144-45
Generic
    copy example, 53
    words, 144-45
Geometry in Motion, 270, 275
Giftware cataloger, 108-9
Gloves example, 186, 189
Golf bag example, 50-51, 59, 199
Golf ball example, 55
Golf club example, 272, 278
Golf instruction videotape
    assignment, 143
Grammar, 48-49, 108-11, 114-15,
    235, 271-72
Grammatik (software), 159
Graphic
    -copy relationship, 48-49
    description example, 54

H

Halogen lighting example, 214-15
Hamilton, Alexander, 117
Hammacher Schlemmer Institute,
    35, 187-88
Hanging folders
    assignment, 219
    example, 222
Hat example, 236, 240
Headings, 87-93
Headlines, 76-83
    assignment, 75
Headset example, 160
Hercules, 68
Herrington, 48
Hit-and-run copy, 66, 284-93
Hogan, 272
Home example, 33
Household products catalog, 237,
    241
HU-MAN, SEVEN STAGES OF,
    195, 229, 324
Huxley, Aldous, 114
Hyphen v. *dash,* use of, 271

I

I am the greatest copy, 11, 35,
    184-86
IBM-AT, 312
Ice cream scoop example, 25
Illustration/copy match, 311
Image, 314
    all the way copy, 7-8, 23
    selecting type of copy, 12
    and types of catalog copy, 3-37
IMPLIED IMPORTANCE RULE,
    173, 321
IMPORTANCE DETERMINATION
    RULE, 174, 231
Important, use of, 156
Incredible, use of, 157-58
Inducements, 313
Information, 315
INFORMATION SATURATION,
    RULE OF, 286, 322
Informational/educational copy, 10,
    28-31
Inmac, 45
Insect killer example, 197
Inside-the-cover letter example, 67,
    72
It is v. *it's at,* use of, 115
ITS/IT'S LAW, 322

J

Jackson, Bo, 48
Jacobsen, Peter, 199
Jargon, 312
Jeans example, 191-92
Jes' folk copy, 4-5, 13-14
Jewelry cleaner example, 92
Jonson, Ben, 112-13
Jordan, Michael, 48

K

Key selling point, 315
King Tutankhamun example, 171-73,
    176-77
Kitchen shears example, 92
K-Swiss shoe example, 178

L

Lamp example, 234-35
Lands' End, 90-91, 196
Lapel pin example, 93
LAW OF ABSOLUTE
    CONFUSION, 233-45, 318
LAW OF COMPETITIVE
    SELECTIVITY, 185, 319
Lawn mower example, 50, 58
Levitating globe example, 287, 290
Lie v. *lay,* use of, 114
Limited edition
    concept, 169
    watch example, 260-61
Lindbergh, Charles A., 260-61
Line breaks, 78-79
Lingerie pouch example, 221, 225
Literacy, 108-19
LIVE ENCOMIUM RULE, 145,
    150-51, 322
Logical sequencing, 300-1
Longines watch example, 260-61
Luggage cart
    assignment, 183
    example, 183, 187-88
Luxurious v. *luxuriant,* use of, 115
Lyon, Patrick, 244

M

Magalogs, 221
Mailbox example, 45, 279
Marlowe, Christopher, 252
Massager example, 42-43
Masters Tournament (1988)
    videotape example, 147
Mechanical device example, 30-31
Megalomania, 313
Men's wear catalog, 236
Micro-computer example, 46
Microwave example, 92, 139-40
Might have v. *might of,* 115
Minimalist example, 3, 9, 26
Mondrian, Piet, 103
Morgan, Julia, 22
Motivation, 310
Muddy writing, 45-46, 64-65, 77-78,
    83
    example, 56

Museum of Modern Art (New York), 284
Musician example, 24-25

N

Nairobi™ hat example, 236, 240
Narrative copy, 8-9, 25
Necklace example, 43, 89
NEGATIVE RULE OF PARTIAL DISCLOSURE, 259-66, 322
Negatives, positives of, 220-21
Networking, use of, 243
Newman, Edwin, 109
Nike, 168
  training monitor example, 207
Nominative heading, 87
Nondescriptive words, 41, 53, 155, 208-9
No-risk membership example, 209, 213
Novelty example, 287, 290

O

Obscure word use, 77-78, 83. *See also* Muddy writing
Oil derrick example, 89
Olive oil example, 34-35
Opening, 3
Order form, 312
Orthopedic pillow example, 35
Overcomplication, 43
Overfamiliarity, 269-80
Overused words, 155-63
Oxymoron, 242, 291

P

Palmer, Arnold, 143
Pants example, 31
Papyrus Institute, 171, 176
Papyrus painting example, 207-8
Partial disclosure, 260-66
Penny loafer example, 293
Personalization, 253, 313-14
Pet Vac example, 116
Phone/clock/radio example, 253
Picasso prints example, 220

Pillow example, 35
Pilot-Bold example, 117
Plain vanilla copy, 11-12, 36-37, 93
Planter example, 256
Pocketknife example, 124-25
Poetry, 112-13
Portable fireplace example, 223
Positioned descriptive heading, 88, 92
Positioned nominative heading, 88, 91
Positioning, 183-92
PRE-ESTABLISHED ATTITUDE RULE, 185, 322
Prejudice, dissolving, 50-51
Prepositional sentence ending, 111
Price
  justification, 167-79
  reduction, 169
Product
  description, 237
  knowledge of, 219-29
Promise phases, 123-24
Proofreading, 65-66, 107-8, 113-14, 119
Publicity, 169
Puffery, 43, 169
PUFFERY-DEFEAT INEVITABILITY RULE, 173, 323
Pumas, 168
Punch bowl set example, 285, 289
Purse-size mirror
  assignment, 249-50
  example, 255

Q

Quartz-watch example, 24
Questions, 309-15
Quietly upscale descriptive copy, 7, 20-22, 63, 69
Quill Office Supply catalog, 196
Quintessence, use of, 75, 101-2

R

Radio example, 203
Reader rapport, 195-203
Reason to buy, 133-39, 226

Reeboks, 168

References, 67

Regardless v. *irregardless,* use of, 115

Repetition, 310

Retail catalog cover, 17

Rewriting, 47-48

RightWriter (software), 159

Rocker example, 179

Romantic descriptive heading, 88, 92

Romantic nominative heading, 88, 91, 93

Rose-lovers example, 29

Rowenta Cool Touch toaster example, 175

Rules. *See specific areas*

Run-in bullets, 139-40

Running shoes example, 178

Ruth, Babe, 48

S

Salesmanship, 49-50
  example, 58

Salsa copy examples
  all the facts, 9
  down home, 5
  I am the greatest, 11
  image all the way, 7-8
  informational/educational, 10
  jes' folk, 4-5
  minimalist, 9
  narrative, 8
  plain vanilla, 12
  quietly upscale descriptive, 7
  shout, 6-7
  snob appeal, 10-11
  touchstone, 8
  you-you-you, 6

Salt and pepper mill
  assignment, 133
  example, 137

Sandals
  assignment, 3
  example, 208

Santa Claus example, 78

Scrabble (game), 100

Scrimshaw example, 76-77

Sculpture example, 270, 275

Sears catalog, 18, 64-65, 108, 198

Seat cover rewrite assignment, 123

Security system example, 137

SELLER/SELLEE EQUIVOCATION EQUATION, 286, 323

Senet (game) example, 265

Sensational, use of, 208

Sentence length, 311

Shadow copy, 271-72

Shakespeare, 114

Shalimar example, 235-36, 239

Sharper Image, 48

Shetland sweaters example, 302-3

Shirt example, 138, 146, 162

Shout copy, 6-7, 17-19

Silver polish example, 92

Slammin' Sam's Secrets videotape example, 147

Slippers example, 42

Snob appeal copy, 3, 10-11, 32-35

Solar kit for children example, 271-72, 276

Solo mailing, 48-49, 198

Sound monitor example, 235

Space ads, 48-49

Speakers
  assignment, 63, 269
  example, 63, 69

Special-interest example, 71

Specific descriptive copy, 211-12

Specific pitch, 310

Specifics, 143-51, 285

SPECIFICS SUPERIORITY PRINCIPLE, 198, 277, 323

Speed, 48-49

Sporty's, 196

Squall jacket
  assignment, 87
  example, 90-91

Stadler, Craig, 272

Stereo system example, 156-57

Striped tunic example, 68

Stylebook, 111

Subhead, 259-60

Suit example, 250-51

Superiority claim, 185-86

Superlative use, 155

Sweater example, 101, 103, 252-53, 302-3

Sweatshirt example, 93
Syntax agreement, 116

T

Tactile blending example, 83
Target market, 310
Teach v. *learn,* use of, 115
Telephone
  assignment, 155
  answering machine assignment,
    283
  example, 128-29, 276-77
Tennis shoes example, 167-68,
    177-78
Terry-cloth robe
  assignment, 41
  example, 57
The, use of, 183-84
Thrill, use of, 163
Tie words, 99
Time, 315
Timeliness, 314
Toaster
  assignment, 167
  example, 175
  -oven broiler example, 300
TOP-END CATALOG FIVE WORD
    NAIL EXEMPTION, 321
Touchstone copy, 8, 24-25, 169
Travel bag example, 302
Travel-accessory case example, 135
Trousers copy/photo mismatch, 236
Trug, use of, 280
Truth in advertising, 262-63
Try to v. *try and,* use of, 115
"20 Questions," 309-15

U

Ultimate, use of, 156, 160-62
Underdescription, 269-80
Underscoring, 156
Upscale copy. *See* Quietly upscale
    descriptive copy
Upscale fashion catalog, 114
Use description, 123-29

V

Vegetables example, 228
Vocabulary, 48-49
  suppression, 68, 97-104
Vol-au-vent cutters example, 77
Voltage adapter, 76
Vuitton, Louis, 32

W

Ward's catalog, 64
Waring Professional toaster example,
    167, 175
Warming container example, 125-26
Watch example, 260-61
Watt, James, 46
Weaseling, 213
WEASELING, FIRST RULE OF,
    174, 323
Welcome letter, 311-12
WHOSE MESSAGE IS IT
    ANYWAY? RULE, 64, 66, 68,
    111-12, 114, 323
Wine chiller example, 284, 288
Wine-lover's catalog example, 20-21
Wolfe, Tom, 219
Wood finishing example, 128
Word
  choice, 109
  -color, 68-69
  misuse example, 82
  power copy, 161
  selections, 41-59
WORD RE-USE RULE, 158-59, 324
Writing
  discipline, 48-49
  test, 43-47

Y

Yamaha, 272
YELL-OUT-BARGAIN RULE, 6,
    324
You-you-you copy, 5-6, 16